Clinical Evolutions c Superego, Body, and Gender in Psychoanalysis

M000233134

Patients in psychoanalytic treatment present with a variety of problems that reflect contemporary cultural issues and values. *Clinical Evolutions on the Superego, Body, and Gender in Psychoanalysis* explores the effects of such societal changes on psychoanalytic theory and clinical practice, covering topics such as greed, envy and deception, body narcissism, gender roles, and relationships. Janice S. Lieberman includes numerous clinical vignettes and insights into working clinically with changing norms.

Lieberman explores how changes in values and norms of behavior in the world beyond the consulting room have influenced what is now heard by analysts within it, using clinical data to demonstrate the psychological underpinnings of the values promulgated by current trends in politics and in society more widely. She explores what she observes to be "a new superego"; where deception abounds and often goes unpunished, where greed and envy have arguably increased and there is an enhanced emphasis on the body and its appearance. Traditional gender roles have been challenged in fortuitous ways, but a certain amount of chaos and confusion has ensued. Relationships are found and maintained using technology, yet many feel lonely and empty. She writes about the clinical dilemmas she has faced and offers suggestions for resolving them in working with today's patients. Lieberman also sees parallels for these developments in several artists' lives and in their work.

Clinical Evolutions on the Superego, Body, and Gender in Psychoanalysis will be of great interest to psychoanalysts and psychoanalytic psychotherapists.

Janice S. Lieberman, PhD, is a Training and Supervising Analyst and Faculty member at the Institute for Psychoanalytic Training and Research in New York City. She is the author of *Body Talk: Looking and Being Looked at in Psychotherapy* and served on the Editorial Board of the *Journal of the American Psychoanalytic Association*. She is a Member of the International Psychoanalytical Association Committee on Sexual and Gender Diversity Studies.

Clinical Evolutions on the Superego, Body, and Gender in Psychoanalysis

Janice S. Lieberman

Routledge
Taylor & Francis Group

LONDON AND NEW YORK

First published 2019
by Routledge
2 Park Square, Milton Park, Abingdon, Oxon OX14 4RN

and by Routledge
711 Third Avenue, New York, NY 10017

Routledge is an imprint of the Taylor & Francis Group, an informa business

British Library Cataloguing-in-Publication Data
A catalogue record for this book is available from the British Library

Library of Congress Cataloging-in-Publication Data
Names: Lieberman, Janice S., author.
Title: Clinical evolutions on the superego, body, and gender in
psychoanalysis / Janice S. Lieberman.
Description: Abingdon, Oxon ; New York, NY : Routledge, 2019. |
Includes bibliographical references and index. Identifiers:
LCCN 2018018234 (print) | LCCN 2018021784 (ebook) |
ISBN 9780429490699 (Master) |
ISBN 9780429955679 (Web PDF) |
ISBN 9780429955662 (ePub) |
ISBN 9780429955655 (Mobipocket/Kindle) |
ISBN 9781138590854 (hardback : alk. paper) |
ISBN 9781138590878 (pbk. : alk. paper)
Subjects: LCSH: Psychoanalysis. | Superego. | Body image. |
Sex role–Psychological aspects.
Classification: LCC RC506 (ebook) | LCC RC506 .L534 2019
(print) | DDC 616.89/17–dc23LC record available at https://lccn.
loc.gov/2018018234

ISBN: 978-1-138-59085-4 (hbk)
ISBN: 978-1-138-59087-8 (pbk)
ISBN: 978-0-429-49069-9 (ebk)

Typeset in Times New Roman
by Wearset Ltd, Boldon, Tyne and Wear

For Gideon, Jonah, Jackson, and Griffin

Contents

Acknowledgments

I would like to acknowledge the following:

I am extremely grateful for the confidence and encouragement given me by my family, colleagues, students, and friends during the writing of this book. I know that I was less available to them on many occasions and I hope to remedy that with this book's publication.

I want to thank those with whom I worked developing some of the previously published chapters. Helen Gediman, my coauthor of *The Many Faces of Deceit* taught me how to think more deeply, to find the "red threads" of connection, and how to construct a book. I want to thank Brenda Berger and Stephanie Newman, Editors of *Money Talks,* who encouraged me to write about "the new superego." Deep appreciation goes to Paula Ellman and Nancy Goodman for including me in their conference and book on *The Courage to Fight Violence Against Women.* I also want to give tribute to the late Alan Frosch, who included my work in his book, *Absolute Truth and Unbearable Psychic Pain.*

I am extremely grateful to Rosemary Balsam, Arlene Richards, and Danielle Knafo, who have served as role models and mentors for my work on the female body and art and for my writing efforts over the years. To my cousins and close friends Judy and Steve Levitan, you are the source of my strength!

I want to thank Kate Hawes, the Chief Editor of Routledge, for her encouragement, and the superb Charles Bath, Assistant Editor of Routledge, for his patience answering the countless questions I had in the preparation of the manuscript. I want to thank Katie Finn, the Production Editor and Matt Deacon, Senior Project Manager of Wearset, for shepherding this project through. Abbey Frawley in New York was a wonderful help to me as I was preparing the manuscript. I was blessed with the assignment of a brilliant copy-editor Anastasia Said, who was a pleasure to work with.

I am grateful for all the opportunities I have had over the years to present papers based on most of the chapters of this book. I want to thank the Program Committees of IPTAR (the Institute for Psychoanalytic Training and Research), CFS (Contemporary Freudian Society), The Metropolitan Center, PANY (Psychoanalytic Association of New York), the IPA (International Psychoanalytic Association), Psychoanalysis Division 39, and the American Psychoanalytic

Association. Special thanks go to Herb Stein, Editor of the *PANY Bulletin*, Anna Fishzon of *The Candidate Journal*, Batya Monder of *The Round Robin,* and Margarita Cereijido of the Washington Baltimore Center for Psychoanalysis, Inc.

I also want to acknowledge my long running study group in Art and Psycho-analysis led by Francis Baudry as well as the Education Program of the Whitney Museum of American Art, where I have been a Docent for 29 years. I have learned so much from all of you!

Permissions acknowledgments

Every effort has been made to contact the copyright holders for their permission to reprint selections of this book. The publishers would be grateful to hear from any copyright holder who has not been acknowledged and we will undertake to rectify any errors or omissions in future editions of this book.

Chapter acknowledgments

Chapter 1 has been adapted from J. S. Lieberman (2012) "Analyzing a 'New Superego': Greed and Envy in the Recent Age of Affluence" in Berger, B. and Newman, S. (Eds.) (2012) *Money Talks: In Therapy, Society and Life,* New York: Routledge, Chapter 4. Reprinted by permission of Taylor & Francis, LLC.

Chapters 2 and 16 have been adapted from J. S. Lieberman (1996) "Patients Who Lie" and J. S. Lieberman (1996) "Omissions in Psychoanalytic Treatment" and J. S. Lieberman (1996) "The Imposturous Artist Arshile Gorky" in Gediman, H. and Lieberman, J. S. (1996) *The Many Faces of Deceit: Omissions, Lies and Disguise in Psychotherapy,* Northvale, N. J.: Jason Aronson, Inc., Chapters 2, 3, and 6. Reprinted by permission.

Chapters 6 and 7 have been adapted from J. S. Lieberman (2000) *Body Talk: Looking and Being Looked at in Psychotherapy,* Northvale, N. J.: Jason Aronson, Inc. They were first published as Chapter 5 "The Therapist's Rush to Metaphor" and Chapter 6 "Working with Women Obsessed with Thinness" in the author's book, *Body Talk: Looking and Being Looked at in Psychotherapy*, Northvale, N. J.: Jason Aronson, Inc., 2000. Reprinted by kind permission of Rowman & Littlefield Publishing Group.

Chapter 8 has been adapted from J. S. Lieberman (2012) "Some Observations on Working with Body Narcissism with Concrete Patients" in Frosch, A. (Ed.) (2012) *Absolute Truth and Unbearable Psychic Pain,* London: CIPS/Karnac, Chapter 8. Reprinted by permission of Taylor & Francis, LLC.

Chapter 11 has been adapted from J. S. Lieberman (1991) "Issues in the Psy-choanalytic Treatment of Single Females over Thirty," *Psychoanalytic Review*, *78*(2), pp. 177–198. Reprinted by permission of Guilford Publications, Inc.

Chapter 15 has been adapted from J. S. Lieberman, (2017) "Violence Against Women in the Work of Women Artists" in Ellman, P. and Goodman, N. (2017) *The Courage to Fight Violence Against Women: Psychoanalytic and Multidisciplinary*

Perspectives, London: Karnac, Chapter 20. Reprinted by permission of Taylor & Francis, LLC.

Image acknowledgments

Figure 15.1: *Pee Body* (1992), wax and glass beads (23 strands of varying lengths, 1 in to over 15 in long); $68.6 \times 71.1 \times 71.1$ cm ($27 \times 28 \times 28$ in). Harvard Art Museums/Fogg Museum: gift of Barbara Lee; gift of Emily Rauh Pulitzer; and Purchase in part from the Joseph A. Baird, Jr., Francis H. Burr Memorial and Director's Acquisition Funds, 1997.82. ©Kiki Smith. Photo: Imaging Department ©President and Fellows of Harvard College. Reproduced with permission.

Figure 16.1 is by Arshile Gorky (ca. 1902–1948), *The Artist and His Mother* (1926–ca. 1936). Oil on canvas 60×50 1/4 in (152.4×127.6 cm). Whitney Museum of American Art, New York: gift of Julien Levy for Maro and Natasha Gorky in memory of their father 50.17 ©2018 The Arshile Gorky Foundation / Artists Rights Society (ARS), New York. Reproduced with permission.

Figure 17.1: *Guitar Lesson* (1934) is by Balthus. Oil on canvas 163.3×138.4 cm. Every effort has been made by the author of this book to contact the private collection, which is now believed to own this image.

Introduction

Loss of integrity in contemporary culture and contemporary psyche

Introduction: loss of integrity

As a psychoanalyst in private practice for over forty years, I am often asked what changes I have seen in those coming into treatment and how the changes in the world outside the consulting room have impacted my patients as well as myself. This book is an attempt to answer these questions. A traditional Freudian tenet is that the "stuff" out of which psyches are made is constant and universal, independent of social reality. This is only partly correct. I have seen vast changes in the psyches of those coming to treatment today from those who came 40 years ago. This is a different world from that of the 1970s. I trained as a Social Psychologist before I became a Psychoanalyst and I use that lens along with my psychoanalytic lens with which to view my patients and the world around us. The patients I see today in psychoanalysis and psychoanalytic therapy present, for the most part, with reduced ego resilience, and different values and morals. They have absorbed the stresses and strains of our contemporary culture.

I am writing this book in 2017–2018 at a particular time in history. Every era has had its own social, economic, and moral problems. The two World Wars, the Holocaust, 9/11, and their aftermath were imprinted on the psyches of those living in those times. These eras have been well-documented and well-addressed by psychoanalysts and social scientists. In this particular period of time, although the majority of the patients I see in my consulting room suffer from the traditional symptoms of guilt, anxiety, depression, and inhibition. I have chosen to write about the less acknowledged, more ignoble issues *some* of my patients present that our culture, in this particular time, has fostered. It is a time in which psychic emptiness, powerlessness, and despair are prevalent. Culturally approved strategies and goals have proved ultimately to not be satisfying. The news coming from our media—"fake news," "alternative facts," sexual harassment and pedophilia, income inequality, body modification, the digitalization of relationships, and the exportation of immigrants—is not good and has made sick people sicker and healthy people sick.

I would like to make the following observations about the "outside world" in which today's patients live: Today's patients, along with the rest of the population, are greatly affected by socioeconomic inequality and gender inequality, especially those who are part of the broadening scope of gender identity. Gender identity is no longer considered to be binary, but fluid, and on a continuum. In addition, today's patients are affected by increasing job demands and job insecurity. They are especially affected by the unsettling "climate of deception" that trickles down from leaders at the top with poor character to other authorities (teachers, employers, politicians, etc.) I postulate a "new superego." As I note in this book (Chapter 1, p. 14),

> It has been my observation that "the new superego" is based on a different, more narcissistically based morality: for many in our culture today attaining one's high ideal and even "goodness" is reached through physical exercise, diet and fitness. It also comes from acquiring wealth. It does not have to come from altruistic deeds or kindness to others or what has been traditionally regarded as "moral" behavior.

I have witnessed a widespread belief that there is in our culture a tolerance of lying and other forms of deception, even corruption, as if it were commonplace, to be expected, and that there is little to do about it. Reactions range from rage to moral indignation to "taking a blind eye" as a way to manage disappointment and disgust.

When I opened my private practice in 1974, the Women's Movement had dynamically engaged both women and men. Many had been "hippies," protesting the Vietnam War, smoking marijuana, and doing drugs. Their idealism was fiery, but seemed adolescent in nature. Most of these protesters eventually had to adjust to "the real world" and take on adult responsibilities. Marriages were renegotiated and impassioned conversations took place privately and in "consciousness-raising groups" about the role requirements for each gender. Some marriages did not survive this scrutiny and either broke up or remained in difficulty. Women who had left the workforce in order to have children now felt entitled and empowered to go back to work. For many years child-rearing was chaotic, shared by couples who each thought the other should do more, or by untrained babysitters.

What was a "family" was itself being redefined. Women who could not find suitable partners to marry began to choose single parenthood. Some fared better than others. Artificial means of reproduction has enabled many who cannot conceive their own children or do not want to adopt children, to have children. It has become more and more possible to choose to not have children and not be poorly judged by family and friends.

Today many women feel comfortable going to work, having careers, even if there is no financial need for them to do so. They can leave their children in daycare or private care with (mostly) women who have made caretaking a profession and who often have taken courses in child-rearing. In many sectors of our working and political worlds, women have broken through or challenged "the glass ceiling." Men are taking more and more responsibility for raising children, cooking, although most women feel they still have the majority of household tasks to do.

Concurrently, the Gay Rights Movement brought many gay men and women out of "closets" filled with shame to places of pride, from marginality to inclusion. He (or she) (implied henceforth when I speak of "he") who had married a member of the opposite sex to keep his gay identity hidden is now able to divorce and find someone of his own sex. He is able to marry again and publicly show his love for someone of his own sex. Legal means have been established that enable gay couples to have children. In certain schools in our larger cities, many children have two mothers or two fathers.

More recently, due to the various successes of the Gay Rights Movement and a change in attitudes about sexual differences (as well as legal support), those who are transgender in identity have been more and more "normalized." Some live in pretty conventional families raising children, celebrating holidays, etc. Terms e.g., "transgender," "queer," "cis-gender," as well as new nouns and pronouns e.g., "they," rather than "he" and "she," have been added to our lexicon. Unfortunately, those who do not assume traditional lifestyles and clothing are still made to suffer discrimination and even violence. At the time I am writing this, the Trump administration is working to remove many of the rights of gay and transgender people causing them considerable stress.

Technology has changed the way we write, think, and communicate with others. When I wrote a paper in the 1970s, I did so on a typewriter with many carbon papers and used scissors and scotch tape to relocate paragraphs. Snail mail took several days or sometimes weeks to reach recipients, as contrasted with the mere seconds provided by e-mail. Photos were taken with cameras loaded with costly film that had to be developed in a slow costly process. Many fewer photos were taken to be in those days and were shared with fewer friends and relatives over time. This contrasts with today's speed when photos are shared via e-mail, messaging, communication to followers by way of Facebook, Instagram, and Twitter. Today, books can be found or purchased online, and journals are to be found online, sparing the reader trips to the library or bookstore. There are, of course, those who are unhappy with this change. Patients once brought to their sessions love letters or breakup letters to read. Today they bring in phones with texting dialogue to review with me and photos for me to see. They manage to do this even while on the couch! Some couples and families sit around the kitchen table texting rather than talking. Love and sex are often to be found online rather than in social situations.

Entertainment used to be found primarily outside the home. Families and couples went to the movies, sporting events together, as they still do. Or families would watch television shows and televised sports together in one room. Today there is much more isolated entertainment as family members individually watch shows on their devices communicating perhaps about where they are as they, as an example, binge-watch various Netflix or Amazon series. This puts pressure on me too to watch some of these series so that I can understand what my patients are talking about when they refer to them. My patients' dreams and associations are filled with the movies and videos they have seen. My younger patients primarily watch science fiction and horror movies, which do not seem to scare them.

Technology has brought us closer to our leaders, their personal lives as well as their policies. Events are broadcast instantly around the world. Idealizations are no longer possible. If they ever were, they are short-lived. The flaws of Franklin Delano Roosevelt, John Fitzgerald Kennedy, and Martin Luther King were revealed after their deaths. Not so the case with Clinton, Spitzer, and Trump, where the media feel free to expose every flaw the minute it appears. As one Hillary ad asked, "Do you want your children watching this?" Whereas most of my patients talk in their sessions about their addiction to the news, how scary it is, how unbelievable it is, how overstimulating it is, others refuse to watch, or read the news. The news overwhelms and frightens them.

The greatest change I have seen over the years, due to the advent of the Internet and digital devices, is their impact on relationships all through the life cycle. Sherrie Turkle (2011) has, in her various books, and talks, noted this tendency to "rather text than talk." Parents, especially working parents, often get child-rearing information from the Internet rather than from friends in the playground. Some of this is misinformation. When I opened my practice, parents were concerned about their children, but managed to have adult social lives and interests apart from them. Today we have "helicopter" and "Velcro" parents armed with Internet and "chat room" advice. In many cases, the children are not just the focus but the "bosses" of the family. Some grow to be "terrorist" adolescents and young adults, often bartering their presence at family gatherings for money and material possessions.

When I began my practice, I worked with my patients to emotionally and financially separate from their parents. I helped them to have "zones of privacy" about their finances, their love lives, and their sex lives. Today many of my women patients regard their mothers as "their best friend" and have several conversations with them every day, telling them everything. There are fewer boundaries between parent and child. Parents have less authority even when footing the bills for their adult children. Many adult children lack a "filter" and feel entitled to express whatever is on their minds and to repeat to others whatever anyone has told them regardless of its consequences. Among those who "fail to launch" there is less privacy, since their whereabouts, and companions are on Facebook and Instagram for all to see! They would not have it any other way.

I wrote in my review of Sarah Usher's (2016) book, *Separation-Individuation Struggles in Adult Life: Leaving Home* that 40 years ago:

> separation-individuation issues seen in adults were not so widespread nor were they so culturally and economically entrenched. Today's increasing costs of higher education and housing and a real scarcity of good entry-level

jobs for post college-educated children has resulted in many of them moving home. There is a feeling among therapists that many young people feel "entitled" to what their parents earn and own. As a result, helping them to separate and individuate has become a much more complex task. Forty years ago children were expected to live on their own and support themselves once they reached the age of 21. They were expected to marry and have children soon after. Not so today. Parents of adult children (and grandparents too) are caught between their own needs to hold on to their children too long (for companionship, to feel young, to serve as buffers in a bad marriage, etc.) in a culture in which/parental (and grandparental) subsidy of apartments, vacations and psychotherapy(!) is common. This "holding on" conflicts with more rational desires to see their children "launch" into adulthood.

(Lieberman, 2017, pp. 227–228)

Many of my younger patients have never been alone. Beginning with the time they were teenagers, they began to link up with a series of partners ("serial monogamy") to whom they became sexually and emotionally attached. Often the partners were not what they would regard as suitable mates. Both members of the couple feared being alone. The women in these couples "all of a sudden" in their thirties realized that they wanted to become mothers and had difficulties breaking up with the partner they were not going to marry. They also became aware of the diminishing pool of appropriate men to marry as they approached the reality of their biological clocks.

Concurrent with this, what has not changed is the value placed on marriage, especially for women. Single women, no matter how successful, and independent, have the same pressure to marry, "to be taken care of," even if their potential husbands earn less and are less capable than they are. In the 1970s brides wanted small intimate weddings. Today it is the custom to have large diamond engagement rings, many pre-wedding events that culminate in large expensive, even if unaffordable, extravaganzas. I have observed over and over rather unassuming young women turn into bridezillas when engaged! Their outrageous demandingness is considered to be "normal" by friends and relatives.

Today there is less stigma placed on divorce if two people feel they have made a mistake by marrying. They get out of early marriages undertaken because of the pressure I just mentioned relatively unscathed. Not so the case when children are involved. Not so when they are middle-aged and the wives have a reduced chance of re-marrying. Some stay in very unhappy marriages fearing single status.

More and more the old idealize the young. Due to the social changes just referred to, the young feel there is less to learn from their elders that are relevant to their lives. Hence, the effort on the part of the middle-aged to look young longer. (They know too that their lives will be prolonged longer than ever before.) Advanced technology used for body and skin modification, for face-lifts, and tummy tucks, have collapsed the differences in appearance between young and old. Despite some media efforts to downplay it, the focus on bodily appearance, on exercise, and on efforts to be thin, have changed the nature of guilt. Rather than feeling guilty that one has hurt another person, today's expression of guilt is often about having eaten a cookie, and about not going to the gym. "You are what you eat." "You are where you eat" (restaurants are ranked for status among the more affluent) are identity themes. This is of course manifest content.

Professions and jobs were once clearly defined. One worked hard, studied hard, and the work one chose usually provided some form of security. If one was unhappy in one's job one could speak up about it. If there was no change in working conditions, one could leave, and find another one. Not so today. I find myself cautioning patients to be careful, whereas I supported their assertiveness 40 years ago. They may not find another job. I believe that a certain amount of adaptiveness in responding to cultural demands and values is necessary for a good life and I convey this to my patients. In general, I am neutral, but I do not sit back in silence if a patient is about to act out in blatant or latent self-destructive ways that he may not have a chance to repair.

In this book, I will be covering these themes that I have found to consistently recur in my private practice. I see in psychoanalytic therapy and psychoanalysis predominantly white heterosexual men and women, a lesser number of homosexual men and women, and equal numbers of single and married men and women. Their incomes vary greatly and my fee varies with their income. They are representative of the middle class and upper middle class population of New York City. To my regret, very few persons of color have been referred to me, although I have supervised the psychotherapies of quite a few. A portion of my patients are psychoanalysts and psychotherapists. I do not write about them. I am grateful to my talented supervisees and students, from whom I have learned about many different kinds of lives.

Psychoanalysis has been criticized as a therapy for the affluent and the "worried well." This is not entirely so. Some insurance policies pay for 3 and 4 times-weekly psychoanalysis and most of us reduce our fees greatly to treat Candidates. However, for someone to profit from psychoanalysis, he or she must have "an affluence of inner fantasy" and the ability to access the inner life, and enough freedom from economic challenges and family problems to focus on himself or herself.

Some have asked whether my practice on the Upper East Side of Manhattan can possibly reflect more universal practices. I regularly present papers in many different parts of this country as well as internationally. I have found much commonality and agreement, which what I have observed. I am constantly told by many psychoanalysts that they are pleased that I am writing about the issues I do. So few address these issues. I have been told that I am "brave" to write about issues that have not received attention. Some have regarded me as a bit of a "scold," seeing me as prone to "moral indignation." I regard myself as one who hopes that what is "moral" is to be considered. I also want to remind the reader that this book is about patients who come to psychoanalysis and psychotherapy with problems in their emotional lives, work lives, and relationships. I have devised some new ways of working with them, especially those with problematic body narcissism. It is a clinical book. The clinical problems I work with are embedded in and affected by our culture today.

In her Foreword to Laura Greenfield's brilliant book *Generation Wealth* Juliet Shor (2017) writes that: "photographer Greenfield has captured a singular era in modern history—a period of rampant materialism and wealth obsession, a world where conspicuous consumption and intense bodily focus reign supreme" (p. 6). She compares this decade with the mid-20th century, where people compared themselves "horizontally" with others of similar status. Starting in the 1980s, identifications became vertical, with those at the bottom trying to be like those at the top. Shor describes "a social milieu in which consumer presentation is all that counts for identity, status, and a basic sense of self ... but it becomes a destructive addiction that takes on a life of its own" (p. 9).

I begin this book with chapters in Part I that deal with clinical problems I have found working with patients who are greedy and/or envious of others, who lie, who omit important information. I also address the analyst's superego and her responsibility to her patients. In Part II are chapters on body and gender, body narcissism, working with concreteness, skin concerns, body modification, femininity, and masculinity. The chapters in Part III are about working with single women over 30, loneliness, the search for love, and oedipal, and preoedipal factors that lead to difficulties finding love.

I have lectured on contemporary art at the Whitney Museum of American Art for 29 years. That experience has enabled me to compare visual representations of human emotions and problems with what I hear in my office. Furthermore, since a good portion of art today is politically oriented, I have an additional perspective with which to understand the world my patients and I live in today. I have included a series of chapters on psychoanalysis and art in Part IV that reflect themes of deception and morality, income inequality, body narcissism, misogyny, sexual harassment, and pedophilia. Most of what I have written years ago seems relevant today. The reader will find a mix of formal and informal chapters, some scholarly and previously published, and others presented and less scholarly.

This book is written in 2017–2018 shortly after the election of Donald Trump to the Office of President of the United States (U.S.). For several months, the majority of my patients, educated liberals, could speak of little else but their shock, disappointment and chagrin, their moral outrage, their empathy for those to be deported, their fears about their own healthcare, the fate of abortion laws and all manifested a generalized anxiety about the future.

But Trump's values are not new. I have been writing about their manifestations for over twenty-five years:

1   The freedom to lie and deceive without consequence ("alternative facts" "fake news").

2   An amount of greed beyond anything the average person could imagine, also without consequence. Income inequality has activated hopelessness in some and malignant envy in others.

3   A tremendous value put on physical appearance, necessitating plastic surgery, especially for women, who must look "perfect," thin, muscular, well-coiffed, expensively dressed, or be mocked by men.

4   Despite the educational professional advances made by women in the last 60 years, some are still groped and raped, and are fearful of reporting their attackers. The harassment of women (and some men) in the workplace and on campus is ongoing.

There are those who believe that this is not new. In his book *Fantasyland: How Americans Went Haywire: A 500-Year History,* Kurt Anderson (2017) states that:

> People tend to regard the Trump moment—this post-truth, alternative facts moment—as some inexplicable and crazy new American phenomenon. In fact/what is happening is just the ultimate extrapolation and expression of attitudes and instincts that have made America exceptional for its entire history—and really from its pre-history.
>
> (p. 11)

This view is in contrast to what was said in a speech on the U.S. Senate floor by Jeff Flake, then Senator from Arizona on October 24, 2017. Speaking to what has been called "the new normal," he said:

> We must never adjust to the present coarseness of our national dialogue with the tone set up at the top. We must never regard as normal the regular and casual undermining of our democratic norms and ideals ... we must never meekly accept ... the flagrant disregard for truth and decency.
>
> (Flake, 2017, p. A14)

Many have asked me to explain the minds of those who support Trump and his values, who turn a blind eye to his lies and misdemeanors. In *The Dangerous Case of Donald Trump: 27 Psychiatrists and Mental Health Experts Assess a President* edited by Bandy Lee, there are serious attempts to explain Trump's mind despite the fact that none of them had him in treatment or met him personally. I believe that examining the psychodynamics of patients who lie, who are greedy, who are misogynistic, as exemplified in the various chapters in this book, will provide important clues. I worry, as do my colleagues and friends, and certain of my patients, about what kind of world this will be for young people to grow up in. Children are aware at too young an age about power and corruption. They are not growing up with idealizations of authority figures—presidents, governors, mayors, and teachers—quite the opposite.

Prevalent in our society today is the expectation that others will lie and cheat. Today's therapists admit more and more that their patients may lie—about reasons for absences, income, affairs, shameful memories, and addictions. They lie about being in therapy and about past therapies. Today's therapists know that these lies are a barrier to progress, but may continue until Trust is established. We are becoming more and more sophisticated about the psychological underpinnings of lies and omissions, seeing them more and more as due to splits in the psyche.

I find quite problematic the basic assumption on the part of university administrators and professors that students are prone to cheat. College professors have software to check whether their students have plagiarized, and students taking standardized tests must leave watches and cell phones—even candy bars—outside the room in which the tests are given.

I believe that there has been a loss of value put on integrity, good character, and good deeds; values those of us born in the mid-20th century were taught to revere.

References

Anderson, K. (2017). *Fantasyland: How America went haywire: A 500-year history*. New York: Random House.

Flake, J. (2017, October 25). And so, Mr. President, I will not be complicit or silent. *New York Times*, p. A14.

Lee, B. (Ed.) (2017). *The dangerous case of Donald Trump*. New York: St. Martin's Press.

Lieberman, J. S. (2017). Review of Usher, S. F. (2016) *Separation—individuation struggles in adult life: leaving home*, London: Routledge. *Canadian Journal of Psychoanalysis, 24*, 227–230.

Shor, J. (2017). Foreword. In L. Greenfield, *Generation wealth* (pp. 6–9). New York: Phaidon.

Turkle, S. (2011). *Alone together*. New York: Basic Books.

Part I

Superego/character issues

Deception, greed, and envy

Chapter 1

Analyzing a "new superego"?

Greed and envy in the recent age of affluence[1]

In my psychoanalytic practice, which, I believe, is to some extent a mirror of the outside world, over the past decade I have witnessed a "new superego," a companion to "the new ego," a term that was used some thirty-odd years ago in discussions of "the widening scope." Those of my patients who reflect this "new superego" seem to be far less guilt-ridden (at least consciously) and governed by a different set of values, ideals, and standards of behavior from those who reflect the "old classic superego." Concurrently, I have listened to, and worked with, considerably more vocal, and ego-syntonic expressions of greed and envy than ever before. Colleagues and supervisees have observed the same phenomenon both in clinical practice and "out there in the world."

I contend that "the new affluence," the fact that the world my patients live in consists of large numbers of peers who have become very wealthy and who lead wealthy lifestyles, is instrumental to the activation of greed and envy. There is a wide gap between the "haves" and the "have-nots." I will limit myself to the issues of greed, envy, and "the new superego" as they pertain to matters of money and material possessions. I do not intend to address what they symbolize on a deeper, more unconscious level: love, the penis, the breast, the womb, etc. Papers published in edited volumes by Roth and Lemma (2008) and Wurmser and Jarass (2008) fully address these issues.

I have done an extensive review of the existing psychoanalytic literature on greed, envy, and the superego. Unlike the work of the ego psychologists on "the new ego," which adumbrated specific ego functions and how they could become arrested or problematic due to intrapsychic conflict, I have found the major papers on greed, envy and, especially, the superego, to be highly abstract, and nonspecific. It did not seem to matter *WHAT* the patient so greedily coveted or *Who* he envied or for *What*. Similarly with the concept of the punitive superego: it did not seem to matter *What* the superego selected to punish the patient for or *WHAT* kind of punishment was meted out.

The superego is supposed to perpetuate the culture. But *What Kind* of culture is it perpetuating? Manifest content for the most part has been disregarded and it is unclear as to how inferences about latent content were made. It has been my observation that the superego appears wearing a very different cloak from the days when Freud developed his theories of the mind.

Freud developed his theories about the superego over many years. In 1914 in "On Narcissism," he conceived of it as derived from the standards of behavior set by the parents and from parental criticism. In "The Ego and the Id" (1923) he saw it as formed from the repression of the Oedipus complex and as standing for conscience in its entirety. According to Loewald (1980):

> Insofar as the superego is the agency of inner standards, demands, ideals, hopes, and concerns in regard to the ego, the agency of inner rewards and punishments in respect to which the ego experiences contentment or guilt, the superego functions from the viewpoint of a future ego, from the standpoint of the ego's future that is to be reached, is being reached, is being failed or abandoned by the ego.

(p. 45)

As Lansky (2004) puts it so well, superego punishment is manifested in "self-defeating, self-harming, and self-sabotaging thought or action" (p. 15). We psychoanalysts were taught to assume that our patients had well-formed egos and to first analyze the harsh, punitive superego. We were not taught how to work with superegos that are weak or have lacunae. Those with superego lacunae were thought to be unanalyzable and/or untreatable.

The traditional definition of "superego" as consisting of the "conscience" and the "ego ideal" is based on a generalized model that is highly ethical, moral, and uniform. It has been my observation that "the new superego" is based on a different, more narcissistically based morality: for many in our culture today *attaining one's high ideal and even "goodness" is reached through physical exercise, diet, and fitness; it also comes from acquiring wealth.* It does not have to come from altruistic deeds or kindness to others or what has been traditionally regarded as "moral" behavior. The oft-heard expression "no pain, no gain" is used by trainers and physical therapists who have in many cases replaced psychotherapists as well as priests, ministers, and rabbis. Excessive exercise and self-starvation creating temporary or permanent damage to the body seems to me to be a 21st century replacement for the self-flagellation and fasting of yore.

When back in 1925, F. Scott Fitzgerald wrote in *The Great Gatsby* of the difference between the rich and others, he was referring to a hidden world of a privileged few that most people did not see or even read about in their daily lives. In recent years, the socioeconomic pie has been reconfigured. Not only are the rich getting richer, but there are many of them, and many of them are known to you and me. This has been well-documented (Frank, 2007; Sorkin, 2007). Even in the recent years of recession the media: *New York Times, The Wall Street Journal,* CNBC, have been replete with stories about 45 million dollar apartments, 50 million dollar paintings, and those who use their private jets to travel to their multiple homes. The newly rich hire an increasingly large army of experts to tell them where to donate their money and what to give to their children. In our major cities live large numbers of men and women in their 20s and 30s who have earned millions in financial arenas and in the better law firms; some have already retired. They inhabit the increasing number of high-end expensive coops and condos being built, eat in four and five star restaurants, and their indifference to any thrift or questioning of bills has driven the price of everything upward in the neighborhoods in which they live. The term "affluenza" has become part of our parlance. In these years in which our economy has been in difficulty, the gap has only widened.

There is a clear demarcation between these "haves" and the "have-nots" of their own age. At this moment of time, among the "have-nots" are the higher educated university professors, scholars, scientists, doctors, psychiatrists, psychoanalysts, and social workers: *ourselves and the bulk of those who we see in clinical practice*. Those among us who have in treatment a number of the "haves" privately complain to one another that our wealthier patients often present greater fee collection issues than those who do not have so much money. Some of our wealthy patients feel entitled because of their wealth to withhold and make us analysts out to be the greedy ones, anxious to collect our fees.

The *New York Times* article (Konigsberg, 2008) about a psychoanalyst who charged his wealthy patients US$600/hour (today this would be US$1,000/hour!), is an illustration of such a countertransference and greed-driven enactment. Frosch (2008) reminds us that Freud (1913) linked money with sex. Freud's loss of control around money influenced his technical position about fees and charging for missed sessions. Frosch's own experience around money and missed sessions leads him to believe that many analysts are filled with shame over being dependent upon their patients for their livelihood. I would add to this the shame that is felt in some cases when the analyst finds himself or herself in much more reduced financial circumstances than his or her patients. The potential for reduced circumstances of psychoanalysts who are dependent for their livelihood on patients who have lost or might lose their jobs has increased the potential for countertransference problems in these patients' treatment.

I will address some of the interrelations between the socioeconomic fact of the recent affluence, the activation of greed and envy and a new set of superego values, the contents of which are quite different from the values most psychoanalysts, including myself, hold. A degree of *concrete specification* is needed. I present clinical examples that are illustrative and make some speculations about a shift in child-rearing at the end of the 20th century that I believe has resulted in what we are finding in our clinical practices and observing in our personal lives today.

Kohut (1971) made a distinction between traditional "guilty man" around which Freudian psychoanalysis has been organized around and the more recent "tragic" "narcissistic man." The former has an internalized superego, formed as an outcome of the resolution of the Oedipus complex. Kohut believed that the central preoccupation of people today is not guilt or moral conflict, but boredom, and dissatisfaction. Traditional psychoanalysis has usually begun with a softening of the harsh, strict superego that punishes the person with unbearable feelings of guilt and depressive affect when he falls short of his ideals and values. *It is my observation that traditional superego definitions do not relate to a certain number of people today, some of whom are our patients.*

Greed and envy are on the short list of "the seven deadly sins" along with their companion's lust, gluttony, sloth, wrath, and pride. By contrast, in this age of "narcissistic man" and the recent affluence, we observe a lack of guilt over greed and envy, little apology for hurting others and/or the analyst and a history of a lack of consequences for bad behavior. The outgrowth of the "age of narcissism" is an "age of entitlement." Since this kind of behavior (formerly regarded as "misbehavior") has become so prevalent, and government figures no longer provide us with role models for "good behavior," it is not really possible to label those feeling "entitled" as "the Exceptions" (Freud, 1916; Kris, 1976; Blum, 2001). They are getting to be the norm!

I believe that such social change and a new social reality have had a strong impact on the psyches of our patients as well as ourselves. *I do not consider this to be "old wine in new bottles."* It is my thesis that what is intrapsychic can be stimulated and amplified by social reality. Waelder (1936) of course emphasized this point with his "principle of multiple function." His inclusion of "external reality," the outside world, as a force on the ego, on the psyche, is something I take quite seriously in my work. But what we call "the relevant social context" is seldom considered in our writings unless it is "early 20th century Vienna" or "the Holocaust." The state of the world post-1950 is taken for granted rather than examined as a causative factor.

A brief example will illustrate how times and my own view of the world have changed. About twenty years ago, a 40-year-old investment banker came into treatment with me. He lived in a Westchester suburb and commuted to the city for work. He discovered that his wife was having an affair with her trainer and that she had asked him for a divorce. He was especially upset about the potential sale of their home and the dividing up of his wealth. He cried because his daughter would no longer have a bowling alley, as they did in the basement of their house, and he was afraid that because of this she would no longer be popular with her friends at school. He believed strongly that with less money he could not possibly attract the kind of woman he desired—a physical "10." Despite my keen awareness of his inner narcissistic issues at that time I had difficulty imagining or relating to his world. It was difficult to feel empathic with this man in order to really help him. Twenty years later, the media, and what I have personally witnessed in my private life and have heard from my patients, have made it so that I can imagine it, although I am still as far from it in my own life financially and value-wise as I was then.

We psychoanalysts can no longer consider ourselves to be upper echelon earners, if we ever were. The realities of managed care, medication as a solution to dysphoria, a world in which people have little time for personal introspection, are some of the factors that have reduced the number of hours that we psychoanalysts can book. We psychoanalysts have good reason to worry about the future, particularly because of the recent economic collapse. Many of us use a certain amount of denial in order to not ruin our days (see Dimen, 1994; Josephs, 2004). Furthermore, psychoanalysts' ability to accrue any wealth is limited by the number of hours we work. (I am not referring to those who have been born into or have married into wealth.) Psychoanalytic patients who are in many other fields have had real opportunities to amass wealth. Some have had no wish to do so. And some, due to neurotic reasons, do not do so, even when they consciously wish to do so. Warner (1991) has addressed this topic quite frontally. He asserts that such situations have potential for serious countertransference acting out. He notes that:

> most analysts have middle-class origins. They may share in the frequently found middle-class covert hatred or envy of the rich ... To cover it up the analyst can either show a reaction formation and be excessively ingratiating or act out this hostility by putting down the rich patient.
>
> (p. 590)

Dimen (1994) in her thoughtful paper on money reminds us that Freud referred to his wealthy patients as "goldfish"!

Josephs (2004), in a similarly thoughtful article, has observed that: "It is increasingly assumed that being a psychoanalyst in the United States can no longer consistently provide for the attainment of the current normative American standard of middle class affluence" (p. 391). He, like myself, has seen a number of young patients who do not know what to do with themselves, are irresponsible, and who are reliant on their parents to support the treatment. They are envious of his fee. Their parents regularly inquire why the patient needs to go more than once/week. Others have parents who will not give them any money. Josephs remarks that: "These patients are barely on speaking terms with their parents" (p. 400). A few months ago a woman patient from Argentina told me that she became so angry with her mother who was visiting for a week because she felt she could not afford to buy her an apartment in the West Village that she could not talk to her mother for days.

Most of us who conduct psychoanalysis rely intrapsychically on inner values and are sustained more by the quality of our relationships and experiences than we are by material things. (There are exceptions, of course!) We pretty much accept and make the best of our lot in life. To what extent should our personal values be expressed to patients with different value systems? In a world in which those who "go for the money" are more valued than we ourselves, do we do our patients a disservice if we attempt overtly, or more likely, covertly, to shape them according to the way *we* are? To those of us who have supported ourselves since we were in our 20s, adults who feel entitled to parental financial assistance and refuse to work seem disturbed and are disturbing to us. Today, women who insist that their husbands support them and refuse to work seem also to be disturbed, or at least greedy, and spoiled. But one can ask whether they are just coming with another set of cultural values. I believe that these are important issues for us to ponder.

The 1980s were a great time on Wall Street. In Oliver Stone's film by that name, the main character, Gordon Gekko, declared that: "Greed is good. Greed works, greed is right, greed clarifies, cuts through and captures the essence of the revolutionary spirit." A new era was launched. Those born between 1960 and 1980 grew up with a new value system. It was a time of prosperity in which there was also much self-examination. (In our field too, Freud was dissected, and deconstructed, and parts of his theory reassembled by Kohut, Kernberg, Greenberg and Mitchell, and others). Whatever was previously considered to be sacred was challenged: the Vietnam War, the institution of marriage, and in particular, gender roles. When I began my practice in the mid-seventies, antimaterialism, *The Greening of America*, autonomy and self-sufficiency were valued (Reich, 1970). It was a time of feminist uprising: mothers went back to school, back to work, and some divorced. For a longtime there was little or no back-up mothering. Unlike today, when we have in place an army of professional caregivers and excellent daycare centers, the parenting many children received was uneven at least. Latchkey children were met at the end of the day by mothers too tired to give them needed attention. Mothers and fathers felt guilty that their children had two parents working. Some were guilty that their children had to witness divorce and live in two different places. Misusing psychological and psychoanalytic advice and expertise, they often tolerated the excessive demands of their children, many of whom we are seeing as adults in analysis and therapy today.

Let me fast-forward to the first decade of the 21st century. The kind of separation-individuation most of us worked at in our youth and worked at 20 or 30 years ago with our patients is no longer desired. (Freud too, unwillingly, left Brucke's lab when Brucke told him to "get practical." He was engaged and had to earn a living! [Makari, 2008]). Today, many families are more often or not enmeshed. Children, adolescents, and grown children dominate their parents, who are fearful that their children will hate them and/or especially, abandon them. Whereas in the 1970s "terrorist" adolescents or "twenty-somethings" were involved in political causes, in this decade "terrorist" adolescents and "twenty-somethings" demand money and material things from their parents. We have in our practices young adults who were both emotionally deprived and overindulged at the same time. I have coined the term "masked deprivation" to describe what I have witnessed: material things are provided, but not the kind of psychological attunement needed for children to develop optimally. Many young adults today do not have the necessary ego strength and frustration tolerance to seek work that will support them. They observe their friends' parents supporting them, buying them apartments, and finding them jobs, and partners. They do not leave home even when they have physically left home and are tied to their parents all day long by cell phones, BlackBerrys, or iPhones. I have seen in my clinical practice, as well as in my private life, the seduction, and courting of young married couples, who are taken by the parents of one member of the couple on expensive vacations, promised country houses near these parents, and many other luxuries in an effort to keep the family together and in some cases to see that the *other* family does not get to see the couple or their future children as much.

All the more problematic for psychoanalytic treatment, the parents often pay for and thus, compromise, or try to control the treatment. In his paper on the children of wealthy parents, Warner (1991) noted that: "their sense of reality can become distorted because if they get in trouble they know they will always be 'bailed out' and never have to face the consequences of their actions as others do" (p. 579). They externalize, get their doctors to tell them what they want to hear. "Another significant transference problem is the attempted seduction of the analyst through the affluent patient's money, charm or power" (p. 590) (see also Rothstein, 1986). As we know, Freud himself was not immune to this as he sought funds to support his psychoanalytic endeavors. As Kirsner (2007) in his paper entitled "'Do as I say, not as I do': Ralph Greenson, Anna Freud, and superrich patients" has noted, Greenson, who wrote a Bible of proper technique, not only stretched the boundaries with Marilyn Monroe, but with a number of superrich patients.

At this juncture I want to make the point that the majority of those I work with, whose parents were able to cut emotional and financial umbilical cords when they graduated from college, do not seem to be plagued by these issues. They found jobs, and if they have conflicts in work or love, these are not encumbered by envy or greed. I can describe them as having *fiber*, moral fiber, something that seems to be lacking in the ever-increasing number of patients I am speaking about. They have reasonable mature superegos and suffer from failure to live up to overly idealistic and unrealistic ego-ideals. Those with "the new superego" on the other hand, often were sexually active at a much earlier age, sleeping with their partners in their parents' houses. If they were lazy, rude to their parents, or teachers, there were little, or no consequences. Their parents (and their culture) set the bar for good behavior at a very different level from that of previous generations.

Despite the considerable advances women have made in the world at large, some of my young women patients seem to be in particular difficulty. Overgratification and prolonged dependency on parents has resulted in their limited acquisition of basic skills for functioning independently: cooking, furnishing a home, purchasing clothing, and paying bills. We have a generation of young women who hire lactation specialists to help them to nurse, specialists to plan weddings, wrap gifts, set tables, choose colors for rooms, personal shoppers to choose a wardrobe and create their "style," and personal assistants to do it all. Spas have multiplied as this generation demands constant soothing and massaging of every part of their bodies as a way of coping with poor anxiety tolerance, the end result of the combination of early over-gratification and neglect. Coupled with the expectation that they have successful careers and gorgeous homes is the social expectation that they look perfect and have perfect bodies, requiring hours at the gym and rigorous dieting, further reducing their energy. When I hear about this day after day I long nostalgically for the days of *The Greening of America* (Reich, 1970) in the late 1960s and early 1970s, when Dr. Spock advised future parents that they could put the new baby in a dresser drawer if they could not yet afford a crib. A far cry from the designer furniture every newborn has to have today. Part of "the new superego" admonitions is that newborns be provided with the best of everything or their parents will or should feel guilty.

Some of the young men I have seen in my practice have suffered from having had parents who were often absent when they needed them, but now as young adults expect them to achieve. They are watched over like hawks, and at the first sign of faltering, their parents take over, writing applications to colleges for them, making phone calls, and pulling strings to get them into jobs. These efforts are not private, but public, and the young men exchange the shame of potential failure for the shame of letting their parents take over. One male patient, 45 years old, spent hours on the phone with his mother, who counseled every minute of his business deal hoping that his business success would take him off the dole. It was my contention that the exact opposite effect would occur.

Greed

At this juncture one might ask just what is greed and what makes an analyst think that his patient is greedy? The assessment of greed from manifest content is problematic because it is so culture- and value system-specific. "Affluence" is also culture-specific. I recall a supervisor of mine in the early 1970s calling a patient of mine "greedy" because she and her friends celebrated her birthday at an expensive restaurant. I assessed this as finally "letting herself have things!" Paradoxically when I needed another control case this same supervisor referred to me as suitable for analysis an educated young man who arrived wearing a t-shirt that said "OUTRAGEOUS." He hoped to pay me US$5/session and to come 4 days/week. He was a graduate student who was about to marry a wealthy woman. Her father was paying for their honeymoon doing the Grand Tour of Europe and staying in five star hotels and had also purchased an apartment for them. He had no plans to work for years.

What happens in the treatment when the analyst's personal values, the analyst's notions of what is right or wrong, differ from those of the patient? It creates a complication in the analysis that must be thought about on an ongoing basis. It is difficult to work with sensitivity without seeming judgmental.

One woman patient Helen, came to treatment because of her over-spending many thousands of dollars every month on clothing she did not need but was desperate for. When she walked in the street and she saw a woman better dressed than she, wearing some stylish article of clothing she had not thought to purchase, she suffered a panic attack due to the intensity of her envy. She could not rest until she had purchased a similar item. The sudden realization that she had the wrong point on her boots or handle on last year's handbag would send her into a panic, which was then followed by a shopping spree to try to set things right.

Helen was particularly susceptible to the selling techniques of a luxury department store personal shopper. No amount of analysis, e.g., asking her about her thoughts, fantasies, and moods just prior to a shopping spree, could enable her to check her desire. She was conscious of worrying that her spending was putting too much pressure on her husband and that he might die. She was unable to access her unconscious death wish toward him. Her husband (whom I suspected of having an affair) was unable to assist in her curbing her expenditures either. I surmised that he tolerated it due to his own guilt, but perhaps he was as greedy as she was, since in some couples one member of the pair acts as the agent for the other's less conscious desires.

Helen reminded me of Joan Riviere's (1932) patient for whom "*all pleasures for her must be acquired and enjoyed at some other person's expense*" (p. 198) purchasing expensive clothes so as to deprive her husband and children. Riviere discovered that under the jealousy of her patient, who needed a triangle in which to operate, lay a "dominant phantasy." She had to seize or obtain from some other person something he desired, thus robbing, and despoiling him.

The countertransference pitfalls when working with such a patient are obvious. Steiner (2008), in a recent paper, has noted:

> the enormous pressure on the analyst to take sides in an argument in which the moral aspects of the situation come to the fore ... we tend to step into a superego role which conforms to the patient's internal superego as it has been projected into us.
>
> (p. 45)

For another patient Eleanor, immersed in the world of "affluenza," eating large numbers of sweets did make her feel very guilty, but the other behaviors did not. Her closets were so filled with the clothes that she had purchased at bargain prices that she had to rent storage space to contain some of them. The contents of her superego were very different from my own. Greed as a sin originally had to do with gluttony. In today's world, overeating is a sin whereas purchasing four houses is a subject for admiration. The Duchess of Windsor's motto: "You cannot be too rich or too thin!" has become a superego injunction.

Envy

Josephs (2004) writes: "it is vastly underreported in the clinical literature how much session time college-educated professional patients, especially in New York City, spend ventilating their financial insecurities" (p. 390). I have had similar observations. In my practice I hear patients express envy of their wealthy parents (with Oedipal overtones), successful siblings, friends, colleagues, and neighbors.

A number of my patients are chronically envious of me. Their envy serves as a chronic resistance and at times leads to a negative therapeutic reaction. They envy my fee, my professional standing, where my office is located, etc. When there is a genuine difference between my material reality as seen and that of the patient's, it makes it difficult to help the patient to observe the transferential aspect of her reactions. When I first began my practice, I worked with a young married professional woman who seemed to admire me as a potential role model. She was very limited in what she did other than her work and had never been out of New York. One August, the session before my vacation, she casually inquired where I was going. In spite of everything I had been taught I told her that I was going to Russia, hoping to inspire her to stretch her own geographical boundary. In September she returned and told me she was terminating. If I had been to Russia that meant I had been everywhere else and that she was too envious to work with me. There was no talking her out of this and I never saw her again. What I hoped for as a positive identification was totally naive. At that moment I became aware of the destructive and often hidden envy that can stumble any treatment. And why an anonymous stance is usually the best one to take! When thinking about this, years later, I believe that I had unconsciously participated in her inner world's need for an object she could be envious of and destroy.

The *Random House American Dictionary* (Block et al., 1968) defines envy as a "feeling of discontent or mortification, usually with ill will at seeing another's superiority, advantages or success" (p. 402). Laplanche and Pontalis (1973) do not list greed in their compendium and they reference envy as limited to penis envy. (Freud wrote often of jealousy and less about envy, which he too limited to penis envy placing it in the phallic phase.) But they worked and observed in times different from ours. For Freud, envy was a cognitive event, whereas for Klein it was first an affect and then linked with a perception. Klein noted the confusion between envy and jealousy. Envy is the earlier and more primitive affect. She (1957) defined envy as:

> the angry feeling that another person possesses and enjoys something desirable—the envious impulse being to take it away or to spoil it. Moreover, envy implies the subject's relation to one person only and goes back to the earliest exclusive relationship with the mother.
>
> (p. 181)

Klein agreed with Abraham's idea that envy is oral-sadistic and anal-sadistic. She conceived of primary envy of the breast that is constitutional and that does not have to do with frustration (Roth & Lemma, 2008) As part of the death instinct there is envy of the breast's "intolerable goodness." Envy arises at the moment when "good" is "not-me."

Klein (1957) viewed "greed as mainly bound up with introjection and envy with projection." Kaplan's (1991) reading of Klein is that:

in greed, as contrasted with envy, there is much less recognition of the object and the focus is on possession and supplies. On an unconscious oral level, greed aims to suck out and devour the breast, essentially robbing it of its possessions. While envy has this aim, it additionally seeks to put bad parts of the self into the mother/breast. In this sense greed relates more to introjection and devouring mechanisms while envy is closely associated with spoiling aspects.

(p. 512)

Whichever comes first developmentally, I have observed a close connection between greed and envy. Clinically I have observed greed to be born out of envy. The envious feel empty. As they approach getting what they want, they become so greedy that they destroy it. Boris (1990) has noted that: "the conversion of greed into appetite is an event of the first importance. Appetite ... is susceptible to satisfaction. Greed is not. In greed ... *any gratification only further stimulates the greed* [emphasis added]" (p. 130). According to Klein (1957):

another defense against envy is closely linked with greed. By *internalizing* the breast so *greedily* that in the infant's mind it becomes entirely his possession and controlled by him, he feels that all he attributes to it will be his own. This is used to counteract envy.

(p. 218)

Spillius (1993) concurs: "Greedy acquisition can be a defense against being aware of envy of those who are what one wishes one had or were oneself" (p. 1199).

Margery

With the following vignette taken from the 4 times-weekly psychoanalysis of Margery I will try to demonstrate the inter-connections between greed, envy, and the superego: Margery presented with many issues, both on a neurotic level and on a character disordered level. She was self-reflective and conscientious, an excellent patient. I just present here the severest of her character pathology in order to illustrate clinical manifestations of envy, greed, and the superego.

Margery lied on her resume, cheated on her expense sheet, and abused salespeople, and employees. She shoplifted as a teenager, and her mother seemed as if she did not notice that Margery had a continual change of new clothes. She envied her sisters and most of her friends. Each and every one had all the things she wanted and felt deprived of. She stole small things from the apartments of one of her sisters and a greatly envied friend. For many years, the only way she was able to be with me in the room was to regard me as a "nothing," having nothing she wanted. Although she spent many of her hours speaking of her envy of various figures in her life with whom she would become obsessed, when I inquired from time to time, she told me that she had no thoughts about me when she left her sessions. She averted her gaze entering and leaving my office, never looking at me. I analyzed her sadism, her aggression gone amuck in her life outside my office. The transference was for the most part displaced.

Margery had no man in her life for many years. When one year a kind man from her past came on the scene and confessed that he had secretly been in love with her in college, her sadism, and greed re-emerged. She made outrageous demands of him, that he buy her jewelry, that he take her to expensive resorts, and that she would only fly first class. He became hostile, and then exploded with rage at her. They broke up and she was back to square one.

Margery grew up in a wealthy suburb of Chicago. As she described it, her mother was unresponsive to her real needs and her father was preoccupied with his business. Her parents were "keeping up with the Joneses," decorating and redecorating their home and taking fancy trips. Thus, her parents both served as greedy identification figures. In a dream of the first year in analysis she pictured her mother as a whale: "There was this big fat whale with fins on it. I was holding onto one and someone else to the other. Someone was jabbing a large point into it—maybe me." Her associations:

> The whale is my mother, me attacking her and her attacking me. She eats everyone up around her. I hate her enough to kill her. I feel like my whole body is filled with anger and hatred—a limitless well. I feel so much hatred it could kill me rather than her.

When treatment began, Margery did not want to work. She held a series of low level jobs while waiting for a man to come along and support her. Once when out of a job she remarked how tired it made her to respond to "want" ads at night. When questioning her why she did not do that in the morning when she was feeling fresh, she snarled: "I don't do mornings. I go to the gym in the morning." Margery's unhappiness was palpable and her mother tried to pacify her by buying her a television, clothes, and a fur coat. Nothing worked. She spent her weekends in department stores and when she had worked up a large debt managed to persuade her father to pay it off. The Oedipal implications of this scenario were not lost on me—Margery wanted what her mother had. Her failures and her guilty self-flagellation (for not having married a wealthy man as did her sisters, for not having a perfect body) seemed to be less from punishment of a structured superego than an unconscious beating fantasy used by sadomaso-chistic patients (Novick & Novick, in Wurmser, 2004).

In her treatment she would not permit me to talk very much. "Let me finish … you are interrupting … it's my session … I am paying you to listen." But she was "hungry" for her sessions, came exactly on time 4 times/week for years. At times, working with her felt like being in a lion's cage. If I moved close she could bite me. The envious person cannot take as if taking would be a gift to the giver. (Cairo-Chiardini, 2001) Her sense of inner emptiness was profound. At times, Margery cried in pain that she was so lonesome: she had no friends and was not close to her family. Both sisters had married wealthy men and her mother preferred them to her.

Despite the emotional difficulties of working with her, requiring constant monitoring of the countertransference, I was engaged in the treatment because I saw positive gains in certain areas. Within two years of one another, each of her parents died, and they were no longer available to give her material things. Their enabling her pathology ceased with their deaths. Margery started a small business that grew and grew and she began to have interactions with a wide range of interesting people. Her self-reflection increased and she developed a sharp sense of humor. She began to travel and go to museums and concerts. She did, however, continue to abuse her underlings (a displacement from the transference among other things). She greedily overworked them so that eventually they would sabotage the work or leave her. She was periodically nasty to me and her response when confronted was: "I pay you, so I can do what I want with you." This abated over several years of reflecting back to her what she was doing with me. I began to receive apologetic phone calls after such episodes, which I regarded as a psychological advance.

Concluding remarks

Conducting psychoanalytic treatment with today's greedy and envious patients is a considerable challenge when the content of the psychoanalyst's superego—the notions of right and wrong, the ideals, and values—are so very different from theirs. The countertransference must be monitored on an ongoing basis so that the psychoanalyst does not give into the temptation to say: "You are greedy," or "You are envious," "What makes you think that your father should pay your rent?" or "You should not treat your sister so badly because she has just become engaged." These patients are quite provocative and the analyst must resist the temptation to retaliate. They are also narcissistically quite fragile and keep a tentative attachment to the treatment and to the analyst. On the other hand, the analyst must also not hang back with stony silence, detaching from the patient with sanctimonious disapproval. These patients are in treatment because they are suffering, feel empty, and are trying to fill themselves up with what does not fulfill.

I have had some success when I ask the patient to anticipate the reality consequences of his behavior. "What do you think will happen if you do this?" I have asked: "How do you think (your sister) feels when you say that?" "Does that matter to you?" I have remarked: "It might bother another person to come late for dinner at her sister's house. It does not seem to bother you. How come?" That is, I work with greed, and envy by asking the patient to think about his actions and his thoughts, fostering a capacity for self-reflection. My stance is neutral and empathic. I have also, when material possessions are so coveted, learned to stay with the concreteness and not attempt to ask what the coveted leather chair stands for or the desired coop apartment means on a symbolic level. By staying with the concreteness I have found that within time, sometimes many years, these patients feel attuned to and the narcissistic repair effected by the treatment enables them to eventually think on a more symbolic, metaphoric level (see Lieberman, 2000). Working with greed, envy, and superego that appear in dreams and in the displaced transference further enables these patients to face themselves and to reflect on themselves.

My description of these patients might lead the reader to think of it as a judgmental rant. It does contain some of my frustration working with them as well as with the predominant materialism of our times. I struggle as I listen to them with their maladjustment. I question what would make for optimal "adjustment" to our culture. What is a "healthy" conscience? What is a healthy, reasonable "ego ideal"? I examine my own superego, its conscious aspects. I was trained with the adage: "Where id was, there ego shall be; where superego was, there ego shall be." The id today seems to have obtained more supremacy in the psyche as it is allied with "the new superego." Again, the "new superego" insists that one exercise, diet, focus on the body, and its appearance, and amass material possessions, and wealth. Profound states of loneliness and emptiness seem to be the outcome along with increased reliance on mood-altering drugs, legal and illegal, as well as alcohol.

I wonder what Freud would think about our times? At the end of his life he spoke about the superego's acting:

> the role of an external world toward the ego, although it has become part of the internal world. During the whole of a man's later life it represents the influence of his childhood, of the care and education given to him by his parents, of his dependence on them—of the childhood which is so greatly prolonged in human beings by a common family life. And in all of this what is operating is not only the personal qualities of the parents but also everything that produced a determining effect upon them themselves, the tastes and standards of the social class in which they live and the characteristics and traditions of the race from which they spring.
>
> (Freud, 1940, pp. 122–123)

Would Freud think the tastes and standards of these times to be allied with the death instinct he was so pessimistic about? Or would he see the psychoanalyst as the combatant of false and shallow values and possibly a conqueror?

Note

1 This chapter first appeared as Chapter 4, "Analyzing a 'New Superego': Greed and envy in the Recent Age of Affluence," in *Money Talks: In Therapy, Society, and Life* edited by Brenda Berger and Stephanie Newman, Routledge, 2012. Reprinted by permission of Taylor & Francis, LLC.

References

Bloch, B., Bloomfield, L., Fries, C., Cabell Greet, W., Lorge, I., & Malone, K. (Eds.) (1968). *The Random House American dictionary and family reference library.* New York: Random House.

Blum, H. (2001). The "exceptions" reviewed: The formation and deformation of the privileged character. *Psychoanalytic Study of the Child, 56,* 123–136.

Boris, H. N. (1990). Identification with a vengeance. *International Journal of Psychoanalysis, 71,* 127–140.

Dimen, M. (1994). Money, love and hate: Contradictions and paradox in psychoanalysis. *Psychoanalytic Dialogues, 4*(1), 69–100.

Fitzgerald, F. S. (1925). *The great gatsby.* New York: Scribner Classics.

Frank, R. H. (2007). *Falling behind: How rising inequality harms the middle class.* New York: Basic Books.

Freud, S. (1913). On beginning the treatment. *S.E.* 12.

Freud, S. (1914). On narcissism. *S.E.* 14.

Freud, S. (1916). Some character-types met with in psycho-analytic work. *S.E.* 14, 309–333.

Freud, S. (1923). *The ego and the id.* Strachey, J. (1960) trans. J. Riviere. New York: W. W. Norton & Co.

Freud, S. (1940). An outline of psychoanalysis. *S.E.* 23.

Frosch, A. (2008). Discussion at panel on money. The New York Psychoanalytic Institute. 5/8/08.

Josephs, L. (1994). *Seduced by affluence: How material envy strains the analytic relationship.* The William Alanson White Institute, 389–408.

Kaplan, H. (1991). Greed: A psychoanalytic perspective. *Psychoanalytic Review, 78,* 505–523.

Kirsner, D. (2007). "Do as I say, not as I do": Ralph Greenson, Anna Freud, and superrich patients. *Psychoanalytic Psychology, 24*(3), 475–486.

Klein, M. (1957). *Envy and gratitude: A study of unconscious sources.* London: Tavistock Press.

Kohut, H. (1971). *The analysis of the self: A systematic appraisal of the psychoanalytic treatment of narcissistic personalities.* New York: International Universities Press.

Konigsberg, E. (2008, July 7). Challenges of $600-a-session patients. *New York Times.*

Kris, A. (1976). On wanting too much: The "exceptions" revisited. *International Journal of Psycho-analysis, 57*(1–2), 89–95.

Lansky, M. (2004). Conscience and the project of a psychoanalytic science of human nature: A clarification of the usefulness of the superego concept. *Psychoanalytic Inquiry, 24*(2), 151–174.

Laplanche, J., & Pontalis, J.-B. (1973). *The language of psychoanalysis.* New York: W. W. Norton.

Lieberman, J. S. (2000). *Body talk: Looking and being looked at in psychotherapy* Northvale, N.J.: Jason Aronson, Inc.

Loewald, H. W. (1980). Superego and time. In H. W. Loewald, *Papers on psychoanalysis* (pp. 43–52). New Haven and London: Yale University Press.

Makari, G. (2008). *Revolution in mind: The creation of psychoanalysis.* New York: Harper Collins.

Reich, C. A. (1970). *The greening of America.* New York: Random House.

Riviere, J. (1991). Jealousy as a mechanism of defence. In A. Hughes (Ed.), *The inner world and Joan Riviere: Collected papers 1920–1958* (pp. 104–115). London: Karnac (Books) Ltd.

Roth, P., & Lemma, A. (2008). *Envy and gratitude revisited*. London: The International Psychoanalytic Association.

Sorkin, A. R. (2007, December 6). A movie and protesters single out Henry Kravis. *New York Times*, C4.

Spillius, E. (1993). Varieties of envious experience. *International Journal of Psychoanalysis, 74*(6), 1199–1212.

Steiner, J. S. (2008). Transference to the analyst as an excluded observer. *International Journal of Psychoanalysis, 89*(1), 39–54.

Waelder, R. (1936). The principle of multiple function: Observations on over-determination. *Psychoanalytic Quarterly, 5*, 45–62.

Warner, S. L. (1991). Psychoanalytic understanding and treatment of the very rich. *Journal of the American Academy of Psychoanalysis, 19*(4), 578–594.

Wurmser, L. (Ed.) (2004). The superego: A vital or supplanted concept? *Psychoanalytic Inquiry, 24*(2), 141–339.

Wurmser, L., & Jarass, H. (Eds.) (2008). *Jealousy and envy: New views about two powerful feelings*. New York and London: The Analytic Press.

Chapter 2

Lies and omissions in psychoanalytic treatment[1]

The psychodynamics of patients who lie to their analysts in psychoanalytic treatment have not as yet been examined thoroughly, despite what seems to be the substantial incidence of such behaviors on the part of some of our patients. Analysts usually trust that they are being told the conscious truth and willingly suspend disbelief as they struggle to make sense of their patients' narratives. If they did not do so, their work would be almost impossible to conduct. Although lies are expected of psychopaths, as Weinshel (1979) has written:

> there is a comparable "expectation" that the so-called neurotic, healthier patient will not lie deliberately to the analyst, and the idea that the patient will be assiduously "truthful" with the analyst is a more or less commonly accepted element of the analytic relationship.
>
> (p. 504)

Freud (1937) instructs analysts that "we must not forget that the relationship between analyst and patient is based on a love of truth, that is, on the acknowledgement of reality, and that it precludes any kind of sham or deception" (p. 266).

Yet, Freud himself reported a number of lies and lying dreams that were told to him by his own patients (1913, 1920). In *Two Lies Told by Children* (1913), he writes of a case in which a woman's boastful lies masked her feelings about a disappointing father, presenting him to the world falsely as supremely effective. Admitting her deceptions would have been tantamount to admitting her hidden incestuous love. In fact, themes of lying and gullibility are to be found throughout the history of psychoanalysis. The first psychoanalysts in Vienna initially believed that their patients were lying about being seduced as children. And Masson (1984) essentially calls Freud a liar for suppressing the truth about the real seductions of his patients so as to further the acceptance of his theories about the importance of internal fantasy. Eissler's trusting attitude toward Masson, who betrayed him, illustrates the extraclinical gullibility of at least one noted analyst (Malcolm, 1983a, 1983b).

I define conscious lying as Fenichel (1939) did: "an untruth in which the subject himself did intend to deceive others with his assertions and did not believe the assertion himself" (pp. 130–131). The kind of lie to be discussed here is entirely *conscious* and *intended.*

In their excellent review of the psychological and psychiatric literature on lying, Ford and colleagues (1988) summarize a myriad of reasons for telling lies: to maintain autonomy, to hurt others, to avoid hurting others, to avoid humiliation, or punishment, to gain love, to gain power, to create a better story, and so on. Although the consensus is that, in general, lying is pathological; it can be adaptive in certain instances and may have originated as an adaptation to a pathological situation. Tausk (1933), for one, notes an adaptive function of the lie:

> Until the child has been successful in its first lie, the parents are supposed to know everything, even its most secret thoughts. The striving for the right to have secrets from which the parents are excluded is one of the most important factors in the formation of the ego, especially in the establishing and carrying out of one's own will.
>
> (p. 456)

The psychoanalytic literature to date contains references to psychopathic lying and to lying that supposedly emanates from patients' unresolved conflicts organized at the oedipal phase of development. Lies are treated as defensive phenomena. Fenichel (1939) likewise understands the economics of "pseudologia fantastica" to be a warding off of the knowledge of instinctual events. The liar thinks, "As I now take in others, so it may be that I was only taken in when I saw what I was afraid was true" (p. 137). He reports the case of a woman patient, a compulsive masturbator who was fearful of burglars and murderers. Her lies consisted mostly of sexual and self-glorifying boasts. For example, as a child, she lied to her teacher that her class was planning to attack her and that she had seen a ghost. The psychogenesis of her lies was found to be based in having heard horror stories from the family cook. She focused on these stories instead of her own primal scene fantasies. Her father had long talks with her that resulted in her sexualization of talking. Her mother shielded her and helped her ignore reality. In this paper, Fenichel attributes the nonspecific gratuitous lies of the obsessional patient to a substitution of small *changes* and omissions for unconsciously wished for much *greater changes.*

One classical position has been that lying about general matters at large symbolizes specific lies about the genitals. When Mack Brunswick's (1943) male patient accused her of lying, it was as if he were saying, "It is not I who need to deny the facts, but you. And you must deny them for me, for I cannot bear the fact that you 'have no penis' " (p. 461).

Weinshel (1979) interprets the lies of neurotic patients as enabling them to reenact aspects of the oedipal conflict. Pregenital factors are present but not considered by him to be essential. The lies permit partial recovery of old memories and unconscious fantasies, in some cases screening oedipal and primal scene fantasies. One patient's lie was that she had "nothing" to say, which covered over certain sexual secrets. One such secret was related to her fantasy that the analyst had a crush on her. She felt her parents had lied to her when her mother told her that she and her father were speaking about "nothing," which she equated with their sexual secrets. Another patient circulated little lies about the analyst: that he never said anything, that he said too much, that he told funny stories, that he wore outlandish clothes. Some were partly true, others not. She involved Weinshel in a lengthy analysis of a symptom, of the meaning of a genital itch, and then revealed to him that she had lied about the date of its onset and had distorted other data so as to mis-lead him. Weinshel understood the genesis of her lie as related to fetishism and negation wherein the lie negates the truth. His theory of lies thus, stresses the centrality of fantasies about genital sexuality.

In Blum's (1983) famous case, a male patient about to begin an analysis phoned him and said he could not get to the initial session because "my mother died and I will be in touch with you after the funeral." The patient recontacted Blum a year and a half later to begin treatment and admitted that he had told Blum a lie. His mother was still alive, although his father had died when he was 10. Blum wondered whether this patient was analyzable, but decided to commence the analysis because a preponderance of factors spoke in favor of analyzability. Blum's classic oedipal phase-centered analysis reveals multiple meanings of the lie. For one, it reveals the lie to be an unconscious confession of matricidal wishes as well as an ambivalent identification with a depressed, withdrawn mother. It enables the patient to deny the oedipally charged memory of his father's death. Blum also understands the lie as a sadomasochistic provocation, aimed at deriding him, and making him out to be a fool. Related also are feelings about the patient's mother's colitis. As a child, he often found excrement on the floor when she could not get to the bathroom on time. Her incontinence was met by silence and shame in the family. She also gave herself and the patient enemas. Blum writes that one of the meanings of the lie is "a repetition of the enema trauma, a submission to the therapeutic process followed by defying and deceiving me with the pseudo-production of 'bull shit.' As a fecal object, the lie was 'living shit' and dead loss" (p. 24), a fleeing from homosexual submission. The patient had an inconsistent superego, failed to master traumatic states, and was burdened by separation-individuation issues.

This patient's history and development were typical of deceptive patients. That is, in deception sadomasochism is prominent, anal fixations are important, superego development is sporadic, and identifications with deceptive parents occur frequently. More recently, work done by object relations theorists call into question the higher developmental level previously attributed to patients who deceive the analyst. O'Shaughnessy (1990) argues that these patients are organized at more primitive levels:

> Because it presents itself in speech, lying must seem to be a relatively mature pathology. Analytic investigation reveals, however, that the fundamental

problem the habitual liar is bringing to analysis by lying is primitive, and primarily involves not the truth and falsity of propositions but the truth and falsity of his objects, their genuineness or deceitfulness.

(p. 187)

The important roles of separation-individuation, preoedipal conflict, fixations at the oral and anal phases of development, and failure of ego integration in the genesis of lying must be emphasized. Those who lie to their analysts do not seem to have a particularly high level of ego and superego structural development, even though the content itself may be at times oedipal. That is, many turn out to be more primitive in structure and function than they may seem initially. The illustrative examples of this early ego pathology, which follow, are drawn from two cases in which patients in psychoanalytic psychotherapy lied to the analyst. Conscious lying to the analyst can be diagnostic of severe pathology. Better integrated patients, more suitable for classical analysis, usually suppress, and repress, rather than omit, and lie about what is too painful to admit.

O'Shaughnessy (1990) reports several cases in which she became involved in chaotic transferences in which the patient experienced her as her lying mother who could not mother properly. One patient asked to change the time of his session because he supposedly needed to meet the plane of a cousin who was flying to his city. In a subsequent session, this excuse then changed to needing to meet the sister of an old friend who was coming for an abortion and then to the sister of an old friend who had only one leg! The analyst's feeling of being provoked by these lies was additionally exacerbated by her discovery that her patient had given her a false address and phone number. He told her that he did not want to be "rung up and told there was no session." O'Shaughnessy (1990) documents the sadomasochistic gratification of such patients, who experienced her interpretations as beatings. Lies have also been understood as having as their underpinnings fantasies of sexual revenge, as they facilitate the discharge of sadomasochistic impulses. The liar experiences considerable excitement in the telling of lies, in getting away with it, in being found out, in telling more lies, and in the subsequent threat of punishment.

The lie is aimed directly at the one being lied to. It is of course aimed consciously and unconsciously at other figures as well.

The patient who lies makes certain assumptions about the analyst's vulnerability and gullibility. He or she may assume, for example, that analysts are more concerned with the genesis of distorted perceptions and less with the kinds of cues others use to assess a person's character. But it is mainly the nature of the work and the work ethos that predisposes analysts to a vulnerable gullibility. Various conditions of the analytic situation foster vulnerability to deception, such as the requirement for adopting multiple perspectives.

Analysts' gullibility can be supported by the belief that they possess special knowledge of what goes on in others' minds. Farber (1975) has written that:

one of the curiosities of gnostic certainty is that it renders the believer so gullible. There are psychoanalysts who will believe absolutely anything a patient tells them about himself provided it is sufficient testimony to his morbid or pathological condition.

(p. 23)

The gullibility of the analyst is a special form of gullibility that is not necessarily pathological, but is related more to the life experiences, personality structure, and professional requirements of those who become analysts. The analyst's gullibility is based on the nature of the analytic task, which is to suspend disbelief. It can also be based upon a lack of personal experience with liars and with lying, for the better integrated analyst may lack an internal frame of reference to permit a quick and easy grasp of the sadomasochism or the lack of trust of the patient who lies. Nor can most analysts really understand from inside themselves why such patients lie to them, especially when their lies are gratuitous. The analyst usually does not have an inner frame of reference enabling him or her to really empathize with such patients in their efforts to sabotage the treatment. Instead, he or she must understand the genesis and meaning of their lies from a strictly intellectual framework.

The following case material illustrates some of these points about both the lying patient and the gullible analyst. The lies told to the analyst in our examples seem to be innocuous when compared with the egregious lies cited by Weinshel (1979), Blum (1983), and O'Shaughnessy (1990), and they might even be construed as part of the psychopathology of everyday practice. They proved, however, in each patient, to be reflective of problems, of splits in the ego and superego, and of other serious pathology that had not been addressed in the early phases of treatment, before they were sufficiently understood.

Miss Alexander, a marginally anorexic-bulimic woman, was in a twice-weekly psychoanalytic psychotherapy with a relatively inexperienced analyst. The patient was charming, attractive, and bright, but she suffered greatly from low self-esteem. After several months of treatment, she acknowledged to the analyst that she lied to others regularly, compulsively, and quite gratuitously. The analyst asked her if she had ever lied to her, and from time to time, in the context of the patient's speaking about her lying, the same query was repeated. She vehemently protested, "No, that would be counterproductive." The analyst, she said, was sane, and she lied only to others who were crazy. Those others would get angry were she to tell the truth and the analyst would not. The analyst wished to believe that her patient really did experience her differently from others. Two years passed, during which time Miss Alexander made considerable progress in the areas of consolidating her identity, raising her self-esteem, and improving her relationships with others.

One day she arrived quite late during a severe rainstorm. The analyst had glanced out from her office window and happened by chance to see her alight from a taxicab with the regal, gracious air that recalled the pathological grandiosity she had manifested from time to time in some of her sessions. She entered the office in a most apologetic manner. She explained that she was late because she had been standing on her corner for a long time, could not find a taxicab, and had walked 20 blocks to the analyst's office.

The analyst was puzzled about the best mode of addressing this falsehood. The lie in this case seemed meaningful and could represent, from what her analyst already knew of her, a masochistic fantasy in the transference in which she needed to present herself to her analyst as pathetic and impoverished while secretly she could bolster an inner grandiosity by putting something over on her. This self-presentation also represented her way of maintaining separateness from the analyst, by contradicting her assertion that she always told her analyst the truth and was having a *different* kind of relationship with her. Miss Alexander lied compulsively to others, but somehow managed to convince her analyst, who had a not too uncommon countertransference fantasy about "rescuing" some of her patients, that she told her the truth.

Momentarily disarmed, and defending against the signal anger and the disappointment aroused in her by Miss Alexander's lie, the analyst did not address this lie during the session. She waited, instead, for the next opportunity, in which she raised the issue of Miss Alexander's ability to pay a small fee increase. Her fee initially had been set at a very low rate because Miss Alexander protested that she could not pay more. Yet, her lifestyle, as revealed in treatment, seemed discrepant with her reportedly low income. When the discrepancy was pointed out, Miss Alexander precipitously broke off treatment and would not deal with her analyst's rather tactful questioning of her veracity. It seemed that the only way she could continue to stay in treatment was if she could fool her analyst as she did the rest of the world. Her precarious psychic balance depended upon her having gullible objects, whom she used in repeated attempts to restore her injured narcissism. In her case, these issues were far more pressing than any dealing with conflict, so that attempts to analyze any possibility that she was disappointed about her analyst's gullibility or was guilty about having put one over on her were to no avail.

As a child, Miss Alexander was a poor eater and her mother force-fed her. She would refuse to eat and instead would sit before a cold and unappetizing plate of food for hours. When her mother succeeded in forcing her to eat, she would vomit, and then her mother would force her to eat the vomit. As an adult she would starve for days and then binge in secret. If her roommate came home while she was on a junk food binge, she would stuff the food into her handbag, kept at her side especially for that purpose. In her fantasy, eating in front of another would lead to engulfment; a revival of feelings connected with her mother's smothering response to feeding.

Since in the transference she experienced her analyst as the force-feeding bad mother who made her eat her own vomit, her lies possibly represented her wish that her analyst, in a reversal, would become the one who ate the bad food. O'Shaughnessy's patient lied in a similar fashion: the lying symbolically represented a wish to feed her bad food. Her interpretation of a dream containing this wish was: "The two pigs you feed stand for me, whom you feed with your talk. In this dream you are bringing your fear that I won't know the difference between your real communications and the other stuff, the rubbish" (1990, p. 187).

Miss Alexander was conscious of a fear that others would be angry with her if she was to tell the truth and envious of her if she admitted to having anything good. But once again, her narcissistic vulnerability outweighed her guilt and conflicts about duping her analyst, and interpretations close to O'Shaughnessy's paradigm could not reach the basic character pathology in which her lying was embedded. Unconsciously, the lies kept her at a safe distance from others, who represented her engulfing, and force-feeding mother. The lies also enabled her to repeat a chronic experience of guilt over having been such a bad daughter. Harsh superego lacunae were the analog of her weak ego structure. Like other patients who deceive, Miss Alexander's narcissism was quite impaired. She told the analyst that she would feel like a "nothing" if she did not lie. Lies helped her maintain control over others. She said, "It's the way I have power over them. I control the impression I make on them. If I were to show myself as I am, I would lose control."

As a result of the work accomplished during the time she was in treatment, Miss Alexander was able to meet and to become engaged to a young man whom she experienced as kind and quite suited to be a potential mate. However, she felt that she had to conceal from him the fact that she was in treatment. Final interpretive efforts centered around the various meanings of her lying about her ability to pay and about her need to lie to her fiancé, who evidently was to replace the analyst as her gullible object.

A second patient, Mrs. Boxer, grew up in a family in which she was grossly neglected and at times physically abused. As an infant she was sent to live with an aunt, for her mother was unable to manage her care along with the care of her older children. She came for twice-weekly psychoanalytic therapy in order to deal with the breakup of her marriage. She was unable to work even though she had had sufficient education to find employment on a professional level. She did, however, seem to be able to provide good enough care for her young son. Through an unconscious identification with her son, she was attempting to provide for herself a second and more benign childhood.

Mrs. Boxer reported panic attacks and migraine headaches at home alone or when driving in which she became convinced that she was going to die. She would then cease all activity and enter a state of withdrawal. Analysis of this defense revealed that rather than take active steps on her own behalf she would, as she put it, "kill herself off," deaden any spirit or initiative, and enter into a private world of fantasy. She began doing this as a child, when she was virtually imprisoned in a room all day adjacent to her bedridden, poorly groomed, chronically depressed mother. As she began to tell the analyst about her split-off fantasy world, she increasingly became able to take some concrete action in her life. Fears then emerged that, were she to find a job, she would not have time to live in her inner world, a dream world that was the only place she believed she was allowed to actually "live." The patient's sweet demeanor and her rich associations elicited in her analyst a strong sense of trust in her as well as respect for her courage.

Then the analyst stumbled upon a lie. The patient telephoned the day after a job interview and asked in a pleading voice to be given a later appointment that day, for she was in the nurse's office at her son's school with a migraine headache and could not possibly arrive on time for her early morning appointment. At this point, the analyst viewed the request as an ordinary one, and in fact had at that moment no other time to offer her. A few minutes later, however, another patient canceled his hour and the analyst uncharacteristically, in what she soon understood to be a counterenactment, telephoned Mrs. Boxer at the nurse's office at her son's school in order to offer her the later hour. The nurse said that she had not seen Mrs. Boxer at all that day.

The analyst found herself to be quite unclear as to why Mrs. Boxer had lied or what to do about it. The patient's lie seemed to derive from her ongoing fantasy that she was sick and in need of care. She seemed to be splitting the transference by going to the school nurse instead of to her session for some kind of help. The lie could be further understood from the material of her most recent sessions, which had to do with her anticipated move forward into a good job. By lying, she could shut her analyst out of her world. If she did not need to do this, she could have simply canceled her session. The analyst hypothesized that she did not want her to know where she was as a way of regaining control of her world. In the next session, the analyst told Mrs. Boxer that she had phoned the nurse and reported to her what the nurse had said. Mrs. Boxer said it was the wrong nurse, that when the analyst called, she was in the school cafeteria with a different nurse. The analyst decided not to pursue the matter further, although she believed that Mrs. Boxer was just elaborating on the original lie. She planned to analyze the lie when the patient was in a more integrated state. She did, however, alert the patient that she was aware of the inconsistencies in her story. She also interpreted her need to gain control by avoiding contact with others in the *displaced transference.* Eventually, Mrs. Boxer was able to make use of this understanding of her lies, confirming the interpretations made by the analyst as she began to speak of compensating for shame experiences with stories she told to her relatives about exciting friends and experiences she had had when in fact she had had neither.

Developmental considerations

Most of the writings in the psychoanalytic literature assign the genesis of lying to the vicissitudes of the oedipal phase of development. The lie is understood as serving to maintain repression and as being organized around oedipal phase fantasies (see Blum, 1983; Freud, 1913; Fenichel, 1939; Greenacre, 1958a; Brunswick, 1943; Weinshel, 1979). For psychological studies of the development of lying and deceit, see de Paulo (1982), Peterson and colleagues (1983), and Piaget (1965).

In the cases of Miss Alexander and Mrs. Boxer, however, issues of separation-individuation predominate. These two lying patients feared attachment and tried to avoid feelings of closeness and tenderness with the analyst by maintaining separateness through their lies. The underlying fantasies reflect oral and anal phase conflicts and express a wish to gain control over frustrating, controlling, internalized objects that are at times overly intrusive and at times totally absent.

Patients who lie repudiate any gratification to be obtained from the object, anticipate pain, and seek to separate from the object by means of lying in order to protect and/or maintain self-cohesion. The one who is deceived is then put into the position of holding onto the liar by believing the lie. If the deceived one confronts the lie, the liar will probably leave the relationship. This is an important factor characterizing the basic dyad of liar and gullible one, of deceiver, and deceived.

The liar takes an active stance in his symbolic feeding of bad food to another, as in the example of Miss Alexander. The liar struggles to detach, to separate, and to avoid symbiosis. Supporting this thesis is Greenacre's (1945) explanation of the psychopath's particularly pressing need for separation from the mother, due to the particular kind of narcissistic attachment the typical mother of the psychopath forms with her infant, which arouses aggression, and impedes the internalization process.

Early in the psychic development of lying patients such as Miss Alexander, Mrs. Boxer, and others, some overwhelming trauma, either shock trauma, or strain trauma, occurs. The developing ego is weakened in some way that leads to certain truths becoming too threatening, too intrusive, and too stressful to be assimilated, contained, and absorbed. Miss Alexander was traumatized by being force-fed and ridiculed. Mrs. Boxer was beaten, restrained, and abandoned. They both deployed dissociative defense mechanisms in order to protect their parents from their aggression, which was then displaced through lying to the one deceived. So, as much as lying patients may fear the closeness of symbiosis, they also need to protect the original parental objects. When this particular early preoedipal conflict is handled by means of dissociative defenses, a tie to the analyst as a new object who can be trusted is most difficult to establish, and the success of the treatment is often put in jeopardy. We note that patients who lie often seem to be extremely trustworthy, for the part of them that lies and presents itself to others is dissociated from the part that is aware of the truth.

Rosenfeld (1987) reports a case of a psychiatrist patient, Caroline, who was put in jail for selling drug prescriptions, a side of herself concealed from her analyst:

> The lying in these cases is so complete and so consistent that the analyst is generally taken in and does not know that he is being lied to. With Caroline, one never had the feeling that she was lying. She seemed to have split off

her criminal and murderous self utterly, so that when this was acted out disastrously in real life it was uncontrollable.

(p. 136)

Patients who lie very often suffer from identifications with parents with faulty egos and superegos who have lied to them or disappointed them; they then tend to defensively idealize the parents (Gottdiener, 1982). Bollas (1989), in his analysis of Jonathan, a lying psychopathic patient, finds the lies to function as reparative and control measures:

> It is only in phantasy that Jonathan can evolve a completed experience with an object, as the continuous interruptions by the parents of their potential use as Jonathan's object left him bewildered and compelled to create an alternative world. He lies psychopathically (automatically) because lying functions as another order of self and object experience, an order that consistently helped him to recuperate from the actual absences of the parent.
>
> (p. 179)

Thus, lying is encompassed by living itself. The lie exposes to the other the betrayal by the parents.

Parental complicity in the development of the proclivity to lying is also addressed by Deutsch (1923) who writes of the narcissistic gratification accruing to parents who used their children as extensions of themselves:

> Those [parents] who were lied to by their children took refuge from sad reality in the fantasy structure of their children. The crudest outside assistance was sufficient to cause their morbid imagination to believe in the reality of what they were told. They believed because they wanted to believe, because they saw their dreams realized in the lies they were told. And only an intuitive awareness of this fact enabled the liars to be believed in.
>
> (p. 150)

Although one would naturally assume that lying patients have weak superegos, in cases such as those of Deutsch, the superego *structures* are harsh while the *contents* lack prohibitions against lying. These are in fact cases of harsh superego development with concomitant superego lacunae relating mainly to content that give a misleading overall picture of superego laxity. Patients whose parents encouraged lying unconsciously seek punishment when their lies are discovered and by this means fueling their chronic sense of guilt about having told the lies. Superego lacunae are evident in cases where parental gratifications from the child's lying interfere with the development of superego contents that forbid them to tell lies, as in Deutsch's (1923) example. Considerable ego impairment is involved, for these lying patients cannot foresee the negative consequences in store for them, including frequent recurrences of negative therapeutic reactions, eventuating in the invalidation, or destruction of their analytic treatment.

Technical issues

Special technical difficulties arise in the psychoanalytic treatment of lying patients, especially in connection with our axiom that lies should be dealt with as soon as they are recognized, within the limits of dosage, timing, and tact. Strong countertransference reactions are provoked both by the lie and the need to acknowledge it and must be analyzed as soon as possible so that a neutral stance can be maintained. Patients who lie are particularly prone to reactions of narcissistic rage, shame, and humiliation and, by their use of projective identification, sudden suspicion of the analyst when they become aware that the analyst is aware of the lie.

Because lying patients typically use dissociative mechanisms, their commitment to treatment is often tentative, and they sometimes precipitously terminate when realistic perception becomes unavoidable and the split-off aggression inherent in the lying becomes accessible.

Analysts work in the context of a contemporary culture in which confronting lies is not generally supported. In Victorian times, it was a challenge to address sexual wishes and fantasies, which were not at the time discussed publicly. Today, the analytic challenge may center more on controversial issues of morals and ethics because we tend not to confront these matters in social settings. Many of us have actually been punished for confronting a liar, especially a parent who lied. In analytic treatment, however, a lie must be called a lie. The impact will be attenuated when the psychodynamic context is permitted to emerge and be interpreted.

We aim in psychoanalytic treatment to help our patients achieve better integration and to avoid further shock to the ego. The issue of timing and dosage is relevant here. We are often reluctant to analyze a lie or a denial of a lie because of the impression that the patient's ego is not strong enough at that moment to tolerate the threat of a fantasized loss of the analyst. We are also reluctant because of our concerns about bringing on depression, as in the case of Mrs. Boxer, the patient who lied about why she needed to have a later hour. Helping the patient gradually become aware, as opposed to forcing upon him a sudden awareness, is the path to take. For example, the analyst can point to inconsistencies in the story as a way of coming closer to confrontation. In this way, the rage toward the analyst that emerges in the form of a displacement from the self or from the object will not be so overwhelming as to disrupt the working alliance. A steady softening of the denial of the lie should enable the patient to avoid experiencing the shock trauma that is often a repetition of past trauma.

Kovar (1975) describes the technical dilemma of the analyst:

> Does he in the service of speaking the truth tear his patient apart, or does he in the service of compassion relinquish his patient to the falsity of the lie?

... In his efforts not to hurt he is aided by a nomenclature which includes a variety of euphemisms for lying and deception. Whether he uses these only to help organize his own thinking, or out loud to help organize his patient's, he is unlikely to think of his patient as lying and even less likely to speak to him about his lies.

(p. 42)

Soon after the analyst becomes aware of a lie, he or she should bring this awareness into the session in a neutral manner. He or she must not withhold, but instead deal actively with the matter. The analyst's withholding of her awareness of Miss Alexander's lie led to the building up of too much aggression, both in the transference and in the countertransference, and may very well have contributed to the patient's premature termination.

Strange derailments in the treatment, unusual or unexplained absences or cancelations, and inconsistencies in the patient's reports might alert the analyst to the possibility that a patient might be prone to telling lies. When a patient seems comfort able with such inconsistencies, it should be understood as a signal that the synthetic function of the ego is impaired.

In making recommendations for the treatment of lies, Kemberg (1975) observes that patients who habitually lie project their own attitudes regarding moral values onto the therapist, whom they then see as dishonest and corrupt. Such patients wish to assert superiority over the therapist, deflect his or her efforts, exert control, and protect themselves from the dangerous retaliation they fear from the therapist should he or she know about matters they wished to hide. They consciously exploit the psychotherapeutic relationship for ends other than receiving help. When such attitudes persist, treatment cannot take place. The analyst must vigorously interpret the lies in the transference. If these attitudes can be changed and a climate of mutual trust instituted, then treatment can proceed.

An assessment of treatability must be made for the patient who has told too many flagrant lies to his analyst (Blum, 1983; O'Shaughnessy, 1990). Reality testing may be too deficient for such patients to profit from psychoanalytic treatment. Lies destroy meaningful interpersonal links, and there is a point at which there is too much meaninglessness to continue. These are issues that bear upon the personality and persistence of the analyst as well as that of the patient.

Weinshel (1979) describes a common reaction of righteous indignation in his patients, along with their allegations that he had violated some pact by confronting their lies. Weinshel does not allow himself to be deflected by this accusation and presses on to analyze the patient's experience that the analytic contract has been violated. In a typical case, he finds that the patient's reaction is a repetition in the transference of a covert pact in childhood when neither the patient nor the parent was ever to speak about having engaged in some kind of forbidden relationship.

In cases in which fees are reduced in order to accommodate patients who enter treatment reporting an inability to pay or who request a fee reduction during the course of treatment, risks of creating a therapeutic impasse are taken, since some percentage of these patients may be lying. The lie, guilt about the lie, and attempts to be consistent with the lie, such as concealing pay raises, purchases made, and trips taken, all serve to defeat authentic treatment. Slakter (1987) discovered his low fee, unemployed patient exiting from a department store laden with packages and then entering a chauffeur-driven Rolls Royce that had his initials on the license plate. Slakter's confrontation in the next session resulted in his patient's tearful relief at being found out. His imposture was due, he explained, to his fear that the analyst and others would only be interested in him for his money. The admission of the lie was couched in yet another lie. We naturally would want to explore these kinds of explanation that could be either extensions of the original lie or new lies to deal with the painful sequelae of older ones.

Countertransference

Countertransference reactions to lying patients can be quite powerful and usually emerge quite abruptly. The ego boundaries of these patients are usually weak and fluid, and they utilize the defense mechanism of projective identification, projecting onto the analyst disowned aspects of the self. Once aware of the lie, the analyst's neutral, benign, passive stance may abruptly shift to one of shock, outrage, or rage if he enacts what the patient is provoking in him.

Bollas (1987) reports feelings of frustration, anger, personal futility, and sadness after being lied to. It is essential that a thorough analysis of the meaning of the lie to the analyst be immediately undertaken so that he can regain his neutrality prior to dealing with the lie with the patient. Gediman (1985) had a similar reaction to her impostor patient: "Why did I let things develop to the point where ... I began to see him as the incarnation of that very evil he had been proclaiming as his ego ideal?" (p. 922).

After the lie is exposed, the analyst must be able to tolerate the sudden perception of himself by the patient as bad, guilty, sadistic, cold, and/or distant. Patients who lie react with righteous indignation when faced with the reality of their lies. They experience the analyst as distant and punitive as they relive and, by way of the transference, project their childhood experiences of lying and/or being lied to onto him or her.

O'Shaughnessy (1990) describes the lie as having damaged her equilibrium, making her incapable of working, depriving her of needed knowledge, and getting her to take the lies as truth, "so that I actually became a partner in a perversion of the analytic relationship" (p. 184). She experienced herself as a "corrupted container."

The analyst's task is to detach enough from his experience of hurt and assault to feel neutral and benign enough to treat the patient. If the analyst remains too angry, treatment may have to be discontinued, for as Blum (1983) notes, the working alliance "develops with difficulty ... where there is a lack of mutual trust and where prevarication provokes countertransference" (p. 18). Those analysts who have heretofore taken pride in their insight into human nature feel caught short by the sudden turn that knowledge of a lie told to them brings. Analysts' work involves knowing, and what they believed that they knew is suddenly invalidated, affecting their own narcissistic balance. Lies are often told to analysts in cases in which they have had to work very hard to supply meanings and synthesis to material that is meaningless and fragmented.

Weinshel (1979) describes our ambivalence about moral virtues:

> Honesty and the capacity to tell the truth are highly venerated moral virtues in our society, but like so many of the moral virtues, our relation to them is both inconsistent and paradoxical. While we respect those who demonstrate these virtues, it is not infrequently a respect commingled with some cynicism and mistrust. The feeling that the truly honest man is somewhat gullible is not a rare attitude limited to the antisocial fringes; and a modern day Diogenes is likely to be viewed as a quixotic figure open to condescension or gentle ridicule.
>
> (p. 523)

Weinshel does not sufficiently take enough into account the *directness* of the aggression toward the analyst in the "real relationship" when he considers that the lies patients tell to their analysts are not moral lapses but useful analytic data as focal points for the reconstruction of early trauma. They are, of course, that, but they are also more than that. This view of lies as purely and solely transferential phenomena denies an aspect of the *direct combat* with the analyst about the worth and validity of truthful discourse and of analysis as a vehicle for uncovering and facing the truth. It also denies that aspect of the analyst's response to the patient as an ordinary person, as described by Winnicott (1947).

The lie may be experienced as a greater assault than other hostile manifestations. The analyst is hurt because the very heart of his or her work is to search for a meaningful narrative for the patient. The lie renders the work meaningless. Because the lie cuts to the quick of what the analyst values most, some analysts defend themselves, perhaps against envy of the patient's freedom from moral prohibition, perhaps against partial identifications with the primitive gratifications to be gained from lying, by being taken in by the lie. It would not be unusual for analysts unconsciously to envy the patient's freedom to lie, for their work ethic, and general moral integrity do not permit them to lie in their work. And so, in the worst case, the perverse dyad of liar and gullible analyst is perpetuated.

Omissions in psychoanalytic treatment

Another related common obstacle to the conduct of psychoanalytic treatment is that of the patient's omissions. Omissions are ubiquitous. Nevertheless, some patients select from the universe of possibilities for free association what is *needed* for the analyst to understand and to analyze them. Others select, consciously, and unconsciously, just so the analyst will *not* really understand them. An experienced analyst expects certain omissions. For example, in the early phases of treatment, many patients are reluctant to talk about emerging transference reactions or about specific subjects or incidents they are ashamed to reveal, such as rejections, abortions, and homosexual feelings. The focus here is on omissions that are unexpected and unanticipated, carry with them an element of surprise, and fall into the category of the deceptive and not the average expectable, as in resistances motivated by shame and guilt.

Riviere (1936), in her discussion of the manic defenses of those with negative therapeutic reactions, notes that "certain patients of this type especially withhold from us all 'evidence' of an indisputable character in support of our interpretations. There are degrees to which this resistance can completely defeat an analytic endeavor" (p. 419). Unexplained latenesses, cancelations, no-shows, or sudden vacations may signal the possibility of omissions.

As beginning psychoanalysts, we were instructed to attend to and to analyze as fully as possible our patients' associations, memories, fantasies, and dreams, and to attend to what they *leave out* in their communications to us. We were privileged to have Freud's brilliant mind as a role model and to be able to follow its intricate workings as his thoughts and analytic acumen turned to the various meanings of the myriad gaps and omissions in the associations of the obsessional Rat Man (1909). Freud alerted us to the significance of unconscious omissions, but did not deal sufficiently with omissions that were quite conscious and intentional. In present-day practice, we are accustomed, as part of our legacy from the early days, to working more with what is brought in and acted in, than with what is not brought in and acted out. The idea that patients consciously and deliberately omit significant material can make analysts uncomfortable. Analysts at times are overly dependent upon or take too much solace from certain assumptions, for example, (1) all will eventually emerge in the transference, (2) there are often periods of time in every analysis when the material is chaotic and not yet understandable, and (3) all events that are dynamically central at a particular time will be reported honestly and around that time. We challenge the usefulness of these assumptions in the treatment of certain patients who are prone to deception.

The psychoanalytic literature "omits" the topic of conscious omissions with but a few exceptions. Fenichel (1939) considers omissions as "negative lies" and stresses the obsessional's tendency to omit. Kris (1956), in his paper on the personal myth, writes about the way in which certain individuals use exaggeratedly positive autobiographical memories as a protective screen against painful experiences, with the benign outline and rich details of their mythic creations covering over significant omissions and distortions, "Only after omissions have been filled in and distortions have been corrected, can access to the repressed material be gained" (p. 653).

At the onset of treatment, often in the initial interview, some patients present their life histories in such a way that the analyst has a full view of who they are. Others present just a slice of life, and the analyst is often left to infer what has not been presented or is put into the position of having to ask a question about why something in particular has not been mentioned. This is, of course, a standard technique of resistance analysis that is equally applicable to the analysis of omissions. Patients then may feel that free association is no longer free, and the matter becomes complicated with the fantasy that they are being put on the spot, influenced, and coerced. The analyst's neutrality becomes compromised by the selectivity involved in asking the question. Some patients are aware of the kinds of information the analyst needs to know in order to help them. They are often referred to as gifted analysands. Others are more involved in a selective process of impression management. Still other patients may assume and fantasize, consciously, or unconsciously, that their analysts are omnipotent and omniscient, and know everything regardless of whether or not they put their ideas into words. Others experience the analyst internally as a parent who decathected them and did not need to know or care to know. Some withhold in order to protect themselves from the analyst as an intrusive parent. Omissions thus, have a myriad of meanings with respect to object relations and transference.

A patient who omits reporting important life events—for example, his discovery at age 18 that he was adopted—or who omits something extraordinary that happened the very morning before a session—for example, his having had intercourse with his ex-girlfriend whom the analyst thought was out of his life—often seems unaware of the deleterious effect the omissions could have on the treatment. That is to say, the omissions interfere with, and seriously stifle the potential therapeutic impact of the myriad connections the analyst could otherwise be making, as, for example, between affects that appear incomprehensible and the events that triggered them and that would make them comprehensible in context. These patients need help, have entered treatment ostensibly to receive it, but cannot, or will not communicate to their analysts what they need to know. That patients render their analysts helpless to help them is a naggingly familiar problem and one that takes on special meaning in the case of deception by omission.

Omissions can be confused easily with certain mechanisms of defense, particularly repression, suppression, dissociation, and splitting, all of which serve as resistance. Yet, omissions seem to merit a category of their own. What is selected via conscious and unconscious choices spans a range of clinical pictures that are full or narrow band with respect to the normality or pathology of the process of omitting and the content of the omissions. Examples of how one judges the significance of material that is left out is presented below.

Freud's (1937) instruction that the analyst takes a neutral attitude and listens with evenly hovering attention leads us to assume that *all* relevant material will eventually appear and that our patients will cooperate in a corresponding manner by free associating and providing us with all the necessary pieces we need to work with. As a way of encouraging us, Freud wrote in *Constructions in Analysis* (1937) that the analyst works under more favorable conditions than the archaeologist. For his task of reconstruction, "all of the essentials are preserved, even things that are completely forgotten are present somehow and somewhere, and have been buried and made inaccessible to the subject" (p. 276). One year later, however, in *Splitting of the Ego in the Process of Defense* (1938), Freud presents another point of view: "The synthetic function of the ego, though it is of such extraordinary importance, is subject to particular conditions and is liable to a whole series of disturbances" (p. 221). He was acknowledging the advances of ego psychology in understanding the variations in functioning of a broader range of latter-day patients who could not be expected to be as amenable to the classic treatment approaches. Freud did not shrink from asking numerous questions of his patients. Looking back, this could have been his effort to counteract the effects of the character pathology underlying conscious deception. Modern trends toward less active questioning could encourage more omissions and gaps than Freud's more actively vigilant stance. The work of Poland (1985) is a welcome addition in its advocacy of an active analytic stance needed to pursue the possibilities of omission.

Omissions raise important issues about ego structure and ego strength, and about superego structure, and superego strength, which bear significantly on technique. Kernberg (1992) speaks of transferences of dishonest communication and issues of character. "To tell the truth, the whole truth, and nothing but the truth" is an implicit maxim for both members of the analytic dyad, and both understand that the truth is slow in emerging. Patients are instructed to say whatever comes to mind and not to censor. For some, particularly those prone to deception, the trust that is involved in following the fundamental rule of free association and of establishing a good working alliance is difficult to achieve. Analysts disagree about whether patients should or should not be urged to tell everything on their minds, thereby following the basic rule. They weigh the benefits of having a seemingly good working alliance against the patient's experiencing the analytic situation as a confessional or courtroom, with the analyst as intrusive, judgmental, or punitive and the analysis as one more time and place in their lives in which their autonomy is threatened. Yet, the working alliance is compromised if omissions are overlooked. Such transferential reactions are to be analyzed rather than to be avoided and counteracted in ways that analysts sometimes falsely presume would preserve autonomy and freedom.

Omissions in everyday social relationships can be adaptive, and being selective about what one imparts to others can be regarded as a sign of maturity. This is not so in the analytic situation. Omissions are a form of deception, of selective reporting, similar to but different from lies. A lie told to the analyst, as defined earlier, is an untruth told consciously with an intent to deceive (Blum, 1983; Fenichel, 1939; Gediman, 1985; Lieberman, 1991; Weinshel, 1979). A piece of reality is consciously distorted or invented: a lie is an act of *commission*.

An omission, on the other hand, distorts reality by leaving a gap, but it does not create a fictitious reality. It reveals something about the drives: perhaps a wish to rebel against following the fundamental rule. As was just stated, it also reveals something about the superego, perhaps a character defect around issues of honesty. And the omission reveals something about the patient's object relations, such as ambivalence, and a wish to devalue the person consulted for help. Finally, it says something about the patient's narcissistic balance, perhaps that omissions restore the self-esteem that is damaged by having to reveal while the analyst is permitted to conceal. Conscious omissions of material that later is brought into the analysis are eventually analyzable in most cases. That is, the emergent material often reveals analyzable motives to distort reality, to avoid pain, to achieve pleasure, to express aggression, to maintain narcissistic balance, and to hold onto the object, as well as many other motivations that are to be explored throughout this book.

Clinical illustration

Miss Atlas, a 24-year-old, bright, attractive art student, the daughter of a high school teacher and an extremely successful advertising agency executive, was referred for psychoanalytic psychotherapy. She found herself unable to make a real commitment to her boyfriend or to her work, and she constantly wondered whether another career would suit her better. She also found herself unable to concentrate. Although she was quite talented in several artistic arenas, she would stop short of completing any project, just when the possibility of success loomed before her. Her family had moved a number of times when she was a child, and she had had multiple caretakers, including her mother, nannies, private counselors, and the staffs in various boarding schools. Miss Atlas's parents managed to keep their tormented marriage together by being apart. Her father was usually away traveling for business.

From early adolescence on, Miss Atlas was exposed by both parents to tales of their sex life and her father's affairs. She was coerced by her mother to play detective, ferreting out information about her father's many paramours. Both parents seemed to demonstrate considerable ego and superego pathology. Her father's self-made success, his tremendous wealth, and his widely publicized acclaim made it difficult for Miss Atlas to de-idealize him. To complicate matters further, he performed a mothering function for her, for when he was home he was always pleasant and nurturant. What in most families was kept secret and private was not in her family. On the other hand, both parents harbored myriad secrets, lies, and omissions.

During the first two years of Miss Atlas's treatment, considerable progress was made in her ability to focus and concentrate, in asserting herself with her boyfriend, and in making some career decisions that led to her exhibiting her work in the professional arena. She no longer played detective for her mother and refused to listen to her stories about her father's sex life. She worked analytically, bringing in dreams and memories, and weaving her associations from past to present. She would not, however, come more than twice a week, although she reported that she found the treatment to be quite gratifying. Considerable analysis of her fantasies and conflicts about deeper commitment did not change her refusal to increase the frequency of sessions.

In addition, from time to time she did not come and did not call, leaving her analyst perplexed and unable to discern any consistent patterns in the sessions prior to her absences that could explain such behavior. Her analyst's counter-transference at these times consisted of transitory feelings of intense pain and anxiety about whether her patient would ever return to treatment, feelings induced by Miss Atlas. When she did return, Miss Atlas could not remember why she did not come to sessions. She seemed to be withholding consciously at those times. The analyst treated this behavior as something to understand. It became apparent that Miss Atlas was repeating with her analyst a reversal of her experience of her father's many absences when she was a child. Neither his arrivals nor his departures were ever announced. She learned defensively not to care about his absences and not to wonder where he was. When her father was away, her mother was depressed and angry, and did not give the children basic care, so it was as if both parents were lost.

During the next two years, careful attention to the issue of Miss Atlas's absences revealed that she was extraordinarily depressed when she did not come to her sessions. She never mentioned these depressed affects in her associations. She only later disclosed that she had what she called "a little affair" on those days, eventually understood as enactments of an identification with her adulterous father. She also omitted speaking about several bulimic episodes in which she would take in vast quantities of food, representing the intrusive maternal introject, and then vomit it out. Her not coming to sessions represented, both consciously, and unconsciously, her wish to keep the analyst out. Had the analyst not suspected that the absences represented resistances to talking about transferences, and had she not inquired as to what was going on, on the days of the missed sessions, this important material would most probably never have come up.

Further analysis of Miss Atlas's omissions led to the emergence of a fantasy, heretofore unconscious, that she had a hidden penis that would enable her to win anything she would compete for.

The anxieties about winning and the repression of the fantasy led to her stopping short of success in her work. On the one occasion that she used the bathroom down the hall from the analyst's office in midsession, she returned reporting that she had had the fantasy that the analyst was envious of her, perhaps because of her father's wealth. She then reported the following dream:

Part of my leg was a prosthesis—a plastic part. I don't know if I could take it off or felt it as part of my leg. A woman or a man looked at it and said, "You're suffering from misogyny." None of what I was suffering from was clear in the dream.

Her associations were to the demeaning roles that women are forced to play in society. She spoke of considerable feelings of shame. She felt that she was weird, different from others, and had felt that way since she was a child. She experienced tremendous shame over having lost urinary and bowel control when she was 4 years old, at the time her family moved. As an adult, any rejection, or physical illness became associated with feeling dirty and disgusting.

After her longest disappearance from treatment, lasting 4 weeks, she returned unannounced, and found the analyst waiting for her at the regular time of her hour. She acknowledged her disappearance for the first time. Up until that time she always seemed to have forgotten that she had missed sessions and left it up to the analyst to remind her. She vehemently declared that she hated the analyst and wanted to hurt her as she had been hurt by her father's absences. She recalled that, when he was away, she was left alone with her mother. Her mother, at these times, would psychologically "disappear" into her own shell. When Father was home and she attempted to attract his attention she also felt she was bad, as if Mother saw her as one of Father's girlfriends and hated her for it. It is clear that narcissistic trauma was involved at each of the psychosexual phases of her development.

Miss Atlas manifested considerable ego pathology in certain areas, as in anticipation, and planning. She did not have at hand certain basic information, such as travel directions, and geographical facts. Many facts and memories were stored in fragments. Over time, this pathology began to improve. The treatment proved to be successful, in part because of the assiduous attention to and analysis of the repressed material covered over by the omissions.

Discussion

The case of Miss Atlas demonstrates the defensive function of omissions in patients who initially seemed more intact and integrated in ego structure than proved to be the case. Anna Freud (1946) alerts us to the ego's myriad ways of defeating treatment:

> We are all familiar with the accusation not infrequently made against analysts—that they may have a good knowledge of a patient's unconscious, but are bad judges of his ego. There is a certain amount of justification in this criterion, for the analyst lacks opportunities of observing the patient's whole ego in action.
>
> (p. 23)

She goes on to write:

> The ego is antagonistic to the analysis, in that it is unreliable and biased in its self-observation and, while conscientiously registering and passing on certain facts, falsifies and rejects others and prevents them from coming to

light—a procedure wholly contrary to the methods of analytic research, which insists on seeing everything that emerges without discrimination.

(pp. 31–32)

Schafer (1968) also writes of the variety of ways the ego's synthetic function could operate:

> What has failed to be synthesized, or what has been denied synthesis, may range all the way from superficial ideas that are contradictory or unconditional to major competing suborganizations of the personality.... Through the exercise of logic and objective judgment, the subject may choose from among competing ideas the one that fits best into existing organizations of ideas, and he may reject those that contradict or create tension in these organizations. This is the work of exclusion.
>
> (p. 98)

Schafer's "exclusions" refer to aspects of self-integration, and although they are quite different from what are here called omissions, they are theoretically continuous with them, and can provide us with further insight into the nature of the ego functioning of certain patients. To understand better the phenomena of ego- and self-integration, we can keep in mind some of the following questions as the analytic work proceeds.

- To what extent are a particular patient's omissions a function of defenses such as splitting, suppression, and repression?
- To what extent are they related to more recent conceptualizations, such as Bion's (1959) minus-K (knowing versus not knowing), which is often related to the anxiety aroused by sex differences?
- How are omissions related to Bion's "attacks on linking," in which the links in the relationship between one person and another are destroyed by attacking any meaningfulness in the connection between them, or to Riesenberg-Malcolm's (1989) concept of "slicing," in which meaning is also denuded? These two authors speak of the patients' attacks on the value of meaning, the very meaning *required* for the analyst to do analysis. These attacks then also become assaults on the analyst's sense of reality.
- To what extent is the incomplete reporting isomorphic with the patient's inner experience at the moment? Is the omission due to ego weakness or arrest, or is ego functioning temporarily impaired due to some conflict being defended against? What is the role of internalization? Miss Atlas, for example, omitted in the style used by her parents, identifying with the aggressors in turning passivity into activity.
- One needs to understand adequately the patient's relation both to his or her inner world and the outside world in order to treat the patient effectively. Therefore, two other questions the analyst should think about in treating

patients who consistently omit are: (1) What is the extent of his awareness of others, of the world, of what is happening around him? and (2) What does he scotomatize defensively and then omit?
- Similarly, the analyst must ask about the superego structure whether it is split, fragmented, or intact, harsh, or weak—of the omitter. To what extent does the patient experience guilt or shame over the omission, and to what extent does the omission keep fueling the sense of guilt or shame?

Kernberg (1992) raises important issues about the treatability of those with dishonest transferences who greatly mislead the analyst. He contrasts these patients with others who:

> may insist, over an extended period of time, that there are issues they will not discuss with the therapist ... This honesty in communicating to the therapist their unwillingness to participate in the treatment may permit an analysis over an extended period of time of the reasons for their fearfulness and distrust.
>
> (p. 14)

Note

1 This chapter is based upon two chapters: "Omissions in Psychoanalytic Treatment" and "Patients Who Lie," from *The Many Faces of Deceit: Omissions, Lies, And Disguise in Psychotherapy* by Helen K. Gediman and Janice S. Lieberman, 1996, Northvale, N. J.: Jason Aronson, Inc. Reprinted by permission of Rowman & Littlefield Publishing Group.

References

Bion, W. (1959). Attacks on linking. *International Journal of Psycho-Analysis, 40,* 308–315.

Blum, H. (1983). The psychoanalytic process and analytic inference: A clinical study of a lie and a loss. *International Journal of Psycho-Analysis, 64,* 17–33.

Bollas, C. (1987). *The shadow of the object.* New York: Columbia University Press.

Brunswick, R. M. (1943). The accepted lie. *Psychoanalytic Quarterly, 12*(4), 458–464.

de Paulo, B. M., Jordan, A., Irvine, A., & Laser, P. S. (1982). Age changes in the detection of deception. *Child Development, 53*(3), 701–709.

Deutsch, H. (1923). Pathological lying (abs.). *International Journal of Psycho-Analysis, 4,* 159.

Farber, L. H. (1975). Lying on the couch. *Salmagundi, 29,* 15–27.

Fenichel, O. (1939). The economics of pseudologia fantastica. In H. Fenichel & D. Rapaport (Eds.), *The collected papers of Otto Fenichel* (pp. 129–140). New York: Norton, 1954.

Ford, C. V., King, B. H., & Hollender, M. H. (1988). Lies and liars: Psychiatric aspects of prevarication. *American Journal of Psychiatry, 145*(5), 554–562.

Freud, S. (1909). Notes on a case of obsessional neurosis. In J. Strachey (Ed. & Trans.), *The complete psychological works of Sigmund Freud* (pp. 153–249). Standard Edition (Vol. 10). London: Hogarth Press.

Freud, S. (1913). Two lies told by children. In J. Strachey (Ed. & Trans.), *The standard edition of the complete psychological works of Sigmund Freud* (pp.305–310). Standard Edition (Vol. 12). London: Hogarth Press.

Freud, S. (1920). The psychogenesis of a case of homosexuality in a woman. In J. Strachey (Ed. & Trans.), *The standard edition of the complete psychological works of Sigmund Freud* (pp. 146–220). Standard Edition (Vol. 18). London: Hogarth Press.

Freud, S. (1937). Constructions in analysis. In J. Strachey (Ed. & Trans.), *The standard edition of the complete psychological works of Sigmund Freud* (pp. 256–269). Standard Edition (Vol. 23). London: Hogarth Press.

Freud, S. (1938/1940). Splitting of the ego in the process of defense. In J. Strachey (Ed. & Trans.), *The standard edition of the complete psychological works of Sigmund Freud* (pp. 271–278). Standard Edition (Vol. 23). London: Hogarth Press.

Freud, A. (1946). *The ego and the mechanisms of defense.* New York: International Universities Press.

Gediman, H. K. (1985). Imposture, inauthenticity, and feeling fraudulent. *Journal of the American Psychoanalytic Association, 33*, 911–935.

Gottdiener, A. (1982). The impostor: An interpersonal point of view. *Contemporary Psychoanalysis, 18*(3), 438–454.

Greenacre, P. (1945). Conscience in the psychopath. *American Journal of Orthopsychiatry, 15*(3), 495–509.

Greenacre, P. (1958a). The impostor. In *Emotional growth: Psychoanalytic studies of the gifted and a great variety of other individuals* (Vol. 1, pp. 193–212). New York: International Universities Press, 1971.

Greenacre, P. (1958b). The relation of the impostor to the artist. In *Emotional growth: Psychoanalytic studies of the gifted and a great variety of other individuals* (Vol. 2, pp. 533–554). New York: International Universities Press, 1971.

Kernberg, O. (1975). *Borderline conditions and pathological narcissism.* New York: Jason Aronson, Inc.

Kernberg, O. (1992). Psychopathic, paranoid, and depressive transferences. *International Journal of Psycho-Analysis, 73*(1), 13–28.

Kovar, L. (1975). The pursuit of self-deception. *Salmagundi, 29*(Spring), 28–44.

Kris, E. (1956). The personal myth: A problem in psychoanalytic technique. *Journal of the American Psychoanalytic Association, 4*(4), 653–681.

Lieberman, S. (1991). Technical, structural, and countertransference issues with patients who lie. Paper presented at the 37th Congress of the International Psychoanalytic Association, Buenos Aires, August.

Malcolm, J. (1983a, December 5). I-Troubles in the archive. *Annals of Scholarship. The New Yorker* (pp. 59–126).

Malcolm, J. (1983b, December 12). II-Troubles in the archive. *Annals of Scholarship, The New Yorker* (pp. 60–119).

Masson, J. M. (1984). *The assault on truth: Freud's suppression of the seduction theory.* New York: Farrar, Straus, & Giroux.

O'Shaughnessy, E. (1990). Can a liar be psychoanalyzed? *International Journal of Psycho-Analysis, 71*(2), 187–196.

Peterson, C., Peterson, J. L., & Sieto, D. (1983). Developmental changes in ideas about lying. *Child Development, 54*(6), 1529–1535.

Piaget, J. (1965). *The moral judgment of the child.* New York: Free Press.

Poland, W. (1985). At work. In J. Reppen (Ed.), *Analysts at work* (pp. 145–164). Hillsdale, N.J.: Analytic Press.

Riesenberg-Malcolm, R. (1989). As-if: The phenomenon of not learning. Paper presented at the 36th Congress of the International Psychoanalytic Association, Rome, Italy, August.

Riviere, J. (1936). A contribution to the psychoanalysis of the negative therapeutic reaction. *International Journal of Psycho-Analysis, 17,* 304–320. Also, in M. S. Bergmann & F. R. Hartmann (Eds.), *The Evolution of Psychoanalytic Technique* (pp. 414–429), 1976.

Rosenfeld, H. (1987). *Impasse and interpretation.* London: Tavistock.

Schafer, R. (1968). *Aspects of internalization.* New York: International Universities Press.

Slakter, E. (Ed.) (1987). *Countertransference.* Northvale, N.J.: Jason Aronson, Inc.

Tausk, V. (1933). On the origin of the "influencing machine" in schizo-phrenia. In R. Fliess (Ed.), *The psychoanalytic reader* (pp. 31–64). New York: International Universities Press, 1948.

Weinshel, E. M. (1979). Some observations on not telling the truth. *Journal of the American Psychoanalytic Association, 27*(3), 503–531.

Winnicott, D. W. (1947/1975). Hate in the countertransference. In *Through paediatrics to psychoanalysis: Collected papers* (Chapter 15, pp. 194–203). New York: Basic Books.

Chapter 3

The availability (and responsibility) of the analyst

"Above all, do no harm"

Thank you to the Editors of *The Candidate Journal* for providing me with the opportunity to explore with the psychoanalytic community an uncomfortable topic, seldom discussed, but affecting all of us. We at times discuss the "patient's availability" to come to sessions, but not the "analyst's" availability. I would like to discuss the issue of the analyst's "physical" availability and not so much his "emotional" availability or "mental" availability, even though these are all interrelated.

I pose the following question to debate: After having taken a patient into analysis, on the couch, 3–5 times/week, the process activating a degree of regression in the patient, for how many sessions and for how many weeks of the year is it the responsibility of the analyst to be physically in his office and providing sessions on the agreed upon days and hours? Similarly, for how many sessions, and how many weeks a year must the supervisor of cases in analysis be physically present? I do not think the answer to this is obvious, and I have observed so many variations in practice that I think it worthwhile to consider. I am going to raise many questions and do not have ready answers.

Little has been written about the analyst's "work superego" and his responsibility to his patient other than "analyzing." The focus has usually been on the patient's availability and the patient's resistances to doing the analytic work, paying for missed sessions, etc. I have not seen cases reported in the literature (with the exception of those writing about the disabled analyst and the pregnant analyst) in which the analyst reports when he was present, when he was absent, and for what length of time during the course of treatment reported on.

We all agree that analysts need vacations (and patients need vacations too). But at what length and at what frequency? What effect does "too much absence" on the part of the analyst have on the treatment? We need to define "too much." Can "too much" create an iatrogenic illness or for those patients whose parents traveled or were often separated from them, a retraumatization? Do analysts regularly inform their patients that they will not have sessions prior to vacations large and small? Do they provide sufficient time to analyze how their patients experience these impending absences? Do they analyze the impact of vacations once they return? There do not seem to be standards established around what is considered to be good practice. The tradition begun by European analysts (before air conditioning was available) of taking several months off in the summer, then the hallowed month of August, has now for many become the taking of several short (1 to 2 weeks) vacations scattered throughout the year. We must examine the impact of these practices on the analytic work.

Some world-renowned analysts travel a good part of the year to give papers and workshops, to participate in national and international congresses, and in governance. Do their patients and supervisees suffer from so much absence? Does the narcissistic gain from having a famous analyst or supervisor feel like compensation? Is this analyzed? In some fields, people say that in this age of computers and Skype, they can work from anywhere. Can the analyst work from *anywhere*?

The variations that concern me have to do with my observations and reports of two groups in particular: (1) analysts who are starting their private practices (usually in their 30s and 40s); and (2) those who are older and long established (usually in their 60s and 70s). Some of these younger analysts of child-bearing and child-rearing age take maternity (sometimes paternity) leave of 3 to 4 months. Little has been written about the impact of these leaves of absence. Those in this age group are sometimes the emotional center of "familial sand-wiches" in which they are caretaking their own children, well and sick, and their aging parents, well and sick. They are in training and/or trying to build their private practices. At the other end of the spectrum are older analysts, who often have adult children and grandchildren. They by now earn a comfortable income and have savings. If they still have their health they feel entitled to "smell the roses." I have heard of some taking vacations of 2 weeks or more every few months often for travel. What is the impact of this practice on their patients and supervisees?

I am questioning the practices of those who electively take vacations or cancel blocks of sessions, not those who must take time off due to planned surgeries, cancer treatment, etc. These analysts are in a position to work through the meaning of their absence to their patients. I am not questioning those who are stricken with an illness suddenly and cannot work and often have to have someone else inform their patients that they will miss sessions, often for an indeterminate amount of time. I am talking about what can be controlled, not the uncontrollable.

Other variations in analysts' accessibility to their patients have to do with practices around providing access in between sessions, on weekends, and on vacations. Are patients who perceive themselves to be in crisis permitted to reach them on the telephone, by e-mail, by text, or are they made to wait until their next session to speak to their analyst? Some analysts will do phone sessions if needed while traveling, while some do not provide an e-mail address or the name of a covering colleague. Do these variations have to do with some notions of how analytic work should be conducted, do they have to do with a perception of the psychological needs or transference fantasies of each particular patient, or do they have to do with the personal limitations of the analyst's psyche and how much accessibility he can tolerate?

I have heard anecdotes from colleagues and candidates of variations in access to analysts. Unfortunately, this can differ according to the fee paid or the ease of working with the patient. I have heard of practices in which analysts who need to cancel a few sessions in a day for personal reasons will cancel their low fee patients and see their full fee patients. Or they will cancel those who are difficult to work with and see those who are easier. Low fee patients (and supervisees) are sometimes not given a regular hour. They are asked to call each week to see what canceled hours the analyst has to fit them in. They are what I would call "analytic stepchildren."

The physical availability of the analyst is connected with both conscious and unconscious resistance to the analytic work. Certain patients may reactivate old buried conflicts and the fear of countertransference feelings may result in cancelations.

Another variation is that of the analyst who is "bicoastal" or has practices in two geographically distant cities and spends several months at a time in each, doing telephone, or Skype analysis with the patients who are outside of the city of residence. Here the analysis is split into two distinctly different experiences that have a planned structure. What is the effect on the analysis?

What do we do or should we do when we observe or hear about the work of analysts who do not seem to care about their patients? On the other hand, how much do analysts have to "care" about their patients?

Analysts vary greatly in the number of patients they see each day and the number of hours they work each week. This is not entirely voluntary, since some receive more referrals than others. Some work as many as 60 hours/week, seeing 12 patients each of 5 days. Others work 20 hours/week, seeing 5 patients over each of 4 days. Analysts vary in energy level. What is "too much"? What is "too little"? It takes a lot of cognitive and emotional capacity to "process" so many sessions daily. On the other hand the analyst who has too few hours may feel out of touch with the work, may feel badly that he has so few hours, may have financial worries, and may have to sublet his office, reducing the hours he could be available to his patients. I have heard stories told of senior analysts who regularly fall asleep in their early morning sessions. One patient, who has since left her well-renowned analyst, was told upon awakening him, that her associations were so defensive she made him sleepy. This obviously left a scar difficult to erase.

Is there such a thing as an "analytic superego"? What subset of "rules" has been established consciously and unconsciously on the basis of the analyst's training: observing the behavior of one's own analyst(s), supervisors, teachers, what has been heard in lectures, seminars, and peer groups about the responsibility of the analyst to the patient. Recently the analyst's ethical failures have been examined in the literature of boundary violations. Do some of the practices in this discussion fall into the area of ethical failure?

One can ask about the relationship between the analytic superego and the personal superego? Does the analyst who wantonly cancels sessions cheat on his taxes or his wife? Does the analyst feel guilty about vacations, cancelations, and if so how does his guilt interfere with his ability to analyze? Or lack of guilt? There are no ready answers, but these issues should be considered.

Chapter 4

Construction outside, reconstruction inside

The analyst's office under siege

A number of years ago I saw in analysis Sally, a 45-year-old narcissistic woman whose beauty and charm masked an underlying borderline organization. She was quite paranoid and suspicious. Her skin was extremely sensitive. She could not have contact with many soaps or lotions or she would become ill. Her psyche was a mirror of her skin. I was her fifth analyst. After about a year an idealizing transference emerged and Sally seemed to be much improved. She was less depressed and began to leave her solitary apartment more and more in order to socialize. She told me many tales of outrageous treatment at the hands of her previous therapist, a psychiatrist who was well-respected in the community.

One day, during her session, workmen appeared on the sidewalk under my office. They began using a jackhammer to break up the asphalt. The noise was unbearable and I had to stop the session and ask Sally to leave. There was no sense in trying to talk through the noise. We could talk about it the next day. Sally came the next day and began by berating me that I was not "professional," that I could not protect my patients and that she was done with me. The thin membrane that had formed around us was shattered by the jackhammer. It may be that her improvement was bound to be destroyed by something, but I am presenting this to illustrate a reality issue with the potential to impact the analytic space.

Papers have been written about the analyst's office, waiting room, décor, etc. as a silent backdrop of the treatment that can take on meaning when something out of the ordinary happens that triggers transferences and evokes memories and previous trauma. The maintenance of the office and its serenity is the responsibility of the analyst who must protect the patient from interruptions and preserve the office as a place in which thought and the emergence of deep emotion can take place. This past year, I have from time to time, lost control over that protection.

A New York City building code (1999) requires every building higher than six stories to erect a bridge and to inspect and point every brick every 5 years. Many of these buildings have therapists and analysts' offices in them, usually on the lower floors. My office is on the second floor of my building and for 18 months has faced a bridge and scaffolding that blocks out all views of the street below, reduces the flow of air and light, and becomes an ever-changing, disorganized upsetting sight since it is used to store an ever-changing array of hoists and ropes, cans, garbage bags, steel girders, etc. The workmen feel free to walk back and forth in front of my windows creating unexpected shadows as they do.

This project began as a "temporary" situation expected to last a few months (that included my August vacation); one to be tolerated and then it would be over. Unfortunately, as I learned is often the case, "problems upon problems" were found, and there have been 18 months of assault on my serenity, my ability to breathe well and to assume that on any given day I will have peace and quiet in which to work.

The reader must be asking: "Why not move?" If I had any idea 18 months ago that this would last this long I would have tried to find another office for the duration of the construction. But that would have involved another kind of upheaval for my patients and myself. And these days one cannot predict when construction will be going on inside or outside any building. The lack of information from the Board to the tenants was Kafkaesque. The project had been mismanaged, several construction crews were fired, numerous lawsuits filed against the building and the lack of work done during the freezing winter further prolonged the job. Playing into my denial, passivity, inertia were the many days and weeks when there was no noise and the work was being done far from my office. The project was so disorganized that no one could predict where the men would be working on any given day. In addition, I have worked for many years in my lovely office and that attachment also prevented me from moving. I purchased several costly air cleaners and had my office cleaned more often as partial solutions to the removal of the constant dust that was coming into the apartment.

Early in the construction, when there was no peace anywhere in the apartment, a new patient who was coming in the midst of a crisis arrived just as the noise began. I spoke to her in the hallway. Needless to say, she came for one more session, said she was not bothered by what had happened and then discontinued treatment.

I have a study in the back of the apartment that is larger than my consulting room. After about six months, that room was no longer under siege since the work outside had been finished. I went to work removing all personal items and photos and set up one sofa as the analytic couch. I was thus, prepared for the days when the noise in the front would be so unbearable that patients and I could move to the back. This seemed like a simple rational solution.

It did however, not prove to be a real solution. One week the noise was so bad that, rather than try to cancel sessions at the last minute, I decided to inform each patient that we were going to work in another room that day and would do so in days in which my consulting room was too noisy. Each patient I saw appeared to casually accept the change. The more sophisticated mused about what they saw (many, many books). It seemed as if the sessions moved normally and I asked for thoughts and feelings about the change. Not one patient admitted to being bothered by it. However, of the 8 patients who were invited into my study that day, 4 within a 2-week period abruptly terminated treatment (ostensibly due to money, time, etc.) These 4 were fairly new patients with little self-reflective capacity. I hypothesized that the move could have been experienced as a seduction, as a boundary violation, as an entry into the primal scene. On the other hand, the next week one woman patient, a successful entrepreneur who had been with me for many years, rang the doorbell just as the incredible noise began. She insisted that we walk to a coffee shop a block away and have her session there. I was personally so rattled by the noise that I agreed. (Totally out of character for me!) To my surprise, that worked out rather well and her treatment continued.

I conclude with a vignette: Linda envied her sisters and most of her friends. Each and every one had all the things she wanted and felt deprived of. Although she spent many of her hours speaking of her envy of various figures in her life with whom she would become obsessed, when I inquired from time to time, she told me that she had no thoughts about me when she left her sessions. She averted her gaze entering and leaving my office, never looking at me. I analyzed her sadism, her aggression gone amuck in her life outside my office. The transference was for the most part displaced. The treatment might not have moved as far as it did had it not been for some construction taking place on the street outside my office window. One day, about 10 minutes prior to Linda's session, a jackhammer appeared to break up the sidewalk. The noise was deafening. Linda traveled quite a distance to get to my office 4 times/week. The office is in my apartment. I made a quick decision to walk her to my study, a neutral book-lined room, where we could work in quiet. (The same study I referred to earlier.) She had never been in any part of my apartment but the office and bathroom. She was reluctant to go, but could not think from the noise. (And I too was having difficulty thinking because of the noise.) She entered the study, began to panic, and had to return to my office. After she recovered she said:

> I have enough to deal with just with *me* and not with *you*. I thought the rooms in the back would be small, like my bedroom, but now I know you have a large room and maybe more large rooms and that is very upsetting to me.

The woman who had averted her gaze and seemed oblivious of me had, in the few minutes she was in my study, noticed a child's game in the bookcase. "Now I have to think of you as having children, probably grandchildren. I cannot handle it. It means you have had sex, relationships." Linda came to the next session but would not speak about her reactions. She ranted about her anger at an intern who worked for her, about how he messed up the work. Then she began to forget to come to her sessions, leaving me waiting for her. She wanted to destroy me and the treatment due to her envy.

Now that her envy of me had entered the transference in such a direct way we were both able to look at it. There were prominent Oedipal as well as oral-sadistic components to it. Entering the study felt like a primal scene repetition. Her mother had everything and she had nothing. Similarly her sisters had husbands and she had none. I believed that sending her away would have been experienced by her as a rejection. It took a jackhammer to pierce the defensive skin of indifference to me.

In conclusion, some intrusions on the session become "grist for the mill" and open up the treatment. Some, however, serve to abort the treatment but are unavoidable.

Part II

Body, skin, and gender

Chapter 5

The female body

A discussion of Malkah Notman's 2003 paper

It is both a privilege and a pleasure to have been asked to discuss Dr. Notman's rich and complex paper. She sums up and masterfully synthesizes the last 30 (now 45) years of psychoanalytic discourse on the female body and its relationship to "femininity." She questions Freud's seminal notion that the discovery of the genital difference is pivotal in female development and elucidates what is specific to females that makes them female, for example, the psychological implications of the capacity for pregnancy and childbirth.

Dr. Notman (2003) says:

> Important components of the female body image are created by the sensations and stimuli arising from the body in the course of maturational changes. Relationships with other females also shape a girl's ideas about femininity and cultural values as to how feminine beauty influences a girl's view of herself and how she fits into these.
>
> (p. 1)

I will address and expand upon these two points in my discussion:

1   I will speak about female bodily feelings, what it feels like to be inside, to see from the outside and to possess a female body—not just visually, but kinesthetically, proprioceptively, and olfactorily—all along the course of female development from infancy to old age; these specifically female bodily sensations and feelings are evaluated and incorporated into the positive or negative body image, what we call "body narcissism."

2   I will more briefly speak about a culture that insists that females be thin like young boys even when their bodies dictate otherwise and ask you to think about how in this context positive or negative body narcissism develops and changes over the life cycle in the female due to external cues e.g., looking at herself in the mirror, in photographs or on video; and/or reflected back to her by others, e.g., her mother, father, siblings, other family members, friends, neighbors, and increasingly important, the mass media—television, movies, magazines, newspapers, (today—the social media: Facebook, Instagram, Snapchat, etc.).

I see the female body as very different from the male body, and believe that the experience of being female in a female body differs greatly from being male in a male body.

There are specific pleasures and pains accompanying bodily changes all through the life cycle that will determine how the girl views herself. Each of course can be magnified or diminished by force of unconscious fantasy and intrapsychic conflict. Each deeply affects her ego functioning. I am going to limit myself to the real and the concrete.

From the start: Being female from a bodily perspective can be pleasant, extremely pleasureful, and exciting; mildly annoying or quite painful at times.

- *Vaginal and clitoral sensations:* spontaneous, as a result of being cleaned or examined, and from masturbation, and self-exploration.
- *Menstruation:* cramps, wetness, leaking, odors, edginess due to premenstrual syndrome, bodily, and abdominal swelling; the need to manage the wetness through the use of tampons or pads. How the girl learns to tend to herself from her mother and/or friends colors the attitudes she will have toward these normal bodily processes.
- *Breast development:* her body will feel differently if her breasts are large or small and boys will react differently to her according to their size; her nipples will become sensitive; she must adjust to wearing a bra and finding clothing that fits her breasts as well as her body.
- *Adolescent development:* bodily changes e.g., body hair, perspiration and body odors, acne, and awkwardness. (These changes are not unique—they are experienced by both genders.)
- *First intercourse:* the pain of defloration; bleeding; the pleasures of arousal, penetration, and orgasm; clitoral, vaginal, uterine sensations, wetness; odors: welcome or not; contact with a male body: its form, feel, and smell.
- *Pregnancy:* her inner body feels different due to hormonal changes accompanied by her vision of her swelling abdomen on the outside and sonogram images of the fetus on the inside; her breasts feel heavier and tenderer; her feet swell; she may lose hair or have morning sickness; and the excitement of feeling the baby kicking. Her body needs larger clothing and she may feel awkward and ungainly. The worries, sorrows, and longtime mourning when there is miscarriage, abortion, or stillbirth.
- *Childbirth:* the pains and pleasures of labor, of her water breaking; of pain unlike any other, of the special pain as the baby is pushed out; the sticking pain of the episiotomy and stitches; postpartum highs and lows as the hormones regulate and the milk comes in, often precipitating a weeping spell when she is also so happy. The sorrow and worry when the baby is not born normal.
- *Nursing:* the pleasure of the infant sucking and uterine contractions; the cycle of milk coming in in response to the baby's cry and schedule of nursing; the pains of sore nipples and leaking and mess requiring special

bras and pads and finding clothes that fit. The sadness when there is not enough milk. The discomfort of breast pumps.

- *Gynecological issues:* that bond one to other females; learning that other females have these issues too: yeast infections, chlamydia, pelvic inflammatory disease, fibroids, cysts, and breast lumps; the potential for ovarian, uterine, cervical, breast cancer, dilation and curettages, hysterectomies, and mastectomies.
- *Premenopausal changes:* when the period becomes irregular and so does sleep.
- *Menopause:* when the period ceases and uncomfortable, discombobulating symptoms appear, e.g., vaginal dryness, hot flashes, night sweats, growth of hair on face, loss of pubic hair, weight gain, osteoporosis as well as an adjustment to having to wear different clothes (those that do not make the body warmer than it is) and being regarded as less sexually appealing to the opposite sex. There is a tremendous challenge in adjusting to a body and face that gravity has discovered and is pulling in a downward direction.
- *Old age:* losing sense of one's femininity and sexuality inside and outside the body. Some overcompensate, others give up altogether.

The ability to embrace and to treasure being female will be sustained if the female can really take pleasure where there is pleasure in her body and accept and integrate the pains and discomforts as they accompany the joys and sorrows of love and romance, of marriage, parenthood and grandparenthood, of separation, loss and reconstruction, and these days, fortunately, the joys of her work. I have found in my clinical work that the non-neurotic use of cosmetics, dermatology, and even some plastic surgery can be very helpful as women age, along with reasonable diet and exercise. We have not studied enough in depth the experience of being "female" for the woman who remains a virgin her whole life or who has experienced intercourse but not pregnancy.

Dr. Notman writes that what matters is not just "awareness of genitals but also her feelings about her whole body form ... Her physical characteristics are interwoven with her sense of herself, her expectations of her future in her family and the wider world" (p. 8).

I take this to mean what the girl looks like and how she feels she fits in in her family. Notman mentions her feelings about her height, her physical strength, and very often how her breasts develop. She notes: "Although standards of beauty and normality about breasts vary from culture to culture, nurturance, generosity and plenitude are universally symbolized by the breast" (p. 11). One patient of mine goes shopping with her gorgeous mother and sister, sizes them up, and herself up for how full and pointed all their breasts are. Another has sadly told me: "My two brothers had penises and I was told to wait, I'd have breasts. But they never grew."

Reference

Notman, M. (2003). *The female body*. Presented at the mid-Winter Meetings of the American Psychoanalytic Meetings.

Chapter 6

The analyst as reluctant spectator

Working with women obsessed with thinness[1]

"Do you want them to write on your tombstone: 'She stayed thin'?"

(J.S.L.)

I have had in psychoanalytic treatment a number of women patients whose associations began to center mainly and obsessively on their efforts, successful, or failed, to achieve the levels of body leanness and muscle tone that this society values so highly. Their obsession with these "surface" issues, and their complete disregard while preoccupied with them for other concerns (relationships, family, work, children, even their own history and/or its analysis) I thought at first to be a resistance to reaching deeper levels in the analysis. It induced in me profound countertransference feelings of hopelessness and a sense of being caught in a net of shallowness, silliness, trivia, and trivial pursuits. I was reluctant to join these patients in treating their bodies as "things," and unwilling to be coerced into the role of spectator while these women used their bodies in the ways they did. Furthermore, the sense of "thingness" extended to me: at these times, these patients experienced me as a "thing" too, easily disposable, or interchangeable, rather than as an individual.

One patient, a 55-year-old woman, extremely intelligent and well-educated, and of normal weight, came for therapy at a time when her son was dying of AIDS, her daughter was on drugs, her husband was having an affair, and she had job issues to resolve. What she talked about in her sessions were the five pounds she wanted to lose, and how hard this was for her. She "dumped" or "evacuated" her problems with her children and her husband into me, requiring me to contain them, so that she could then deal with herself. The hidden agenda of her treatment was her need to experience herself as intact; I was to focus on her and not on them—to look at her and admire her and so make that experience possible.

The transference-countertransference paradigm that emerged with this woman felt to me like the phenomenon that a number of authors in recent years have characterized as "perverse transferences" (Etchegoyen, 1991; Fogel, 1991; Bach, 1994; Reed, 1994). In the perverse transference, as I understand it, the patient's (unconscious) aim is not so much to gain self-understanding through an analysis of the past as repeated in the present, but rather to use the analyst in some covert and sadistic way. Whereas in the classical transferences the patient for the most part experiences the analyst as a particular internalized figure in a particular internalized fantasy and eventually becomes aware that he or she is doing so, in the perverse transference, the patient uses the analyst himself or herself as a fetish (Renik, 1992).[2]

The interrelationships between the "perverse" (in the sense of "that which is turned away from what is right, reasonable or good" [Fogel, 1991, p. 3]), perversions, perverse fantasies, and perverse transferences have yet to be fully elucidated or understood. However, the perverse transference paradigm I will describe here emerged in the late 20th century as a reflection in treatment of a particular social context. "Social reality" for many women patients demands that they be extremely thin, and rewards them for conforming to a body ideal that requires their depriving themselves of needed food. Lately this demand has expanded to require muscularity and muscle tone, necessitating several hours of "working out" every day, and sometimes two sessions a day at the gym. When starvation and extensive exercise are not enough, women may turn to such adjuncts as pills (diet pills, diuretics, and laxatives), body wraps, or liposuction, and other forms of plastic surgery. All of this "perverts" and redirects the oral drive, whose purpose under normal circumstances is to satisfy the body's biological need for food (Gamman & Makinen, 1994).

This demand is so prevalent in this society that it is difficult to find anyone not aware of it or affected by it. It is not new. At the end of the 19th century the tubercular, cadaverous woman was the aesthetic ideal: " 'Sois belle et sois triste' (be beautiful and sad), as Baudelaire commanded. A woman who was not child-like and innocent was thought to inspire evil desires, with the result that the poets were fond of confusing women with boys" (Jullian, 1971, p. 42). The Duchess of Windsor was widely quoted as saying: "You cannot be too rich or too thin." Susan Faludi (1991), Naomi Wolf (1991), and others have hypothesized that as women won new freedoms in the late 20th century, a backlash arose in response, reinforcing more than ever such crippling ideals. During one single day in my own practice at the time I was writing this book, one patient had to leave in the middle of her session in order to go to the bathroom because she had taken laxatives in order to lose weight; another reported that her husband had told her that he wanted a divorce because, although she was thin enough, she did not have good "muscle tone"; and the fiancé of a third was organizing their elopement so that the hour of their marriage would not prevent her from "working out" that day.

My observation of these patients leads me to believe that they internalize this demand and treat it as an imperative with moral and ethical authority. From this privileged position it dominates the manifest content of their associations during certain phases of their psychoanalytic treatment. It also appears to me that such women have in common certain fantasies and childhood experiences. They are not diagnostically anorexic or bulimic, as described by Bruch (1978), Sours

(1980), Wilson and colleagues (1987), and Aronson (1993); although they may sometimes starve themselves, binge, or purge, they never get so regressed, or lose so much weight, that they require medical attention, or hospitalization. But they envy, admire, and seek to emulate truly anorexic women. Some of these patients have been rail-thin while others were of normal weight, but all embarked upon psychoanalytic treatment because of chronic unhappiness and blunted affect.

Ogden (1995), described a patient of his as suffering from "inner deadness":

> [S]he subsisted on a diet of fruits, grains and vegetables and organized her life around a rigorous exercise regime that included marathon jogging and the extensive use of a stationary bicycle. The patient exercised vigorously for at least three hours every day. If the exercise routine were in any way disrupted (for example, by illness or travel), the patient would experience a state of anxiety that on two occasions developed into a full blown panic attack.
>
> (pp. 55–56)

Ogden's patient belongs with the group of women I am discussing here. Shortly into treatment, it becomes apparent that they are "consumed" with thoughts about what they will let themselves eat, and how to avoid eating. They rage at themselves when, in the grip of their bodies' drive for survival, they give in, break their self-imposed diets, and eat something—usually a particularly forbidden or "junk" food—which inevitably they do.

These women are generally unaware of the degree to which they idealize men on the one hand and denigrate them on the other. They are unaware of their anger at others. They are chronically tired, yet they exercise several hours daily, and have little time left over for work, friends, or other interests, any of which might help them feel less empty. The media—movies, theater, newspapers, magazines, television—as well as their husbands and boyfriends support what they are doing, and are all too generous in suggesting role models for them to emulate. The social reality sustaining this unhealthy ideal is very powerful, and it presents a considerable problem in psychoanalytic treatment. Adherence to this ideal is entirely ego-syntonic to these women, and it is up to the analyst to make it dystonic. But work with these patients poses countertransference problems for the analyst, who is called upon to address the surface, since these patients have difficulty connecting to deeper layers of the psyche.

In their analysis of asceticism in contemporary culture entitled *The Good Body*, Winkler and Cole (1994) put deliberate fasting and starving into a cultural and historical perspective with moral connotations. They examined the relationship between cultural idealization of control of the self through ascetic practices and rises in eating disorders. In this same volume, Miles described the "pleasure of unpleasure" (p. 60), and Moore addressed the self-denial of abused women who "put lots of energy into trying to figure out what their abusers want, to please them, or to change themselves so their abusers will stop insulting or hating them" (p. 37).

But the women patients I discuss here do not need others to abuse them—they abuse themselves. They suffer from never reaching their unreachable goals of bodily perfection, and they suffer from the "eating crimes" they believe they have committed. I think of them as "junk food Raskolnikovs"—their superegos mete out harsh punishment. They come to their sessions declaring profound remorse and guilt over not having attended an exercise class or having eaten a candy bar or cookie. The analytic couch becomes a confessional to the "mortal sin" of eating sweets, and this sin is not necessarily a repetition connected to such childhood transgressions as stealing cookies from the cookie jar. Yet paradoxically some of these women buy a dress, wear it with the price tags tucked inside, and then return it for a refund, saying that "everyone does that," and feeling no awareness of guilt over such behavior.

As analyst I am witness not just to this "new ego" of our times—one in which deficits in body narcissism impair total ego functioning—but to a "new superego" as well, the contents of which are very different from my old-fashioned model. Continuous countertransference analysis is required in order to maintain the requisite neutrality—I personally do not find the confessed sin (eating sweets) sinful, but I do experience as sinful the one not confessed to (returning the worn dress). Furthermore, until I began to understand what was really happening between my women patients and myself, and found useful ways of addressing it, I experienced the content of the sessions as too trivial for someone with all of my training and expertise to deal with, and I felt guilty about collecting my fee. Later on in this chapter, I will elaborate upon the considerable countertransference issues these patients arouse.

I have come to the realization that the women patients who in psychoanalytic treatment display an obsession with body thinness seem to possess neither adequate intrapsychic internalization, nor adequate cathexis, of their own body surface. I now understand that in treatment they attempt to use me as a trainer, who will help them to focus upon and cathect the body surface, to mirror it, and reflect it in order to strengthen its cathexis. When my analytic patients experience pangs of hunger on the couch from excessive dieting, uncomfortable fullness after a binge, cramps from laxative-induced diarrhea, or pain following upon cosmetic surgeries, I now understand that they are not just communicating an experience of masochistic gratification, but a deeper need for primary narcissistic restoration. They need to be looked at. They are trying to feel something in order to combat inner feelings of deadness and emptiness. Although they report that their efforts are aimed at satisfying the contemporary male's desire for a thin woman, they show, as I have said and will demonstrate on p. 70, much contempt for men, and are in general sexually anesthetic and uninterested in sex. They do seek with men the holding, cuddling, and visual attention that shores up the sense of body boundary. Paradoxically, in what can only be regarded as a split in the ego, many of these women simultaneously embrace both feminism and its valuation of independent women, and this restrictive ideal of staying thin so that men will like them. I cannot say that all of these women belong to the widening scope of psychoanalysis, for much of what goes on in their treatment, which I will not report here, falls into the range of the "average expectable," and is typical of most treatment.

From time to time in the cases I am writing about, there emerges what I think must be described as a "perverse transference," the goal of which is to pull me into certain enactments in which I in my role as analyst was (countertransferentially) reluctant to engage in. My reluctance came in part from the high value that my work as a classical analyst has taught me to place on neutrality, and from my belief that the analyst's task is to bring into consciousness derivatives of inner fantasy and conflict. But I have had to diverge from that stance in order to be effective with the patients described here. In the perverse transferences that emerged in these cases, what was demanded of me was to look at the patient's body surface, and to comment about what I saw. I came to see my role in that context as "reluctant spectator."

The treatment of women obsessed with thinness is usually accompanied by acting out and by splits in the transference. These patients are adept at mobilizing a host of "helpers," in addition to the analyst, in their task of shoring up the body ego. Visits to trainers, nutritionists, chiropractors, dermatologists, and plastic surgeons are part of their daily routine, and these visits are often coupled with the timing of their analytic hours. Hairdressers, manicurists, and facialists are their confidantes, and may well hear their dreams and fantasies before the analyst does.

Psychoanalysts have long struggled with the treatment of narcissistic issues within the context of the more standard drive-related transference issues. To the Freudian analyst, the "body" means the biological drives and object-directed wishes that emanate from them. When Freud (1923) wrote that the first ego is the body ego, he was referring to an inner experience of the body, the body imago. Today, when patients refer to their bodies and to their dissatisfaction with them, they usually mean their bodies as seen from the outside by another—size, shape, muscle tone—and from the inside by critical internalizations.

Barbara, an attractive entertainment lawyer, divorced after a 10-year marriage. She had one daughter, and began psychoanalysis at 41, when she had been single for 9 years and was searching with little success for her next husband. She was chronically unhappy, felt empty, and was puzzled as to why the various men she dated did not wish to marry her. Paradoxically, she did not love, or admire any of them, but nevertheless, felt rejected by them. Early in her treatment, it became obvious that she suffered from an obsessional personality disorder, the symptoms of which were organized around compulsive closet-cleaning, drawer-arranging, and shopping for clothing seasons ahead of time.

Barbara felt chronically empty and as if she had "no life," despite daily reports of her career as a lawyer, her full and active social life, and her many cultural pursuits. She could experience a bit of excitement when introduced to a new man, but she was sexually indifferent. She assured me that all of her lovers experienced her as a terrific sex partner and that she was adept at deceiving them about her lack of enjoyment of sex and her incapacity to reach orgasm. She could have sex with three different men in 1 week or be celibate for months on end without complaint. It was all without meaning to her.

The only consistent pleasure in her life was finding and eating new flavors of ice cream. She would report her finds to me as if she had come across some forbidden and perverse pleasure, and she seemed to want to share the pleasure with me, hoping to "turn me on." She would say, "Today I am into Heath Bar Crunch," or "Today I am into Passion Fruit," in a voice that expressed salivation and a sexualized licking of her lips. She found a low-fat cookie with the brand name of "No-No's." In Barbara's world, sex was not forbidden; it was quite ordinary. Ice cream was forbidden, and ice cream was what counted.

Barbara had had a previous analyst, a man, and at the beginning of treatment it became clear that whatever she had learned from him was experienced by her as superior to anything she might possibly learn from me. Early in the development of the transference I experienced myself as psychically "vomited out," or, as was also evident in displaced transferences to her paralegals and secretaries, "defecated upon." The way she prolonged her profound feelings of emptiness was demonstrated in her unwillingness to take me in, to use me as an object for identification. This began to change only when the negative transference became manifest and could be interpreted. But this took some time, for Barbara, in the style of other patients discussed here, acted quite manifestly grateful for, and involved in, her treatment. She praised my work, and admired the way I looked and dressed and the décor of my office. This flattery covered a deeper layer of basic rejection of what went on between us. Also, if the analysis never ended, she would never lose me.

Barbara came from one of those perfectionistic families described by Bruch (1978), Sours (1980) and Wilson and colleagues (1987). Her parents presented themselves to their children as flawless, encouraged them to repress emotion, and never argued in front of them. She learned early on that she had to stay bone thin in order to be popular and admired. As an adult she was always on a diet. She used laxatives and diuretics, embarked on all kinds of exercise programs, and went regularly for liposuction to remove the evidence of the ice cream binges that collected around her abdomen and thighs. She regularly visited plastic surgeons for consultation, both here and abroad, and had had her facial features remodeled a number of times. She received much social approval from friends who concurred with her opinion that she was being good to herself when she undertook these surgeries. Although she felt emotionally flat most of the time, she became ecstatic when she could "turn one of her friends on" to going to one of her plastic surgeons. Further adding to the ego-syntonicity of her symptoms was the fact that in her social and professional world, there were no role models imparting different values. The task in her treatment was to demonstrate to her that her obsessions, which she considered to be normal, were not in fact normal, and that they were related to fantasies and events in her childhood and her neurotic way of seeking love. As a further complication, Barbara routinely visited a number of physicians in her stated goal of self-maintenance—periodontists, dermatologists, gynecologists, proctologists, and chiropractors—and these figures all served to split the transference and to keep the narcissistic problem intact. Her relationship with one plastic surgeon seemed to be a perverse and sexualized one, as she supplied him with new customers whom she had "turned on."

Constraints of space permit me to present only a small portion of the reconstruction of Barbara's childhood. Through the analysis of dreams, memories, and the transference, it emerged that she had been expected to be a perfect, beautiful, and clean child who was to make no noise and to know nothing of family problems or illnesses. Important issues were never discussed. It became apparent, despite her protestations to the contrary, that she suffered from a lack of "motherliness." Her basic needs were cared for, but in a sterile way. Nothing was soft and warm. I had the sense that there had been "food without food," "mother" without "mothering."

For months on end, in what I eventually came to understand as a perverse transference, her associations were full of empty chatter about clothes, diets, and face-lifts, all presented to me in a way that made it impossible to deepen the material. In the countertransference, I began to feel hopeless, and resentful of having to listen to such a barrage of shallow talk, but I searched within myself to find a way to get through to this patient.

During one particularly cold winter, Barbara's dieting regimen seemed to be breaking down. Frustrated with the treatment and realizing that my neutral classical stance was getting us nowhere I tried something new. I confronted the patient with the way her snacking, bingeing, diuretics, and laxatives were jeopardizing her health. I wondered why she did not stop at her local market, and I named it specifically, buy some dishes of low-fat foods, and provide herself with some nourishing dietetic meals. When she had a cold, I mentioned the possibility of her purchasing for herself a soup or a stew, a "comfort food." In other words, I became very concrete. She brightened up—she had never thought of food as "comfort." In this discussion with my patient I had unwittingly but instinctively filled in some "gap" in the mothering imago—Lacan (1977) would have called this a "suture."

This might seem like a standard supportive intervention, and supportive it was. The concreteness of my suggestions provided something the patient needed at that moment, thus stimulating ego development. It demonstrated the mutative function of what I call "mundane interventions," the kind that most probably take place in many analyses but that do not find their way into the literature.

A few months later progress led to regression. Barbara had her eyes done, an unnecessary procedure that no amount of interpretation could prevent (in this context see an old but still relevant study of poly-cosmetic surgeries by Menninger [1934]). For the next few months as she entered my office she would raise her face so that I could look her squarely in the face before she lay down on the couch. Her associations in those sessions made it apparent that the underlying activated dynamic was not competitive, exhibitionistic, or homoerotic (although it had aspects of all of these), but was connected to a need for my gaze, a need for me to look at her and to confirm that she was intact. Once I realized that need, I began to make occasional concrete references to the new appearance of her face and to the surgery. She was able to experience me as "seeing" her.

Interventions such as these, stimulated initially perhaps by the countertransference affects of impatience, frustration, and boredom, were surprisingly helpful in breaking through the treatment impasse. Barbara became increasingly able to talk of matters of relationship, of caring, of loss, and of meaning. For the first time she began to acknowledge thoughts, feelings, and fantasies about me. Prior to that I had been "just anyone," an "anyone" not to be thought about or missed.

I saw Carol 4 times-weekly in psychoanalysis for over ten years. As in the other cases, a dynamic of "purging of the analyst" occurred, making the work seem interminable. She entered treatment when she was 26, describing herself as "a total mess." She was working as a saleswoman, living in a tacky studio apartment, and feeling badly about her looks and her body, especially about what she perceived to be her large derrière. She also felt deeply ashamed that her breasts were overly large. Carol was of normal weight, but she experienced herself as heavy and was always on a diet. Aside from her sulky expression, she was actually quite pretty. She had been rejected by her boyfriend, who had ended a virtually sexless relationship of 2 years. She felt profoundly rejected by him, even though she had experienced him as physically repellent.

She was the fourth of five children from a socially prominent family. All of her siblings were boys. She, like Barbara, had been raised to be good, beautiful, thin, and socially adaptive, the end goal being to find a rich husband. Instead, Carol was sulky and belligerent, acted like a tomboy, and was much punished for her rebelliousness and her futile efforts to separate from her controlling mother. Her mother forced her to exercise as a preteen in order to reduce the size of her derrière, which was the target of family jokes. Her father referred to her as "Porky" upon a number of occasions. As an adult, Carol's primary concerns were her body and her clothes. Her mother taught her to sleep only in certain positions in order to maintain the tone of her facial skin. She avoided eating good food, and when she cooked she made food that was tasteless in order to avoid temptations that might lead her into putting on weight.

I cannot discuss all the details of the complex analysis of this severely narcissistic and masochistic woman, whose manifest treatment issues centered on castration anxiety, penis envy, and sibling rivalry, and defended against the less conscious ones of oral frustration and thwarting of affection and dependency needs. She was envious of, and competitive with, most of the women she encountered. Her parents encouraged a morbid dependency upon them, rewarding her for being sick. Over the years, as with Barbara, the transference was split, as Carol regularly visited chiropractors, orthopedic surgeons, gynecologists, and dermatologists. Despite these interferences with treatment, some changes occurred. She became able to find work in a field she liked and to attain a high level of competence in it. And after a number of years, she became able to experience sexual pleasure and to become conscious of her sexual fantasies, which excited, and aroused her.

Prior to the "awakening" of her sexuality, a period occurred in which Carol took cooking classes, invited friends to dinner, and cooked with her new boyfriend. This brief period of progression then led to regression. She began to report a fear that she would not be loved because she was not thin. Carol had, during the course of her analysis, a series of women friends from whom she would take advice. I remarked to her that although in her sessions with me she might come to a conclusion about something, she then needed her friends' advice before she would act on it. Her response, a profound belittling of me, was the verbalization of her chronic refusal to take me in, just as she had tried to refuse her mother's influence on her. How could I know anything about sex or relationships, she wanted to know, for I was "a nobody" just like her. The analysis of her sadistic attack on me facilitated real psychic change, along with some transient identifications, heretofore warded off that, furthered psychic growth.

Additional changes occurred when I began, in an enactment reactive to Carol's provocations and ongoing belittlement of me, to alter my technique in certain ways. I had come to doubt that she was "analyzable," and therefore began to let go of my analytic stance. She brought in some photographs of an island off the coast of Maine that she had visited. Until that time, she had never traveled, or shown any interest in anything outside her immediate existence. I commented on the beauty of one photograph of the sea. The following week she reported having framed that particular photo, neglecting, in her usual fashion, to acknowledge that we had spoken of it. It seemed to me that after many years, a process of internalization had begun, due to the relaxation of my interpretive stance and a positive, concrete comment about something she must have experienced as a part of herself.

I then began to make, over time, a series of uncharacteristic (for me) interventions. When she spoke of her body, her exercises, her weight gain, or loss, her frustrating clothes shopping expeditions, all areas that seemed so "unanalytic," I began to acknowledge what I actually saw. I began to express what I concretely, rather than symbolically, understood, and I did not address the issue in terms of its "deeper" meanings or possible genetic links. I would say, for example, by means of clarification or confrontation: "You feel disgusting and sweaty, yet you are wearing a wool sweater on a hot day"; "You say that you cannot find clothes that are elegant because of your wide rear end, yet you ignore the fact that overblouses are the fashion this season"; or "You say that you have no new clothes. Isn't the outfit you're wearing now new? I haven't seen it before."

It was difficult for me to make such statements. I felt the way I imagine an Orthodox Jew who eats bacon must feel. I asked myself: "What is an analyst doing in this territory?" I have since come to understand that interventions such as these are exactly what such patients need. They need to know concretely that the analyst sees what they are doing, that the analyst knows and notices, in a way that their parents did not. After a session in which I made a comment that referred to my gaze and to something I saw about her, Carol brought in the following dream: "We were in adjoining beds. You cut the cord to my white noisemaker." My interpretation was: "Now you are going to let me be heard."

The obsession with thinness has been addressed in the literature from various points of view. Orbach (1978) regarded it as "a flight from femininity." Gamman and Makinen (1994) argued that "some women 'pervert' the oral drive for sustenance to assuage narcissistic feelings of inadequacy in relation to their self-identity" (p. 139). Louise Kaplan (1991) viewed it as an enactment of a perverse strategy; she saw the bingeing and vomiting to be fetishistic.

In my treatment of these patients, I have come to believe that they make use of the analyst as a "spectator" (by which I do not mean a voyeur). The analyst's focus on their bodies helps them to supplement an insufficient cathexis. In the perverse transference that develops, the patient tries to get the analyst to look at him or her in order to repair the feeling of deficit, to "suture" a tear, in the Lacanian sense. In this endeavor the analyst herself is used, rather than her interpretations. This often takes much time in the analysis, since the internalization of a mirroring, approving object is insufficient, and must be both met and worked through before the patient can really work analytically. Statements that indicate concretely to the patient, one's awareness of small body changes, or changes in clothing—that is, of what is on the surface, rather than within the psyche—are the raw materials of this work.

The classically trained analyst usually feels uncomfortable during this phase of the treatment and such feelings must be monitored. This is not a "corrective emotional experience" in the sense that Alexander meant that term. This "confirmation" of what is on the surface, and the use of concrete language appropriate to the developmental period from which the narcissistic problem arose, eventually permits the treatment to progress to issues which pertain to inner fantasy and conflict, the areas the analyst was trained to work with and the discussion of which make her feel that she is "doing her job." It is my contention that the analyst will be "doing her job," when this perverse transference is mobilized, by reflecting back to her patient some of her concrete observations about the patient's appearance (or of displaced related issues, such as Carol's photos).

In an article on a different topic altogether, Caper (1994), described a session with a female patient who dreamed about silk blouses, and who spoke of her preference for wearing skirts that were shorter than the one she had worn to her session on the previous day. Caper wrote: "I said that she seemed to feel that it was too dowdy for her, that she would prefer something sexier" (p. 908). This was experienced by the patient as a "beautiful interpretation." The analyst felt that it freed her to wear sexy clothing, and that he was no longer experienced by her as some archaic superego figure trying to desexualize her. Caper went on to say: "The mind needs reliable information about itself—truth, if you will—just as much as the body needs food" (p. 909). I am in agreement with Caper on this latter point. I believe that what "worked" was his acknowledgment to the patient of what he actually concretely saw—the visual truth of the dowdy skirt of the day before.

In the course of the analysis of patients obsessed with thinness, I have found it necessary at appropriate moments to confront them with my perception that they embrace this societal ideal at least in part because it relates to their own issues. I point out that most women do not pursue thinness to such a degree, or give it the priority that they do. It holds special importance for them because of their need to take in and then to eliminate what is taken in. They need to feel left out, like second-class citizens. Eventually the link between what they say about their obsessions, and the genetic roots that give rise to them, become clear, and they become more able to examine their inner conflicts and fantasies.

These periods of confronting of my patients with my perception that their own issues are part of the problem have proved to be a particular challenge to me. Confrontation arouses anger and defensiveness. For example, one day Mrs. B. presented me with a book on face-lifts, a thinly veiled recommendation. In the countertransference, I am forced daily to confront my own struggle with aging as bodily perfection continues to elude me!

As I work with these patients, I am daily pulled into the terrain of reality, for, as Inderbitzen and Levy (1994) have written:

> Reality is especially well-suited for purposes of defense against unconscious instinctual and moral pressures because of its compelling visibility, its often engaging both analyst and analysand experientially (as in interaction), its here-and now quality, its "socializing" nature, and many other attributes that contrast with the confusing, slippery, and often fantastic quality of what can be inferred about unconscious drive and superego forces during analysis.
>
> (p. 785)

Confronting these patients about their goals can take place at various points. For example, when they complain of fatigue, the analyst can make statements such as: "You are starving your body and that is why you have no energy." Or when they break their diets and enjoy a meal, "Do you see how you feel? Why do you deprive yourself of such feelings?"

It is impossible to analyze these patients more deeply until some of the acting out abates. Acting out may occur in the use of diuretics and laxatives, or in visits to the surgeons and diet doctors, who cut them, touch them, look at them, and enable them to split, even splinter, the transference. Unable, on a deep level, to trust the analyst, or the analytic work, they often rely on an ever-changing "panel of advisors" in whom they can confide and from whom they receive concrete advice. After this phase, the analysis can really progress as they begin to see how their behavior is connected to the wish to be rid of specific inner tensions.

The women patients discussed here shared certain dynamics: They all felt rejected and unloved, and they all received attention from their parents only for their looks. They were quite willing to accept the masochistic gratifications of chronic pain in the form of hunger, body aches, and post-surgery pain. Some had progressed somewhat to the oedipal phase, but were severely let down by their fathers, who made no pretense about their lack of interest in them as little girls, and their preference for their mothers' company. This led to a profound oral envy of their mothers, a refusal to internalize them or what they could realistically provide, and a profound envy as well of other women whom they saw as having what they did not. Fantasies of magic such as: "Some women have that magic touch and can get any man they want" were prevalent. This was associated with the goal of "thinness" as potentially providing the missing something that eluded them. They managed, on an anal level, to turn to feces, to eliminate, and evacuate, whatever they did take in, and their chronic inner experience was one of emptiness.

Notes

1 This chapter has been adapted from Chapter 6 "Working with Women Obsessed with Thinness" in J. S. Lieberman (2000) *Body Talk: Looking and Being Looked at in Psychotherapy* Northvale, N. J.: Jason Aronson, Inc.
2 A fetish can be a non-genital body part (for example, a foot), or an inanimate object (for example, a shoe), that is essential for sexual discharge to take place while contact with the anxiety-provoking genital is avoided. In the common use of the term today, "fetish" or "fetishized" stands for a sexualized and often idealized object, usually a consumer product (for example, a handbag). In the perverse transference, the analyst himself is used rather than his interpretations. In the perversion, a substitute is used instead of normal intercourse, just as the perverse transference implies a substitute for the real thing.

References

Aronson, J. (1993). *Insights in the dynamic psychotherapy of anorexia and bulimia.* Northvale, N.J.: Jason Aronson, Inc.

Bach, S. (1994). *The language of perversion and the language of love.* Northvale, N.J.: Jason Aronson, Inc.

Bruch, H. (1978). *The golden cage: The enigma of anorexia nervosa.* Cambridge, M.A.: Harvard University Press.

Caper, R. (1994). What is a clinical fact? *International Journal of Psycho-Analysis, 75*(5–6), 903–913.

Etchegoyen, R. H. (1991). *The fundamentals of psychoanalytic technique.* London: Karnac.

Faludi, S. (1991). *Backlash: The undeclared war against American women.* New York: Crown.

Fogel, G. I. (1991). Perversity and the perverse: Updating a psychoanalytic paradigm. In G. I. Fogel (Ed.), *Perversions and near perversions* (pp. 1–16). New Haven, C.T.: Yale University Press.

Freud, S. (1923/1960). The ego and the id. In *The standard edition of the complete psychological works of Sigmund Freud* (Vol. 19, pp. 1–66). London: Hogarth Press.

Gamman, L., & Makinen, M. (1994). *Female fetishism.* New York: New York University Press.

Inderbitzen, L. B., & Levy, S. T. (1994). On grist for the mill: External reality as a defense. *Journal of the American Psychoanalytic Association, 42*(3), 763–788.

Jullian, P. (1971). *Dreamers of decadence: Symbolic painters of the 1890's.* New York: Praeger.

Kaplan, L. (1991). Women masquerading as women. In G. I. FogeL & W. A. Myers (Eds.), *Perversions and near-perversions in clinical practice* (pp. 127–152). New Haven, C.T.: Yale University Press.

Lacan, J. (1977). *Ecrits: A selection.* (A. Sheridan, Trans.). New York: W. W. Norton.

Menninger, K. (1934). Polysurgery and polysurgical addiction. *Psychoanalytic Quarterly, 3*, 173–199.

Ogden, T. (1995). Analyzing forms of silence and deadness of the transference counter-transference. *International Journal of Psychoanalysis, 76*(4), 695–709.

Orbach, S. (1978). *Fat is a feminist issue.* New York: Berkeley.

Reed, G. (1994). *Transference neurosis and psychoanalytic experience.* New Haven, C.T.: Yale University Press.

Renik, O. (1992). Use of the analyst as a fetish. *Psychoanalytic Quarterly, 61*(4), 541–563.

Sours, J. A. (1980). *Starving to death in a sea of objects: The anorexia nervosa syndrome.* New York: Jason Aronson, Inc.

Wilson, C. P., Hogan, C. C., & Mintz, I. L. (Eds.) (1983). *Fear of being fat.* Northvale, N.J.: Jason Aronson, Inc.

Winkler, M. G., & Cole, L. B. (Eds.) (1994). *The good body: Asceticism in contemporary culture.* New Haven, C.T.: Yale University Press.

Wolf, N. (1991). *The beauty myth: How images of beauty are used against women.* New York: William Morrow.

Chapter 7

The analyst's rush to metaphor[1]

In this chapter, I will attempt to link some observations about body narcissism with some observations about the way language develops and how it is used in analysis, particularly with regard to the capacity for symbolism and metaphor. The most active period of language development coincides broadly with the original integration of body narcissism. Language and body narcissism are linked at the very least by synchronicity.

In my clinical practice, I have observed increasing numbers of patients, male and female, who present initially, or after some months of treatment with preoccupying concerns about bodily and or facial appearance. Some focus exclusively upon their own looks, some focus with great intensity on the appearance of others, especially present or potential love objects, and some focus on both. These patients do not, in my experience, understand their anxiety about these issues to be "symbolic" of anything (although they may be able to understand other feelings about other issues in more abstract ways). Their worries and questions about the importance of "looks" are concrete, and so is the language they use to describe them.

About twenty years ago, before I had considered the technical issues I am writing about here, I saw a patient with a compulsive wish to have the darkest tan in New York. He spent summer days in the sun, and winter weekends jetting to Florida and Puerto Rico in this quest. He loved the compliments and attention he received from friends and strangers, and he called himself proudly "the Man with the Tan." Nevertheless, the strain of travel and the time devoted to the sun was wearing on him, and he came into therapy to deal with the resulting conflict. He quickly manifested an idealizing transference, and after a handful of sessions began to feel better. He attributed this to me, "the best therapist in New York," and he sang my praises to everyone around.

He began to arrive at sessions in his jogging clothes, and would sit before me deeply tanned, sweating, and half naked. His dreams indicated an intense erotic transference. Just out of training, I tried to interpret what I thought to be these erotic wishes toward me, but my efforts fell upon deaf ears. He terminated shortly afterwards, in his opinion "cured." I did not have at that time the diagnostic and clinical tools that would have enabled me to address the true nature of his problem. I have since learned more about the origin of narcissistic deficits and the adjustment of thought and language, the *linguistic attunement* that these patients require.

I believe, and will try to demonstrate, that disturbances in body narcissism are often reflected in more or less temporary disturbances in the capacity for metaphoric language when speaking about the body, its appearance, and its maintenance. This is not surprising in view of the facts that they develop contemporaneously with each other, and that the developmental deprivations that may influence the one (such as insufficient maternal attention) are also known to influence the other. The earliest registration of form is visual form. And the first representations of self and other are registered non-verbally: by sight, smell, hearing, and touch. Mothers and other caretakers teach the beginnings of language by looking at, touching, and naming, the infant's (and their own) various body and facial parts. Positive or negative affects connected with the body and its parts are communicated in these very basic exchanges. Children with depressed, narcissistic, or otherwise unrelated mothers may not experience this close connection between looking, naming, and caretaking, and the resulting deficits may manifest themselves across all three fields.

This correspondence makes for potential difficulties in the psychoanalytic treatment of such common developmental disturbances. They (the difficulties) are a result of the conflict between the concrete language of that developmental period and the established mores of analytic communication. Contemporary psychoanalysts value metaphor. "Where symbol was, there metaphor shall be" was the way Wright (1991, p. 165) put it. The capacity for "higher-level" abstract thought is so highly valued in our field that it has long been held as a criterion by which to select those suitable for analysis (Arlow, 1979; Levin, 1979; Borbely, 1998).

One reason for this preference is the undoubtedly greater capacity of metaphoric language for grasping and conveying subtle and complicated psychological constellations. Our own analyses were conducted in the language of metaphor, and our training in highly conceptual language. We are used to metaphor as the vehicle for elaborating psychological experience, and our work feels more stimulating and meaningful when conducted in abstract discourse.

However, there are some dangers in this preference. The first is that, as we know, abstraction can be used as a defense against more immediate kinds of experience. As Riesenberg-Malcolm (1999) says, "Using symbolic language bypasses the depths of the transference experience. It destroys the live contact between analyst and patient and turns the analysis into *talking about* unconscious phantasies, rather than experiencing them in their crude impact" (p. 51).

A second danger is that metaphor, being multi-layered and multi-faceted, is also open to multiple interpretations, and is much more likely than a concrete statement to be understood differently by the patient and analyst—sometimes without the awareness that this has occurred. I will have more to say about this shortly.

The third and most serious danger is the dismissal of concrete speech as either not relevant to analyzable patients, or not capable of communicating anything important. In fact, however, many analysts have expressed the opinion, and supported it strongly, that the use of concrete language may be an important part of the analytic process.

I caution analysts to not "rush to metaphor," by analogy with O. J. Simpson's attorney, who cautioned the jury to not "rush to judgment" in assuming his client's guilt. Especially with educated patients, we tend to assume that they share with us a common language and common symbols. I have found that many times this is not so, especially when issues about body narcissism arise in the treatment.

Patients in analysis regress to troubled points in their development, and this sometimes means regressing to less mature forms of mental representation. Lecours and Bouchard (1997) noted that "clinical observation confirms that each patient displays certain specific emotional 'dark zones' that are less mentalized and others that are more mentally elaborated, partly independently of their character organization" (p. 871). They observed further that "the desired evolution in the levels and forms of mental elaboration during analysis seem to imply a prior necessary activation and working through of dynamically more regressed and often less mentalized drive-affect material" (p. 870).

They were referring specifically to the acting out of borderline patients who cannot maintain stable mental images, but I believe this formulation to be true for narcissistic patients as well. In addition, Borbely (1998) has noted that trauma affects the capacity for metaphor; only people who can tolerate strong emotional experiences can use metaphor. "Trauma reduces the polysemy of experience due to overwhelming anxiety and leads to a fixed meaning of the experience ... during psychological trauma ... the fabric of semantic relations gets skewed or torn apart" (p. 930). "Cure" results from letting the analysand regain metaphorical potential. Prior to that, "the individual is forced to resort to idiomatic, rigid analogical thinking" (p. 930).

Busch (1997) has addressed this topic also, and his work has greatly influenced me. As the ego undergoes changes in the analytic process, he maintains, it becomes temporarily less available for abstract thinking. Concrete thinking may appear in the patient's area of conflict, and the analyst must wait until, with integration of the changes, the patient's ego becomes once again available for abstract thinking. He wrote:

> In making my interpretations, I often repeat the patient's themes and sequencing ... the practice is based on my observation that in areas of conflict patients' ways of thinking are concrete and limited to a "before the eye" reality (Busch, 1995b), similar to a type of thinking seen in children at an age when conflicts become formed (eighteen months to seven years). Thus my interpretations rely, wherever possible, on what is most tangible, concrete and observable–that is, the patient's own thoughts.
>
> (p. 413)

Busch has criticized any uses of metaphor that do not take into account the current state of the ego and its readiness at that time to work with metaphor.

If in fact, therefore, certain psychological situations tend to be characterized by concrete rather than abstract thought, the question arises of how the analyst should address them.

Gedo (1979) has noted that "the majority of psychoanalytic clinicians probably have not experienced much discomfort about the loose fit between their theoretical tools and their *patients'* associations" (pp. 161–162). More recently (1996), he wrote that "in regressive states, analysands often become unable to process the intended meaning even of syntactically and lexically clear messages—unless these meanings are amplified by paraverbal indications of affect" (p. 14).

These things being so, it seems that a patient (temporarily) limited to concrete thought and speech, and an analyst operating on his accustomed highly symbolic plane, may not always be understanding each other, however well they may communicate when the patient is in comfortably metaphoric mode. They may not always recognize when misunderstanding occurs. Further, the analyst may misinterpret an actual misunderstanding as psychologically-motivated resistance.

Levin (1979), for example, has a great interest in and appreciation of metaphoric language for psychoanalytic communication. He takes pains to describe the complexity of metaphoric language, which involves what he calls "switching" functions, as well as ambiguity, multiple meanings, symbolism, and thinking by means of similarities. He notes that metaphors manage both to surprise us and to bridge experiences by their capacity to bind unexpectedly conjoined concepts. However, I am not convinced that we all agree on what constitutes a metaphor in clinical work. I will use one of Levin's own illustrations to exemplify the kind of possible misunderstanding I am talking about.

He offers the following example of what he considered to be a metaphoric communication. The patient, Mr. A., had lost father, grandfather, and uncle while young. Levin is describing how the patient's mourning process continues:

> Having had some of his clothes stolen from a laundry, he spoke one day of his outraged embarrassment and his impulse to immediately replace the lost articles. Unfortunately, he would have to order new clothes in a slightly larger size since he felt he had gained weight. He mused about having someone assist him in relation to this loss. I suggested that he needed a tailor and asked him if he knew any way to mend the situation. This ambiguous metaphor was a reference to his major loss in childhood, (father) who was a tailor; to his recent loss (of clothes); and to myself in the transference as one who mends or helps him to mend himself, etc.
>
> (p. 234)

My own impression of this encounter is that his patient was thinking concretely, and that Levin himself was speaking in both concrete and metaphoric modes.

Obviously I am not necessarily right, but this is a good example of a communication that is ambiguous as to its concrete or metaphorical nature.

As I will show, my experience with patients like this leads me to think that the therapeutic gains that Levin reports could as well be attributed to the concrete statement that the patient needed a tailor as to a metaphorical connection between the lost father and "mending the situation." It is not always clear what is concrete and what is metaphor. There can be mixtures of both in the same phrase, and different people read the phrases differently.

Another example: when I first read Silverman's (1987) widely studied and discussed clinical report in *Psychoanalytic Inquiry*, it seemed to me the patient was a quintessential "concrete" patient. She would, when Silverman spoke symbolically, and metaphorically, follow him cooperatively wherever he led her. In my opinion, however, she was located in a different cognitive and linguistic world where concrete reality dominated. When she spoke about a problem in tipping her hairdresser, Silverman told her that she was avoiding sexual excitement, that scissors and fingers in her hair sounds "sexual." She replied that she had "no problem tipping her manicurist." This kind of exchange is characteristic of concrete patients. (Silverman's patient, by the way, like many of the patients I will discuss in this paper, presented in her associations preoccupying concerns about her looks.)

Ogden is another analyst with a great interest in metaphor who has done us a service in studying its place in analytic thought. In a series of articles on the analyst's reveries (1997), he described reverie as a metaphoric expression of what unconscious experience is like, and of the way metaphor is created. He praises the use of metaphor: "Without metaphor, we are stuck in a world of surfaces with meanings that cannot be reflected upon" (p. 727). Ogden values the use of metaphor highly, but he also appears implicitly to devalue concrete language. He does not (at least in his clinical reports) apparently use concrete language himself in talking to his patients, and he presents material from several cases in which he and his patient worked very well with metaphor.

In one example, however, he describes a failed attempt to elaborate upon a metaphor. It seems to me likely that this is another good example of a case in which the analyst was in one place and the patient in another, and where misunderstanding ended up getting misinterpreted as resistance.

> In a recent analytic session, the analysand, Mr. H, said, "Last evening I didn't leave the college [where he teaches] with anyone. While waiting for the bus I was completely alone with myself." I asked, "What was it like being alone with yourself? What kind of company were you for yourself?" The patient replied, "I don't know. I finished almost all of my Christmas shopping yesterday."
>
> (p. 723)

Ogden interprets this response as a defense, which he counters with another metaphor, that the patient regularly feels like an unwelcome guest of the analyst.

The patient then remarks that he is not sleeping well because of mechanical noises—a response that a metaphor-using analyst, I think, would have to understand as a comment that these interpretations were experienced by him as just that, "noises." Rather than adjusting his language to that of his patient, he keeps pushing metaphors.

But Ogden is very interested in these matters, and he in fact provides an excellent description of concrete patients:

> The experience of attempting to work with patients who are very concrete in their thinking and use of language is an experience of communication (or lack of communication) characterized by a paucity of metaphorical language (or more accurately, an inability on the part of the patient to experience a metaphor as a metaphor). For such patients, people, events, feelings, perceptions are what they are: a session cancelled because of the analyst's illness is just that, a session cancelled because the analyst was ill, no more and no less. The event is an event; it is not even felt by the patient to be his experience of an event.
>
> (p. 725)

He also provides some useful references to other analysts' studies of the limitations of metaphor, and their admonitions that the analyst not surpasses the patient, or steal, or creates metaphors, or in an authoritarian way gives the patient the "right" way. He does not, however, offer technical recommendations that might help analysts working with such patients. Although in speaking with clinicians it becomes clear that many do in fact use concrete language with concrete patients, this informal practice has not apparently been much reported upon in the literature, or studied systematically.

A further complication of the technical implications of concreteness is that although its presentation is easily recognized and its results widely discussed, there is no widespread agreement about its causes.

Some analysts consider concreteness a defense; for others it is a defect in a primitive ego that has not yet integrated the symbolic and the abstract. I understand concreteness as Giovacchini (1972) did when he referred to "a mind that is unwilling to deal with both inner and outer experiences in psychological terms" (p. 353). (However, Giovacchini himself views concreteness as a function of ego defects, and/or as controlling manipulations designed to sabotage the analyst.)

So the question remains: how do you increase the capacity for metaphor in patients with whom you can't talk metaphorically? Bass (1997) has addressed directly this dilemma of what he calls the "problem of concreteness." He feels that concrete patients "present derivatives of fantasy material, often in an apparent drive-defense configuration, but cannot make use of interpretation" (p. 642). He sees persistent concreteness as "a particularly inert form of wish and defense working together" (p. 649), and "a result of the process that produces the primary split in the ego, a split between any differentiation that has become too anxiety-provoking and the defensive use of hallucinatory wish fulfillment substitute for it altogether" (p. 659). He goes on to write:

> If one has to believe that one's perceptions provide indubitable knowledge of "reality," the possibility of intervention is pre-empted. To interpret always implies that one thing might mean another. The "concrete" patient paradoxically defends against just this possibility while remaining in analysis.
>
> (p. 645)

Bass discusses dreams as convincing visual experiences. For the dreamer, "seeing is believing." When it is too threatening to deal with the unseen, patients must stay with what they can see. The analyst of concrete patients must bear this in mind.

Lacan (1953–1954), in the context of a distinction between full speech and empty speech, described empty speech as: "caught up in the here and now with the analyst, where the subject wanders about in the machinations of the language system, in the labyrinth of a system of reference offered him by his cultural context" (p. 61).

If the task of the analyst is to help the patient achieve "full speech," the problem of technique that confronts him or her is how, as long as necessary, to conduct the analysis without it. A wall of so-called "empty" words must be penetrated. How can we talk to these patients?

It is my impression that the need for concreteness of language and thought coincides frequently with times of preoccupation with the external, physical body. The nature of these preoccupations may change. Gedo (1979) has observed that "in the aftermath of Victorian prudery, Freud taught the victims of the discontent produced by a civilization simultaneously moralistic and prurient that one must live one's life within the body" (p. 259).

Today issues other than the "moral" use of the body prevail among our patients. Freud's writings reflected his patients' concerns about the "inner body" and the genitalia. Today's patients speak of their concerns about the "external" body, particularly how it looks to themselves and others. Many seem manifestly less concerned with issues of gender and sexuality than with the narcissistic cathexis of the body, and the search for ways to shore up a shaky body ego.

However, whatever the particular bodily concern, it seems to me that it is likely to be associated with a diminution of metaphoric thinking, which becomes profoundly irrelevant, at least temporarily, to the patient. In *The Broken Mirror*, Phillips (1997) deals with body dysmorphic disorder, or BDD. She cites the complaint of such a concrete patient:

> Some of my therapists have tried to convince me that my appearance concerns are just a symptom of other problems—that they aren't my real problem. After years and years of trying to figure this out, I've finally come

to the conclusion that they're wrong. My obsessions have a life of their own. They're a problem in their own right. They're not just a symptom of other problems.

(p. 39)

The body is a concrete object with an actual concrete manifestation and actual physical feelings (as opposed, say, to an idea, or a fantasy). Also, people have to begin to deal with their bodies well before the emergence of abstract thought. For both of these reasons, and perhaps others that will become clear over time, psychological issues about the body appear to require a concreteness of thought that other issues do not. Hinshelwood (1997) has presented some of Melanie Klein's unpublished writings. Klein described the "inner object" in its deepest sense to be a physical being, lodged inside the body with concomitant bodily feelings. In her technical recommendations about addressing such a concept to the patient, she wrote:

> In my experience the more concretely, the more specifically, I should say vividly if this did not have a flavour of dramatization which is unnecessary, we can convey to the patient the content of the unconscious phantasies we see in action, the more effective our interpretations will be.

(p. 895)

I would add to this "the more visually."

As I have said, I think that the contemporaneity of the development of language and the integration of body narcissism, and their joint dependency upon intense maternal involvement, both bodily, and linguistic, gives them a sort of a joint vulnerability. A deficiency in the caretaking environment that affects the one will be likely to affect the other—therefore disturbances in bodily narcissism are likely to be accompanied by disturbances in higher-level thinking and speech. In my experience, concrete thinking is often connected with problems in the development of the bodily self and its boundaries, and tends to be the result of deficits in attention to the body and its care and maintenance. Such problems intersect and interact with the development of internal fantasy, conflict, and defense from early childhood on.

I believe that in circumstances where a patient is dealing concretely with concrete preoccupations about looks concrete responses from the analyst actually facilitate and promote the concrete patient's capacity for symbolic thinking, and that such responses can begin to repair the narcissistic deficit underlying the preoccupation (see three brief examples on p. 89), allowing the ego to grow and further develop. Just as Busch (1997) advocates speaking to the surface of the ego, I believe that in this area of body narcissism the analyst must include in his or her comments to the patient concrete references to his or her observations of the patient's body, of what is revealed at the level of the skin and its covering, clothes. Only apparently superficial, this is very much a way "in," for the external body is the gatekeeper to the inner self, its thoughts, and its fantasies.

The prevalence in some of our patients of thoughts and obsessions about their bodies is evident in the amount of time and effort many of them spend in exercise, on diet and nutrition, and on the selection of clothes. When they appear in our offices in scanty exercise garb, too quick an "understanding" of this as sexually seductive can lead us to overlook the more immediate therapeutic need to be looked at by us. Kohut (1971) referred to the "mirror transference," and he developed from it an analytic technique of reflecting back to the patient important aspects of self. On a concrete level, some of these phenomena may be understood as reflecting the more literal wish on the part of the patient for the analyst to be a mirror telling him or her what he or she quite literally sees.

For Lacan, symptoms are resolved through an analysis of language. An analysis of the language deficits manifested by patients preoccupied with appearance leads to the conclusion that the analyst must use concrete language in order to communicate with them until they are ready to use symbol and metaphor.

Before offering some extended clinical studies of people in whom an upsurge of issues around body narcissism temporarily shut down the capacity for metaphoric analytic work, I want to address the belief that concrete communication is necessarily "simple" and not psychological when it occurs in analysis.

When patients are dealing concretely with issues of body narcissism (as opposed to the times when they are using concern about their looks to symbolize something else, such as castration or Oedipal victory), I think that they must be responded to directly and concretely in the "here and now." This feedback about what the analyst sees provides them with confirmatory, empathic responses that demonstrate the analyst's awareness of their experience of and in their bodies in the moment. But such responses are not necessarily "simple," psychologically uninformed or uninforming, or even unanalytic, and they should not be devalued as part of an ongoing psychoanalytic process. I offer as illustration three exchanges from the analysis of one patient:

PT: "I never feel that I look that great. I never know what to wear. I am so uncomfortably warm today."

A: "It is 90 degrees out, yet you are wearing a wool cardigan and slacks. What about that?"

PT: Complains that she has to go to a business lunch the next day in a fashionable restaurant and has no idea of what people would be wearing.

A: "Why not go over to that restaurant today and have a look?"

PT: (She is envious of me but not yet aware of that, and she always avoids looking at me when she comes into her session.) "My rear end is so large. I am so out of fashion. I haven't the vaguest idea of what people are wearing this fall."

A: "You have the option of looking at people when you are out in the street."

In the first example, I could (correctly) have interpreted the links between the patient's conscious discomfort with the unconscious discomfort of her sexual feelings toward me. I did not, because this patient had demonstrated many times that she could not yet hear or process an interpretation like that, while she could easily comprehend and relate to my more concrete comment. But it is important to note that when I responded to what I saw, my response, although concrete, was not simple. It was informed by long and hard analytic work, in which I had come to the conclusion that there had been a profound lack of concrete maternal attention when this patient was a child. In light of this reconstruction, my "concrete" statement addressed the consequent deficits that I had observed in the patient's capacity to care for herself. My comments were available for understanding on two levels: the concrete one of which she was at that time capable, and the historical/metaphorical one in which I encoded my understanding of her childhood experience.

In the second and third examples, I spoke from another convincing reconstruction—that this patient's curiosity had been suppressed when she was a child. I did not interpret at that moment her envy of me or her not looking at me, but I did interpret *what I had learned about them*, in a displaced form.

A series of interventions such as these, in which looking, and being looked at were facilitated, eventually enabled this patient to purchase a fashionable wardrobe, to feel good about her body, and more importantly for the analysis, to begin to work symbolically again to understand the genesis of her narcissistic problem. She was then able to proceed to talking about issues of envy and competitiveness with me.

Similarly, if the "Man with the Tan" were my patient today, I would not try to interpret erotic transference at such a time of concrete narcissistic preoccupation. I would focus first on the narcissistic issues and speak to him about his tan, the perspiration I observed, etc. That is, I would stay close to concrete bodily issues in my comments. I would say, for example: "You are sitting on the floor in the position you take in the sun."

When a patient has regressed to concrete ways of thinking, it facilitates progress when the analyst reports what he or she actually sees (as opposed to interpreting what he or she thinks it means). However, the analyst will do this in the context of what the analyst knows about the patient's issues with seeing and being seen. The symbolizing analyst must give up symbolic speech in order to communicate with a non-symbolizing patient, but he or she does not give up the capacity to think symbolically, or to be aware of the psychological context. (The temporary regression involved in relinquishing symbolic and metaphoric speech may of course have countertransference implications for any individual analyst.) The kind of consequent "narcissistic repair" demonstrated in the examples above stimulates the ego to grow. If all goes well, eventually the patient will become able once again to communicate in symbol and metaphor.

Many researchers and commentators have maintained that women suffer more about their bodies, and dislike them more, than men do theirs. In my clinical practice I have had a number of male patients, both heterosexual and homosexual, whose predominant concerns have centered on body narcissism. Men tend, however, to displace their own insecurities about the appearance of their bodies onto women's bodies. (Since women have, since time began, been willing to accept such displacements, these practices continue!)

Male and female patients both report concerns about what they look like. Often their communications in analysis are aimed, consciously or unconsciously, at getting feedback about how they look to the analyst, how the analyst sees them, and whether or not the analyst likes their looks. I have had a number of male patients who were obsessed with the looks of the women they were trying to date, were dating, or were married to. They also spent much time in the mirror looking at themselves, trying to reassure themselves that they were physically acceptable, and they used women to buttress their own self-images.

I want to illustrate now what has in my experience been the characteristic clinical presentation of these kinds of issues: the coincidence of a period of intense bodily preoccupation with the loss of a previously-available capacity for metaphoric language. Most began treatment with language and associations that suggested an oedipal level of development. All of them were capable of symbolic thought and speech, all of them were psychologically-minded, and all became quickly involved in the analytic process.

My first three illustrative patients were men. Initially, when they came to analysis, they all wondered whether they were good-looking or not, and reported feeling insecure with women. Each, however, somewhat paradoxically started out convinced that he was his mother's favorite: the "oedipal winner" (over father), the "sibling winner" (over brothers and sisters), or the only child in the family.

In the next phase of treatment, each of these men regressed to a completely syntonic, highly concrete phase in which he experienced himself as extremely attractive, and displayed an intense, and very judgmental interest in the appearance of the women he encountered. During this period, not one of these men was able to search for the meanings of such an attitude in the way he had been able to do, and had been interested in doing, in the earlier phase. My purpose in these examples is less to illustrate the particulars of the verbal process (as I did with the patient above). Instead I want to demonstrate what I consider the characteristic aspects of the clinical presentation and the consistency of this presentation over a number of patients: a regression to an intense preoccupation with body narcissism, and at the same time a loss of the capacity for metaphoric thought and speech.

Mr. H., an attorney, was suicidally depressed when he came into treatment at the age of 37. At that time he undertook and completed several years of analytic work in which symbol and metaphor were used as a matter of course in the usual analytic way. Mr. H. had experienced himself to be the favored child of his mother, although he was the middle one of three boys, and his mother, a physician, was seldom home. However, his treatment focused predominantly on an intense rivalry with his successful, castrating, competitive father.

Mr. H. "took" to his analysis like the proverbial duck to water, and during it he progressed both in his legal career and in his social life. During the difficult times of working through his rage at his father, he had a number of brief homosexual encounters, but he thought these to be compulsive behaviors which he would someday be able to control—he considered himself straight, not gay, or bisexual. He moved in with his girlfriend (despite my challenging this decision, for the relationship lacked passion) and he terminated his treatment believing that it was successful. He felt happy enough and was quite successful in his career.

But 5 years later, Mr. H. returned with an entirely different set of issues. His relationship was in trouble, and he was preoccupied with physical and sexual concerns. It was strikingly apparent to me that his manner of speaking had also changed. It was much simpler, and he no longer used abstract or symbolic language.

Mr. H. was in the middle of a passionate sexual affair with a woman named J., who lived in California and who shared his love of athletics and exhibiting the body. J. wore thong bathing suits and spandex shorts and tops, and could not possibly, said Mr. H., be more unlike his short, plump girlfriend. J. was "hot." He said to me with joy: "Imagine finding someone who looks just like you!" He regarded the lean, long-legged J. as his female counterpart, and he gave both of them high ratings for beauty and firm skin tone.

"Imagine having someone who looks just like you!" His excited tone indicated that he believed that I shared this wish and valued it as highly as he did. He felt contemptuous of those who did not. Mr. H. was furious with his girlfriend for not working out and being "toned." He was clearly turned on by the women in thong bathing suits he saw on the beaches in California and the ones who wore short shorts on the streets near his summer home. Being "toned and fit" had moral value for him.

But J. did not want to leave California, and she attempted to end their affair. Mr. H. decided to work on his official relationship, and he asked his girlfriend to work on her body so that she could please him more. She did not like this request, but she acquiesced. She did a several months' "makeover," from which she emerged as quite a beauty. However, she was still short, and so her transformation did nothing to shift Mr. H.'s interest away from J., who, being tall "looked like" him. He attempted to deal with his disappointment by trying to contact her, but she refused to see him. For weeks he fantasized revenge on her.

A suicidal depression then ensued. He threatened to kill himself by jumping from a bridge, and I was concerned enough that he might do it that I recommended that he take medication. He said that he had heard that Prozac caused weight gain, and he was afraid to gain weight. I responded: "You mean you don't want to be a fat corpse?" He began to laugh uncontrollably, and pulled somewhat out of his depression after that session. The fact that he could laugh at himself indicated at least some degree of self-awareness and ego strength, and I became less concerned about his potential for suicide. For a brief time he did take antidepressants, but what really seemed to affect him and return him to his formerly positive ego state were the concrete statements, like the "fat corpse" one, that I made to him about his body, his attachment to J.'s body, his disinterest in his girlfriend's body, and most important, his concerns about he was going to meet women once he gave up J. and separated from his girlfriend. We discussed concrete options: the personal ads, parties, blind dates, etc. Mr. H. began an avid search for a new woman with excellent body tone and fitness. We discussed together what he wanted in a woman in concrete terms. He said that he did not care about anything beyond her having a good body to match his own. I did not at this time challenge him or ask him to think about "why."

We stayed on this level for a longtime, perhaps a year. It seemed much longer to me, for I continually had to monitor and analyze my negative countertransference feelings about how completely Mr. H. experienced and treated women as objects (I will discuss some aspects of this later on). I followed Mr. H. through the dating and bedding of numbers of women, most of whom were socially and intellectually incompatible with him, but who met his physical criteria. His anger toward women showed in his asking them what they weighed before he met them, or telling them he would not see them again because they were not "toned." I did not address the shallowness of his connections, nor did I ask him to understand his "fear of fat." We had covered this ground with little understanding or psychic change during the year he was trying to work things out with his girlfriend. (I hypothesized privately that the "fear of fat" was rooted in his feelings about his mother's pregnancy during the oedipal years, coupled with her increasing unavailability to him; I also thought that the need for a hard, toned body, along with his obsessive exercise, was an effort to affirm and strengthen his fuzzy body boundaries. However, by then I was convinced that speaking to those factors—i.e., treating his preoccupations as symbolic—was premature and would not be useful.)

I stayed with his concreteness in the sessions, speaking in equally concrete terms about his search for a woman with a perfect body, and his work keeping his own body fit. Gradually, aspects of the sensitive, and thoughtful man I had worked with years before reappeared. A new phase of the transference opened. Mr. H. became intensely curious about me, about what I did and read, about what man might have called me on the telephone, etc. He decided that I must have been divorced recently and that like himself I was out trying to find another partner. He wondered about the men he assumed I was dating. He cited many ways in which he believed us to be alike: we had similar houses, furnishings, work schedules, etc. He began to bring with him intellectual and scholarly books, which he carefully left in my view. He came to many sessions after or on the way to exercise, in shorts, and sleeveless tops. He seemed to be acting on a narcissistic need to have me look at him and admire him, mixed with a wish to seduce me. He wanted to be like me and identify with me. In short, he was becoming more like the person I had originally known, and displaying a much more recognizable transference.

By this time, Mr. H.'s language had resumed its original metaphoric style, and since he no longer seemed to need me to limit myself to concrete speech, I reverted to "normal." My lack of response to his non-verbal seductive and exhibitionistic acting-in led to more bouts of depression, and random homosexual encounters. These were dystonic, for he did not regard himself as homosexual, but he became aware that those impulses emerged when he felt rejected by women. I began to interpret the erotic transference in displacement—in metaphoric, symbolic terms. Mr. H. was now able to engage in this process. He eventually found a loving and caring woman with whom he shared an intense sexual life, but he continued to date others, as he felt that he wanted to wait a while before committing himself. In his final session, joking with me about the women he was dating, he said, "I won't see those who won't sleep with me!"—that is, his analyst!

It can be argued, and I think it is true, that Mr. H.'s concreteness served in part as a defense against the erotic transference, but in itself it was also an issue that had to be worked through. Working through it demanded my participation in the concrete dialogue. I am reminded of Fenichel's statement that "no sight can actually bring about the reassurance which these patients are seeking" (1945, p. 348). This is a correct appraisal of the insatiable nature of the quest, which ultimately can only be satisfied by repair of the internal narcissistic wound.

Mr. K., like Mr. H., entered psychoanalytic treatment in a very depressed state. He appeared originally to be a thoughtful neurotic, but subsequently regressed to a shallow and concrete self-presentation in which he manifested hysterical and obsessional character traits. An architect who loved clean, sleek-looking things, he had been very critical of his wife, who was slightly plump and buxom, and wished (as he felt it) to "spoil" the clean, immaculate look of their apartment by displaying some of her own possessions. Fed up, she had left him, asked for a divorce, and found another man. Mr. K. spent the next few years flooding the analytic couch with tears, dredging up the past in order to understand his inability to get over his loss, get on with his life, and meet someone new. He tortured himself by spying on his ex-wife and her husband, standing outside their apartment until they closed the blinds to make love.

It was obvious that he had been a spoiled child. His mother had favored him over two younger siblings and especially over his father, for whom the whole family had contempt. The primal scene and oedipal implications of the stalking of his former wife were evident both to Mr. K. and to me. After years of crying, he himself likened the endless stream of tears to an endless rope, a symbol that had appeared in his dreams and that represented the umbilical cord—the tie to his mother and to his ex-wife. This metaphor was his last for a longtime.

After this realization, Mr. K. began to go out in the evenings in search of another woman, but he couldn't find one who was "right." He fixated on women who were sleek and slim, like the buildings he designed, but none were up to his standards. He seemed a completely different man from the one who had entered treatment mourning his plump wife. Finally he found an aggressive business-woman who had once been a model. She was tall and slender and he chose her for her appearance, but he admitted that he secretly enjoyed the company and pleasing sight of her dog—a sleek Dalmatian—more.

Several more years of analysis ensued. Eventually, the concreteness of our dialogue shifted and the use of symbol and metaphor was resumed, as was a less one-dimensional personality. Mr. K. ended his relationship with his model girl-friend, became involved in a number of philanthropic enterprises, and eventually met a caring and loving woman to marry.

Dr. L., a professor of physics, became severely depressed when his wife told him, "all of a sudden, without any notice," that she was divorcing him and mar-rying another man. Dr. L. had never suspected that she was unhappy or that she was having an affair. He did not have the energy to go out and try to date and he had never really dated as a young man 40 years ago. He was an only child. He had been doted on by his parents, he said, and had only fond memories of his mother and father. He remembered his mother encouraging him to find a nice girl. He had married his wife for her simplicity, her beauty (she looked like Ava Gardner) and her "goodness." (His conviction of her goodness did not alter, even though she rejected his sexual advances and barely spoke to him during the long years of their marriage.) In his therapy Dr. L. spoke about loss, and his complex relations with his four sons. Gradually the simpleminded idealizations of mother, father, and wife began to break down. Dr. L. was able to come to some real understanding of his marriage, its breakup, and why he had broken down so completely. His splitting defenses altered, and for the first time he realized the depth of the anger he had suppressed for so long.

Dr. L. then began to attend social functions and place personal ads in the newspaper. He received an overwhelming response; hundreds of women sent him letters and photographs. This shy, insecure man turned, within the space of a few weeks, into a "connoisseur" of women. He rated them by looks on a scale from "dogs" to "lookers," and laughed sadistically at the former. Puffed up with himself and his success, he began to sit for hours in front of the university library watching the women pass by—he reported that only "dogs" seemed to attend. His "interviews" with the women from the personal ads were highly stressful because he became extremely jealous to learn that they had ever been with another man or men.

His jealousy was dystonic. I raised the possibility that it had its genesis in feelings about his father's relationship with his mother. Dr. L. denied this, but my having raised the possible connection to his father proved to be helpful. His jealous feelings began to abate to some level of comfort. He began to feel for the first time jealousy of his wife's boyfriend, now husband, which he had hereto-fore repressed, but he was still unable to relate this jealousy to any feelings he ever had about his father.

After this period as arbiter of female worth, Dr. L. began to feel better and to "flirt" with me, trying to find out if I found him to be attractive. Although he maintained that "I don't care what they are about as long as they are good-looking," he seemed also to be searching for a loving woman—more specifi-cally, one who would love him. I worked with him in a concrete manner on his dates. He found a woman who "loved him like his mother did." He reported:

"She loves me so much, her whole life has changed because she has met me. She is just happy looking at me. She sits and stares at me for hours." Every day he hoped that he would love her a bit more. He thought she was "hot." In this case, the narcissistic gratification was so great the patient decided to terminate, happy, but not cured.

Dr. L. returned to treatment 2 years later. His girlfriend had ended their relationship, telling him that he was too selfish for her to bear. This time, in deep pain, he was able to reach into himself and to work more deeply, using symbol, and metaphor.

These three vignettes demonstrate the characteristic alternation of the analytic work from a mode in which it was possible to work in terms of symbol and metaphor to a more concrete one, and then back again. Each of these men came to analysis feeling unloved and empty. Each had experienced object loss either prior to or during treatment, and while in treatment found someone to replace his former love. Each entered treatment in a state of profound pain. As each began to feel better, each regressed temporarily from using metaphor to a more concrete, shallow experiencing of women. For them to feel better, the narcissistic deficits had to be made good—hence the regression to body narcissism, and the feeling better, and the concreteness. When the narcissistic deficits began to be repaired, the ego became capable of more advanced object relations and an increased capacity for symbol and metaphor.

I would like to note here that there are times when a patient leaves feeling satisfied that he has reached another level of psychic organization and compromise formation, but the analyst does not feel satisfied because the patient is not communicating at the level of symbol and metaphor. I have come to understand that what seems like resistance may in fact be regression, and that it is an error to assume that the treatment has not been effective.

I will now offer cases of female patients, also previously capable of metaphoric thought and language, who like their male counterparts shifted to concrete language at times of preoccupation about their looks. The dynamics of the narcissistic issues may be different, but the connection with concreteness of thought is the same.

Ms. S. was 34 and single when she entered a 4 times-weekly analysis. Lovely although somewhat disheveled, she was involved with a man whom her family disliked. They expected that he would jilt her, and they kept warning her of this in no uncertain terms. For the first several months of her analysis Ms. S. was able to use the couch, to free associate, and to bring in dreams and memories. She filled me in about her relationship with her friend T., and she knew that it symbolized aspects of her parents' marriage.

Ms. S. had grown up in Beverly Hills. Her mother, a former actress, was a beauty, but could neither manage her home nor get her children to school on time. She had numerous affairs to which the children were witness. Ms. S.'s father, an attorney for a film production company, was away on business a lot, and had a series of mistresses. Ms. S. described her youthful self as "fuzzy—walking about in a blur" (note that these descriptions indicate the subjective perception of an inadequate visual grasp of the world.) She spent her high school years sunbathing and shopping with friends, running up huge bills over which she and her father battled—it was the way she could reliably get his attention.

Ms. S.'s parents entered her in child and teenage beauty contests, some of which she won. Whenever she gained any weight, her father would take to calling her "Fatso." (He himself weighed close to 250 pounds, but as a man in our culture he felt he was exempt from any criticism.) Ms. S. managed to get through college, majoring in art history. She came to New York and found a job as a researcher for an art gallery.

Before she began her analysis, she had started dating T., a handsome, hard-working, well-educated, rather brilliant man, who, by her reports, both used, and abused her. He was interested in the possibility of working for her father. T. criticized Ms. S. whenever she gained a pound, and although his similarity to her father was not lost upon her, she persisted in trying to please him, and reported that she "loved him to death." (She had some real capacity for self-awareness, but she could not hear the aggression in this metaphor).

Ms. S.'s analysis progressed well for several months. Then she left her job for a lower-paid one that would leave her with enough energy to see T. at the end of the day. By then they were engaged, and she said that she wanted to have the energy available to plan her wedding. She was not interested in becoming a professional woman or in having a career. All she wanted was to be a wife and mother. She cut back to two sessions a week.

My experience during this period was that Ms. S. went from being a "pretty woman" to being a "silly woman." All she seemed to care about was looking good, staying slim, and buying clothes. T. overtly exploited her, making her wait for him for hours to come home late from work, requiring her to drive late at night to pick him up at the airport, and asking that she entertain his friends and relatives even at times when she did not feel well. She reported feeling tired and run-down and suffered from numerous viruses and allergies. My interpretation that she was somatizing rather than verbalizing her anger at T. and her family fell upon deaf ears. She wanted me to serve as "witness" and "container," and frustrated my efforts to examine what she was doing. This was a "perverse transference" akin to Renik's (1992) notion of the use of the analyst as a fetish, where the analyst is used to serve the thinking function.

Ms. S. went home to California to be fitted for her wedding gown. Her father became extremely angry when he saw her in it, and snarled that he didn't like it, that it was "ugly." After the wedding and honeymoon, Ms. S. reported anger at her husband for his egregious behavior toward her on their honeymoon, (playing tennis all day and leaving her alone at the pool) but she found herself unable to speak up and confront him. Then she began missing sessions, calling me on her cellular phone from the StairMaster at her health club. More than once she said that she would feel too "guilty" if she did not exercise and since her husband had invited people home for dinner, she had to miss her session. She could not entertain the interpretation that the "guilt" was really about her anger at her husband and her father.

At this point in the treatment, Ms. S. presented as "empty." She showed little interest in her work or anything other than "looking good" and holding her husband's attention—especially keeping him away from the topless bars he visited after work with his colleagues. She could not see any parallels between her behavior with him and her desperate childhood behavior with her often absent, philandering father. She reported a dream, which she experienced as "gross." "I had a huge zit, but not that apparently large. I squeezed it. There was a huge explosion. A bruise was left." Her associations were to "never be wrinkled" and "a thought of piercing her thigh with a pen to get out the fat." Kaplan's (1991) observation came to my mind: "When I came to the various masquerades of feminine gender identity ... I pointed to the collaboration of the fashion and cosmetic industries with the fetishization of the human body and the trivialization of the female mental and sexual life" (p. 523).

Ms. S. seemed to me to be no longer analyzable or possibly even treatable. At that time, I had not yet considered the issues of concrete vs. metaphoric language that I am raising here. I continued to attempt to interpret her fears of her aggression toward her father and husband, how she was turning the aggression on herself and trying to work it off through exercise. I had some intuitive feeling that Ms. S. needed to be seen face-to-face and asked her to sit up during her sessions. Just looking at her, but not commenting concretely about what I saw, proved to be insufficient.

Ms. S. decided to leave treatment, with the excuse that her busy life permitted only time for exercise and trying to look good. I believe now that if I had been able to discuss with her on her own terms the concrete concerns about her body, reflecting back to her what I saw, rather than interpreting her anger or its roots, face-to-face treatment and an ongoing analysis of the countertransference when the "silly woman" material emerged, most probably would have led to a better result.

Nevertheless, the patient reported satisfaction with the treatment, for she had after all married T., which had been her stated goal from the start. Over the next 10 years, she referred to me a number of acquaintances who remarked on the positive changes they had seen in her as a result of her psychoanalytic treatment. She had three children and she seemed to them to be content.

Mrs. P., a slender banker, began psychoanalytic treatment at the age of 36. She was seductive in her body language and dress, but she was soft-spoken, and her manner was demure. The miniskirts and tight spandex tops she wore did not look like the usual uniform for the conservative bank at which she worked, but she reported that she liked her work, and that she was well thought of there, and was considered successful. She and her husband led a very sophisticated urban life.

Mrs. P. said that she had come to treatment to deal with her marriage of 10 years, since she was feeling uncertain about whether she had married the right man. Soon after, however, the focus of the treatment changed to her feelings about her looks. She was concerned that her husband would find other women attractive, and felt that she lacked "definition" in a crowd of people. (She saw her husband as having that same problem of lacking "definition.") She spent many hours crying about these issues.

She was aware that she was attractive to men, but was obsessed with the idea that as she got older, she would lose this power to attract them. This fear caused her to break down and cry in much the same way she did when thinking about her lack of presence. Her constant need for compliments and attention invaded and diminished her opportunities for conflict-free work and general happiness.

Mrs. P. reported feeling badly from time to time about not being very thin. She felt that very thin women were unattainable and untouchable, and that she "lost power" by not being "rail-thin." She said that she wanted to lose 10 pounds, but that she liked her pasta dinners. Rather than ask her to associate to the meanings of this, I asked her, why, if this was so important to her, she did not diet and lose the weight? I wasn't saying she needed to lose weight, but if she felt she did, there were things she could do about it. My concrete comments were aimed at getting her to engage in a real concrete behavior, as opposed to just endlessly "picking on herself." In the next session, the patient, for the first time, spoke of her mother's "picking on her" and her guilt at being angry at her, which she had suppressed. My concrete "suggestion" about her "concrete" issue gave her ego support and strength, which led her to tolerate the conscious awareness of her mother's sadism.

My careful tuning to Mrs. P.'s very concrete ideas and my oscillating between concrete idea and metaphor resulted in a successful resolution of this case. I reflected back to her my perception that she wore trendy clothes and noted that she had highlighted her hair. Mrs. P.'s chronically ill mother had stayed too close and undifferentiated for her to be able to internalize her and to develop in a normal way. Mrs. P. was able to attain a more distanced and age-appropriate relationship with her mother and to cease the obsessive jealousy that plagued her with her husband. She became more confident about her looks and not so worried about their meaning for her as she aged.

(In a subsequent phase of her treatment, memories came up that clarified the genetic bases of her seductive dressing and its symbolic meaning. She was by then able to understand her seductiveness as a symptom and as a symbol, and with this understanding it abated).

Discussion

Brooks (1993) has most eloquently described the connection between body, language, and thought:

> The body, I think, often presents us with a fall from language, a return to an infantile pre-symbolic space in which primal drives reassert their force....

> Bodily parts, sensations and perceptions ... are the first building blocks in the construction of a symbolic order, including speech, play, and the whole system of human language, within which the child finds a libidinally invested place.
>
> (p. 7)

Unfortunately, there has not been much attention in the psychoanalytic literature to such concrete aspects of the experience of the body. Issues of gender and gender difference have been extensively studied, but not such matters as whether the body is experienced as looking "good" or "bad." Sifneos (1967, 1975) and McDougall (1989) have addressed the difficulties of those who cannot verbalize their emotions and who express themselves through somatic channels. Sifneos has written about "alexithymia," a term describing the way some people define emotions solely in terms of somatic sensations or behavioral reactions rather than being able to use meaningful words. The patients I am writing about here have words, albeit concrete ones, for the body, and its experiences.

Balsam (1996) has noted the neglect in our thinking about the visual aspects of the external body in the development of the young girl. She believes that we do not listen enough for the surface quality of visual and tactile information and its mental representation:

> The literature has stressed a continued internal focus on the mother, for women, as encompassing a "fixation" on her, implying a state to be hurdled if development is to proceed. This attitude could cause the analyst to try to "help" the patient too rapidly past the inevitable fascinations I dwell upon here.
>
> (p. 422)

In her work on daughters' perceptions of their pregnant mothers, Balsam was referring to the patients' fascination with the analyst's clothes, her own clothes, and those of other women—concrete issues. She has addressed some of the same issues I deal with here.

Paniagua (1998) in a paper on the analysis of "acting in," reported that he noticed that his patient, anxious about some job interviews, put her index finger over the bridge of her nose and told her what he saw. She was self-conscious about her nose, which she thought was ugly. He then told her that she was hiding her nose from his view. She reported that his view of her nose from his chair was unfavorable. "This clashed with her wish that I found her ravishing (transferential). She fantasized that, perhaps, touching what she considered the imperfection in her nose would make it disappear magically" (p. 507). His intervention is an example of the technique that I have come to use.

During the course of some analyses, the analyst may be speaking one language (metaphor) and the patient another (concrete). The psychoanalytic literature is replete with the conviction that "listening" is superior to "looking" as the preferred medium of communication between analyst and patient, the use of metaphor being associated with the former mode and concrete language associated with the latter. When patients begin their analytic work in the latter mode they risk being judged as unanalyzable and referred out for psychotherapy, or even considered untreatable. Other patients may begin their treatment using symbol and metaphor, but regress, for a few minutes, or for many sessions, to concrete ways of thinking and communicating that confuse and baffle the analyst.

The effect of translating and abstracting, at least in the case of very concrete patients, may be that we miss what is actually being said, and that our patients in return find us difficult to understand. Our patients understand us best when we speak their language, and it is often difficult for them to tell us that they have not understood. As a matter of habit, for example, we should use statements like: "You don't like you" in preference to "You have low self-esteem." We should use language that refers to the thing itself rather than an abstract essence when that is what the patient is doing. Furthermore, some people become adept at using symbol and metaphor but do not really "connect" with what they are saying. As one patient of mine cleverly put it: "She can talk the talk, but she can't walk the walk." I understand my efforts to be in the same direction as Schafer's (1976) elaboration of an "action language," and Gedo's (1996) efforts to communicate with his patients using tropes and affects. They too were dealing with the analyst's need to use words that reach the patient. However, they were seeking more affective immediacy, and it has seemed to me that this is not the issue in working with the kinds of patients that I describe here; that resonating with them affectively can in fact be too frightening and/or overstimulating. It is their capacity to perceive their concrete selves that is at issue.

I have attempted to demonstrate the style of analytic thought and the kinds of technical interventions that can be used with such patients, with particular attention to *linguistic attunement*, the use of concrete language when narcissistic issues about the external body, whether the body of the patient or the bodies of others, emerge in the treatment.

I also hope that I have demonstrated the danger of a blind preference for symbol and metaphor, what might be called a "rush to metaphor," at times when our patients are not really able to process what we are saying. The analyst must be able to tolerate his own regression and must use concrete language, both for practical, and for developmental reasons, when the patient is thinking and speaking concretely. Only then will the patient be able to use the analyst's interventions, grow with their help, and ultimately develop the capacity to use symbol and metaphor genuinely in treatment. When a patient lacks this capacity, symbol and metaphor can be used by both patient and analyst to defend against primitive or uncomfortable material.

Note

1 This chapter first published as "The Therapist's Rush to Metaphor," in the author's book *Body Talk: Looking and Being Looked at in Psychotherapy*, Northvale, N. J.: Jason Aronson, Inc., 2000. Reprinted by kind permission of Rowman & Littlefield Publishing Group.

References

Arlow, J. A. (1979). Metaphor and the psychoanalytic situation. *Psychoanalytic Quarterly, 48*(3), 363–385.

Balsam, R. (1996). The pregnant mother and the body image of the daughter. *Journal of the American Psychoanalytic Association, 44*(Suppl.), 401–428.

Bass, A. (1997). The problem of "concreteness." *Psychoanalytic Quarterly, 66*(4), 642–682.

Borbely, A. F. (1998). A psychoanalytic concept of metaphor. *International Journal of Psycho-Analysis, 79*(5), 923–936.

Brooks, P. (1993). *Body work: Aspects of desire in modern narrative.* Cambridge, M.A.: Harvard University Press.

Busch, F. (1997). The patient's use of free association. *Journal of the American Psychoanalytic Association, 45*(2), 407–424.

Gedo, J. (1979). *Beyond interpretation: Toward a revised theory for psychoanalysis.* New York: International Universities Press.

Gedo, J. (1996). *The language of psychoanalysis.* Hillsdale, N.J.: Analytic Press.

Giovacchini, P. (Ed.) (1972). The concrete and difficult patient. In P. Giovacchini (Ed.), *Tactics and techniques in psychoanalytic therapy* (pp. 351–363). New York: Science House.

Hinshelwood, R. D. (1997). The elusive concept of "internal objects" (1934–1943): Its role in the formation of the Klein group. *International Journal of Psycho-Analysis, 78*(5), 877–898.

Kaplan, L. (1991). *The female perversions.* New York: Doubleday.

Kohut, H. (1971). *The analysis of the self.* New York: International Universities Press.

Lacan, J. (1953–1954). Le seminaire: livre I. In J. A. Miller (Ed.), *Les ecrits techniques de Freud.* Paris: Editions du Seuil, 1975.

Lecours, S., & Bouchard, M. (1997). Dimensions of mentalisation. Outlining levels of psychic transformation. *International Journal of Psycho-Analysis, 78*(5), 855–875.

Levin, F. (1980). Metaphor, affect, and arousal: How interpretation might work. *The Annual of Psychoanalysis, 8,* 231–248.

McDougall, J. (1989). *Theaters of the body.* New York: W. W. Norton.

Ogden, T. (1997). Reverie and metaphor: Some thoughts on how I work as a psychoanalyst. *International Journal of Psycho-Analysis, 78*(4), 719–732.

Paniagua, C. (1998). Acting-in revisited. *International Journal of Psycho-Analysis, 79*(3), 499–512.

Phillips, K. A. (1996). *The broken mirror.* New York: Oxford University Press.

Riesenberg-Malcolm, R. (1999). Interpretation: The past in the present. In R. Riesenberg-Malcolm (P. Roth Ed. & Intro.), *On bearing unbearable states of mind* (pp. 38–52). New York and London: Routledge.

Schafer, R. (1976). *A new language for psychoanalysis.* New Haven and London: Yale University Press.

Sifneos, P. E. (1967). Clinical observations on some patients suffering from a variety of psychosomatic diseases. *Acta Medica Psychosomatica, 7*, 1–10.

Sifneos, P. E. (1975). Problems of psychotherapy in patients with alexithymic characteristics and physical disease. *Psychotherapy and Psychosomatics, 26*(2), 65–70.

Silverman, M. (1987). Clinical material. *Psychoanalytic Inquiry, 7*(2): 147–166.

Chapter 8

Body narcissism and linguistic attunement[1]

In the documentary film, *Valentino: The Last Emperor* (2008), the great fashion designer asked (as did Sigmund Freud a century ago): "What does a woman want?" The answer was simple for Valentino, but not for Freud, *"A woman wants ... to be beautiful."* I think that Valentino had it right on many levels. The wish to be beautiful is true of many women. Many men too want to be handsome, and many men want to be with a woman who is beautiful. Psychoanalysis has had little to say about the wish for beauty, yet it dominates the thoughts of so many.

In my private practice in New York, I have found that increasing numbers of patients present initially or after some months of psychoanalytic treatment with preoccupying concerns about bodily and/or facial appearance. They do not understand their anxiety about these issues to be "symbolic" of anything. Although they are intelligent and may be able to understand other feelings about other issues in more abstract ways, their worries and questions about the importance of their looks are concrete, and so is the language they use. One university professor confessed that: "When I look in the mirror, I am not sure of what I see and I need someone to tell me what they see."

Many of today's patients come into psychoanalytic treatment feeling ashamed about the way they look, whether the shame has to do with the entire body or it parts: arms, legs, face, nose, lips, hair, body fat, acne scars, tallness, shortness, etc. Others are ashamed of the way their lovers or spouses or parents look. Most psychoanalysts, in classical Freudian tradition, pay little attention to these concrete complaints, assuming that they are manifest content and derivatives of inner dynamics, compromise formations. I have found that working with patients who are ashamed of their bodies by interpreting what I assume must be the underlying fantasies and meanings of the shame either hits a stone wall of un-understanding or in some cases, meets with intellectual compliance with the interpretation, but little alteration of the shame experience.

I see shame as a painful and powerful affect suffered early on at a time when the child lacked the words that would have made the shame experience more bearable and metabolizable. In addition, the bodily and social vicissitudes of early adolescence force one to revisit these early affects and combine with them to produce the language-deficient shame we see in our consulting rooms with adults. Jacobs (2005) has postulated the "adolescent neurosis" as equal to or even more important than the "infantile neurosis." He speaks about early adolescence and its bodily disharmony (ages 11–14) and notes that it is quite difficult to retrieve memories of shame about the body from this time, the teasing and exclusion by peers, because the young adolescent does not have the capacity for metaphoric thought that the later adolescent has.

As I emphasized in my (2000) book, *Body Talk: Looking and Being Looked at in Psychotherapy*, the body is a concrete object with an actual concrete manifestation and actual physical feelings (as opposed, say, to an idea, or a fantasy). We have to begin to deal with our bodies well before the emergence of abstract thought … therefore, psychological issues about the body appear to require a concreteness of thought, other issues do not. I have found that concrete thinking is often connected with problems in the development of the bodily self and its boundaries and is connected with early deficits in attention to the body, its care, and maintenance. Such problems intersect and interact with the development of inner fantasy, conflict, and defense from early childhood on.

Since I published that book I have been able to fine-tune my thinking about the relationship between bodies and language due to a plethora of articles and books subsequently published that confirm and add to my theories. (Among them are Farrell, [2000]; Lombardi, [2003, 2008]; Mitrani, [2007]; and Steiner, [2006]). When I researched my book, I missed the important work of Rizzuto (1988) who noted that: "Psychoanalytic theorizing has not paid enough attention to the function of language in the development of character structure, transformation of object relations, but most important, regulation of affect and self-esteem" (p. 2). She has observed that "the avoidance of communication seems to be a defence against the transference. For these patients, *that is the transference*" (p. 4).

Several recent cases, both in psychoanalysis and psychotherapy, have provided me with more insight into the underpinnings of body narcissism. I have had to think more about the role of shame due to my presentation on a panel on "Shame and the Body" in New York with Riccardo Lombardi in March, 2006. The writings of others have helped me to analyze my countertransference reactions, potentially powerful, and disruptive to treatment. In my work with these patients, I have had to tolerate exposure to abject bodily processes and have had to think about and talk about them. I have had to tolerate constant cycles of need and rejection, provocations to withdraw from the treatment in transference/ countertransference cycles that repeat the early relationship with the mother.

Amanda, a 35-year-old marketing executive, was referred to me for psychoanalytic treatment by the analyst she saw while in college. She had relocated to New York at the age of 25, but had not "psychologically" separated from her mother, with whom she was in cell phone and e-mail contact many times/day. Her parents had been divorced since Amanda was 9. Her mother was their "mainstay." Her father, considered to be quite "crazy," was essentially unavailable. Her mother would stay in a hotel, visiting for a month at a time. Mother's visits (as well as phone calls and e-mails) involved constant negotiations about money. I had the feeling that Amanda wanted to suck her mother dry.

Although I had been told by the referring analyst that Amanda had a serious eating disorder, an attractive, trendily dressed young woman swept into my office. She may have seemed anorectic elsewhere, but was more normal by New York standards! The referring analyst thought she was a virgin still. Amanda reported living with James, an architect, who adored her, and who listened to all of her complaints, soothing her endlessly as he did his mother. He barely earned a living and Amanda was angry that she was their main support. She also described James as a "baby" who could not handle the simple matters of life; it seemed clear to me that she wished that she could trade places with him as the one who played "baby."

Amanda told me that she sought treatment to keep her resolution to do "good things" to her body. She wanted to become pregnant and had been told that she might not be able to do so because she had not menstruated in 8 months, or very much before that, for that matter. She told me that after a boyfriend jilted her at age 16 she became anorectic and had to be hospitalized for a while. Since then her diet was vegetarian only and she had little appetite for many foods. She was an Internet addict, researching every food she ate for problems. I detected considerable grandiosity ("I can only eat the best") as well as paranoia in this matter.

As treatment began, Amanda began to visit a series of dermatologists and was particularly upset by one who "assaulted" her by biopsying several small bumps on her chest. She experienced this as a kind of rape. (The displaced negative transference was thus activated.) On some level I believe that she was experiencing me as attacking her and invading her, but she protected herself from awareness of this through displacement.

Amanda had a slight case of acne and became obsessed with it. She stood in front of the mirror for hours looking at and squeezing the pimples, thus making the irritation worse. She tried all kinds of creams on her face, and then looked up their ingredients on the Internet, concluding that they were "bad" for her. She argued with each dermatologist about the safety of the creams and antibiotics they prescribed. She came to me as "referee" and spent countless hours with her mother on the phone about whether these products would cause her permanent damage. (Her mother seemed to share similar concerns about her own body.) Amanda was concerned that with her anorexia and her treatment for acne she had done "permanent" damage to herself, had permanent scars.

A classic understanding of her problems would be one of castration anxiety and fears of genital damage. My treatment of her was along the lines described in my (2000) book: I spoke with her quite concretely, since she was unable to speak of her issues as if they had any psychological meaning. She wanted me to see her face each session and to let her know what I thought: was it better or worse. She came in suffering. "I've had a miserable weekend. I have driven my boyfriend and my mother crazy." I thought that she wanted to drive me crazy too. She burst into tears the way a 2-year-old might do. In addition to the dermatologists she visited, Chinese herbalists, acupuncturists, and cosmeticians were called on to look at her and give their opinions. She challenged every suggested treatment. I was called upon as another "mirror" to try to soothe the bad image she had of herself. She would come in and confess (in a highly dramatic manner):"I was BAD," meaning that she had picked her pimples. It was high drama, and I was quite aware of the role I had been cast in. I was also willing to play that role, since it confirmed the hypotheses I had developed about working with body narcissism. The kind of aversive countertransference I might have had 15 years prior ("I cannot believe that I am listening to such rubbish!") was quite muted due to my experience with so many of these patients, what I regard as the patients of our time.

A concurrent scenario was being played out on the gynecological end as Amanda sought treatment for what she imagined to be her "infertility." She had been told as a young girl, by a doctor her mother had taken her to that, she would have problems conceiving a child. She pitted several traditional medical doctors against several Chinese doctors. This daughter of divorce trusted no one. She was afraid that the hormones the medical doctor prescribed would damage her eggs and that the herbs given her by the Chinese doctor had aggravated her acne.

I continued to look at her face as she came in and commented about the redness or lack thereof of her pimples. I asked her if she had picked them. My concrete interventions and my taking her complaints seriously began to calm her down after many weeks. She needed reassurance that she had not permanently damaged her face or body. I did not offer it, but did offer attention, and talking. My task, as I saw it, was to look, to be verbally descriptive, affirming, and to avoid any seductive or personal, non-professional compliments, or vocal intonations.

I used my psychoanalytic lens to understand what was going on underneath. She was quite conscious of envying a pregnant friend, the envy being so great that she could not see her friend anymore. As is my custom from time to time to test the current level of my patients' thinking, I tried a metaphoric statement: "The bumps on your face may represent baby bumps." She had no response to this, as if it were nonsense. At another time, I interpreted "picking your face is a substitute for picking on yourself," but this too went nowhere with Amanda.

Somehow the traditional medical doctor's advice prevailed and Amanda took antibiotics and then progesterone for a week. At her checkup she was told that she was pregnant. (In the transference, in which she was a needy child, no mention of sexual relations had been made!) Fleeting moments of pleasure about this fact were soon turned to pain and worry as Amanda feared she had already damaged her baby with the various creams she was putting on her face for her acne as well as whatever was in the little food she was eating. Her visits to the dermatologists now included her obsessive questioning about the safety of their products for pregnant women. They reassured her, but she then found on the Internet that they were not "safe." Her fears of damaging herself then morphed to damaging her baby. She stayed in the house on the weekends because she did not want to be seen with acne.

Concurrent with the treatment in which she was quite regressed, Amanda was working in a very challenging job. She received a considerable salary raise during this time. Her job required a high level of interpersonal as well as other skills. She and her boyfriend kept appointments with the doctor who was to deliver her baby (although she had a second one waiting in the wings!) She consulted with a nutritionist about prenatal nutrition and brought in to her sessions bags of "healthy" food to show me she was taking care of herself in this way. I believe that the transference reflected a regression in body narcissism that had to be worked through with me as a kind of verbal mirror, continually reflecting back to her what I saw.

Although her mother seemed to be quite attentive to Amanda as an adult, there is some evidence of severe neglect when she was a young child. She has a memory of having broken a glass at age 4. Her mother did not have the torn finger repaired properly. One can only wonder what fantasies emanated from this, e.g., castration fears. When in treatment with her former analyst, Amanda developed psoriasis on that very finger, and the analyst interpreted her somatization as due to that trauma. She remembered after many months having to wear a metal bar that connected her shoes while she slept, a method used to correct a slightly displaced hip. When she asked her mother about it, her mother could not remember it.

From the transference, I have concluded that Amanda was a needy and annoying child who her mother tried to appease and then ignore. Her pregnancy gave her the excuse to not return to her hometown that summer. She feared being seen with the acne.

Although she had quite a distance to travel to my office by subway, Amanda came to her sessions until the week she was to give birth. Her skin seemed miraculously better, for she had ceased aggravating it with picking. She was excited and looking forward to the birth process. "Squeezing the baby out" was my metaphor, a replacement for squeezing her skin.

She sent me an e-mail and photos of her lovely baby daughter Emily and was proud of having a quick delivery and natural childbirth. She planned to nurse Emily. Her mother arrived to help her out for the first month. Amanda enjoyed the breastfeeding, but Emily developed colic, and screamed for several weeks. When she was 3 months old, Amanda brought the baby to my office. She seemed quite comfortable caring for her in my presence, nursed her, and was very proud to display her skills as a mother, her child's lovely outfit and her own white, unblemished face. She had to resume her job on a part-time basis and hoped to continue sessions.

Most people experience some shame as the body changes and ages and then learn to adapt to it. Extreme cases of those who do not have been described by Phillips (1996) in her book, *The Broken Mirror*. She coined the term body dysmorphic disorder (BDD) and chronicled the plight of patients she had treated who tortured themselves, like Sartre, in their relationship to mirrors, feeling stuck to them for hours, compelled to stand, and look. One found it hard to function because of the need to comb and recomb her hair. It was difficult for her to perform her work in a hospital because the patients' rooms had mirrors. She tried to conquer this problem by getting dressed without her contact lens so that she could not see and could avoid mirrors.

I will present another example: Robin, an elegant wealthy woman, was plagued by her body, which seemed to me anorectic, yet she worried if she gained a pound. She was 5 feet 5 inches tall and weighed 105 pounds. She was constantly being shamed by others, who told her that she was too thin. Robin was obsessed with her clothes and spent a small fortune every year for her wardrobe. Yet she felt that she had nothing to wear and spent hours in front of her closets in each of her four homes not being able to decide what to wear or what to pack for the house she was traveling to next. Her greatest dread was of the shame she would feel if she went somewhere and confronted, all of a sudden, another woman who was better dressed, who "really" knew how to put her outfit together. She was terrified of being the recipient of envy of the kind she herself experienced and often would not wear her best clothes for that reason.

Robin seemed to suffer from an internalization of an envious critic appearing in the guise of a harsh superego introject. Incidentally, a series of women I have seen in psychotherapy with issues like Robin's have been endless talkers, are on their cell phones a good part of the day, and lead frenetically busy lives. Robin endured ongoing humiliation by her husband, who would not listen to her, she being a "motor mouth" who invited his constant rejection. Robin maintained an exhaustingly busy schedule filled with minutia and chores. She defended against experiencing feelings of shame by NOT THINKING. At the beginning of treatment she brought in lists of things to tell me, clippings from self-help articles, sorting, and shuffling among them in her Hermes handbag, so that I would notice the bag. Once she told me what was in the notes, she threw them away, nothing really being processed by her. She came in once asking to use the bathroom and quipped that it was one of many in the city she used all day. Robin's problems are rather typical of a certain type of woman who seeks analytic treatment but needs a treatment geared to her concreteness.

Rizzuto (1988) noted that patients such as Robin:

> deal with the spoken word as though it is an indispensable but meaningless nuisance that they have no choice but to use. Frequently the affective tone of their voice is a monotone pitch which may disclaim the significance of the content of what they are saying … When the analyst speaks trying to help the patient to understand herself, he or she is frequently met with an attitude of disbelief, skepticism, and rejection of what the meaning might be.

(p. 1)

Farrell (2000) decided on her book's title *Lost for Words*, recognizing that words are problematic for women with eating disorders.

> They are either seen as a useless form of communication, or as tremendously powerful, so powerful that they may drown in them, or be torn to pieces by them. The pre-verbal, concrete way these women often think and relate make words both a dangerous and unwanted commodity.
>
> (p. xiv)

Farrell sees the body for such women as a transitional object. Their mothers have taken *them* as objects rather than the other way around. "She wishes to use her baby both to confirm her own physical boundaries and as a bridge toward whole object relations" (p. 44). This certainly seems to be the case with Amanda.

To conclude: the analysis of body narcissism is a painful and difficult task. It opens up all kinds of fantasies and memories related to shame and humiliation and sometimes mental, physical, and sexual abuse. Too rapid a leap from the concrete can unleash a sadistic attack on the analyst, a therapeutic "bloodbath" from which it may be difficult to recover or more likely, without the words being expressed, an abrupt termination. The analyst's countertransference must be constantly monitored. It is very hard work.

Note

1 First published as Chapter 8, "Some Observations About Working with Body Narcissism with Concrete Patients," in *Absolute Truth and Unbearable Psychic Pain: Psychoanalytic Perspectives on Concrete Experience*, edited by Allan Frosch (published by Karnac Books in 2012), and is reprinted with kind permission of Taylor & Francis, LLC.

References

Brunswick, R. M. (1928). A supplement to Freud's history of an infantile neurosis. *International Journal of Psycho-Analysis, 9*, 439–476.

Caper, R. (1994). What is a clinical fact? *International Journal of Psycho-Analysis, 75*, 903–913.

Farrell, E. (2000). *Lost for Words: The psychoanalysis of anorexia and bulimia.* New York: Other Press.

Freud, S. (1919). The uncanny. *S.E.* 17, 219–256.

Freud, S. (1923). The ego and the id. *S.E.* 19, 3–66.

Gilman, S. (1995). *Picturing health and illness: Images of identity and difference.* Baltimore, M.D.: Johns Hopkins Press.

Jacobs, T. (2005). *The adolescent neurosis.* Presentation at the Psychoanalytic Association of New York.

Jay, M. (1993). *Downcast eyes: The denigration of vision in twentieth century French thought.* Berkley, C.A.: University of California Press.

Lieberman, J. S. (2000). *Body talk: Looking and being looked at in psychotherapy*. North-vale, N.J.: Jason Aronson, Inc.

Lieberman, J. S. (2006). Presentation in panel on "shame and the body." Symposium 2006: Shame. Mount Sinai Hospital, New York.

Lombardi, R. (2003). Catalyzing the dialogue between the body and the mind in a psychotic analysand. *Psychoanalytic Quarterly, 72*, 1017–1041.

Lombardi, R. (2008). The body in the analytic session: Focusing on the body-mind link. *International Journal of Psycho-Analysis, 89*, 89–110.

Mitrani, J. (2007). Bodily centered protections in adolescence: An extension of the work of Frances Tustin. *International Journal of Psycho-Analysis, 88*, 1153–1169.

Phillips, K. A. (1996). *The broken mirror*. New York: Oxford University Press.

Rizzuto, A-M. (1988). Transference, language and affect in the treatment of bulimarexia. *International Journal of Psycho-Analysis, 69*(3), 369–387.

Steiner, J. (2006). Seeing and being seen: Narcissistic pride and narcissistic humiliation. *International Journal of Psycho-Analysis, 87*, 939–951.

Chapter 9

Outrageous women

The "Cleopatra complex"

In this chapter I present some clinical observations I have made in my private practice over the course of the past decade. I find that the issues presented by some portion of the women coming for treatment are *manifestly* different from those I worked with in the late 1970s when I first began my work as a psychoanalyst. Due to a paucity of self-reflection and the ego-syntonicity of the form some of these women's aggression takes, along with my own countertransference reactions, it has become increasingly more difficult to access unconscious fantasies while working with them in analytic treatment. This presentation will therefore seem more sociological and descriptive than reflecting a deep understanding of unconscious dynamics.

Many of the writings of feminist psychoanalysts have indicated that women's morality is based on ideas of non-violence, caring, and nurturing. I have not found this to be the case in my practice.

The social changes of the 1960s and 1970s greatly altered women's lives, especially those of upper middle class educated women. At that time, women's roles as subordinate to men in marriage and work were changing, and many were intrapsychically unprepared to leave their homes and small children to enter the workplace and compete with men. In my analytic work at that time, I consistently encountered passivity, guilt, inhibition over self-expression and self-realization, blurred identity, and masochism. Men were idealized. Marriage and children were the only acceptable goals. One married early and had one's first child by the age of 25, at the latest 30. Women baked cookies, cakes, and pies, and traded recipes with one another. They cooked breakfast, lunch, and dinner, and set the table for dinner parties. Especially in the suburbs they drank a lot. The popular TV series *Mad Men* illustrates the way it was. If women moved around, it was to buy groceries or pick up the children from school. Betty Friedan's *The Feminine Mystique* (1963) chronicled the lives of traditional women and lit the torch that inspired many of the changes we have seen in the 21st century. In the late 1970s, well into the 1980s, women who sought treatment were paralyzed due to conflicts about what they perceived were aggressive moves into the workplace and out of the kitchen. As Joan Hamburg the radio host put it at her 60th Barnard College Reunion: "The only march we knew was the march down the aisle!" (2017).

Fast-forward to my private practice today, I see very few women as I just described. I see a certain number, which seems to be growing, who I characterize as "outrageous." They do not "lean in" as Cheryl Sandberg (2013) advises women to do. They "step on." I think of "outrageous" as including notions of narcissistic, of entitled, but going beyond. The outrageous person's behavior is not to be believed, is not tuned to the mores of others, like a child not yet socialized, and lacks implicit notions of social boundaries. The outrageous are not inhibited. They do what they want. Their *rage* is *out* there. The stereotype of women suffering from an inhibition of aggression does not seem to be very relevant today. It is unclear as to what they want (as Freud asked: "What does a woman want?") and are not getting. There are men like this too, but in the past women have been punished and shamed for outrageous, demanding behavior. I do not think that this is so very true today.

It has been my observation that the social changes of the 1970s liberated women from having to stifle their aggression. Today women are punished less for aggression, for hurting others from birth onward than in the past. In fact in some cases, there is peer pressure to be tough, pushy, and loud. Bullies are often admired.

In history, mythology, and in literature, we have many women who advanced themselves and their causes in admirable, assertive ways: from Athena to Joan of Arc, from Wonder Woman to Princess Leia, from Hillary Clinton, Madeleine Albright, Elizabeth Warren to Michelle Obama. How we admired the women wearing pussycat hats in the January of 2017 March. We also know of outrageous tyrannical women, both fictional and non-fictional: the Red Queen in *Alice in Wonderland* ("off with her head"); Queen Elizabeth I, who beheaded Mary Queen of Scotts; Judith, who beheaded Holofernes; Marie Antoinette ("let them eat cake"); and, of course, Lady Macbeth. In recent times, clear examples are Joan Crawford (*Mommie Dearest*); Leona Helmsley (*The Queen of Mean*); and Martha Stewart, who was said to have run over her gardener in a dispute. Today's television and film heroines are no longer like June Cleaver or Lucille Ball. They are more like Carrie in *Homeland* or Alicia in *The Good Wife* or Hannah in *Girls* or Claire in *House of Cards*. Not to mention the popularity of the "Housewife" programs, programs celebrating bridezillas, etc. There are few shrinking violets or dainty women television personalities. Oprah Winfrey, Barbara Walters, and Ariana Huffington set the trend.

I have been particularly intrigued by Cleopatra, the Egyptian Queen who ruled in about 48 BC (Schiff, 2010). She was the wife of her brother, then Julius Caesar, and then Marc Antony. A wet nurse cared for her, someone chewed her foods first. Nothing was eaten by her that was not tasted for poison (Was this a forerunner of today's food paranoia?) Cleopatra ruled with her older brother Ptolemy XIII and younger brother Ptolemy XIV who she married according to Egyptian custom. Her older brother died, making Cleopatra and her 10-year-old brother joint monarchs. Although married to him, she made it clear that she had no intention of sharing power with him. Her face was on the coins. She had him killed and had herself smuggled inside a carpet into Caesar's Palace. We do not know whether she loved Caesar or later Antony, but from the Roman point of view she "enslaved" them both. Finally, she controlled her own death, bitten by an asp.

I have seen in treatment several modern day Cleopatras.

A brief vignette: When she was 7, Vanessa fought with her 5-year-old brother and hit him over the head with a golf club, an injury that resulted in some form of permanent brain damage. She became pregnant by a random boyfriend at 16. She chose not to have an abortion and gave birth in a home for unwed mothers, giving up her baby boy for adoption. Several years later she married. She fought constantly with her husband, making outrageous demands on him with regard to how he should brush his teeth, where he should put the toothpaste after, how he should chew his food, etc. They had a child, a boy, from whom Vanessa was not able to separate for a moment. (I believe that in her unconscious she feared the aggression toward him she felt toward her brother). Her husband called me to intervene. She had not been in treatment for several years. She arrived, not alone, but with her 2-year-old son. (a surprise!) He immediately turned over a large potted plant in my office, which we had to clean up rather than talk. She did eventually return alone and we were able to continue our work. I want to underline here the aggression toward her brother, conscious and unconscious guilt, and the temporary derailing of treatment.

I have several more illustrative vignettes, but I want to first outline some of the similarities I have found in various "Cleopatra" cases:

1   A symbiotic relationship with mother (similar to what mother had with grandmother). These patients' mothers indulged them with material things in order to pacify them when angry rather than address their misbehavior.
2   Their mothers were idealized by them. Their hostility toward them was latent.
3   They had brothers, usually younger brothers, who did less well in life. Their envy of their brothers was not manifest, but they dominated and bullied them, sometimes abused them.
4   They, their mothers, and grandmothers had pathological relationships with men: their fathers and husbands were passive and accepted their aggression and ridicule. (These women must have fulfilled these men's fantasies of women as castrators, as phallic, as having "vagina dentate.") There were few consequences for bad behavior.
5   They were charming, a mask for their aggression (Joan Riviere's 1929 paper "Womanliness as Masquerade" comes to mind.)
6   They suffered from conscious and unconscious guilt over their unchecked aggression and wish for punishment.
7   In their relationship with me I was from time to time been actually "tricked" or "fooled" into breaking the frame. (Just as Cleopatra fooled Caesar by arriving in a rolled carpet.)

8   Due to a paucity of self-reflection and the ego-syntonicity of the form these women's aggression took, along with my own countertransference issues, it was difficult to access their unconscious fantasies while working with them in analytic treatment. I had to do a lot of speculation.

Balsam (2012) in a chapter called "Brothers and Sisters" in her recent book remarked that:

> Since I started to conduct analyses in the late 1970s, I have noticed that a number of female patients did not fit the stereotype of our literature at all, which regularly presents females with low or dubious self-regard.
>
> (p. 126)

She found these female patients to be ambitious and aggressive. They had brothers who were disappointments to their families. One had a brother who was institutionalized with Down's syndrome. Some were cruel to their brothers, psychologically and physically abusing them. They had internalized their parents' hostility toward their brothers A lack of conflict about this led to exaggerated omnipotence and reified these girls' sense of their own sadism and power. Balsam writes:

> These women had in common a set of features that were associated with a strong proclivity for unchallenged omnipotence. They saw themselves as powerful, and met the world in this way. They expected others to fit into their strategies and their plans for life.
>
> (p. 140)

Clinical example I

Catherine was truly a "Grand Queen." A great beauty when young, she resembled a famous movie star who you could not help thinking about as you looked at her face. She swooped into my office wearing designer clothes and slowly took her coat and jacket off and laid them on the couch with the designer labels from Paris evident for me to see.

She told a sad tale of losing her parents as a teenager and being in charge of a mentally and physically handicapped younger brother. She spent many hours weekly consulting about his well-being with his caretakers in various nursing homes. She had married young, had several grown children, and seemed to "meddle" inappropriately in their lives under the guise of taking care of them. She was divorced from their father, a wealthy politician.

Early in treatment she would arrive early, usually 10 minutes before the previous patient, interrupting his session with the doorbell. She sulked when asked to wait or take a walk. (I believe he represented in the transference her younger brother.) My keeping the frame of her time eventually led to her coming on time. Nevertheless, if she was coming or going and passing the previous or next patient in the waiting area, she managed to say something to me, ignoring the patient! She told me constantly how much she appreciated her sessions and how "wonderful" I was. However, she brought in coffee in paper cups and left them behind her (making me into the cleaner!) At home she could not hold onto help and she needed several employees to care for her huge home, garden, pool, and tennis court, to drive her to the city, and others to care for her city apartment. She either demanded what seemed to me too much of them and/or crossed boundaries, getting herself overly-involved in their personal lives.

Catherine idealized me and made me constant offers that I had to refuse, as I had had to send her away when she arrived early for her sessions: to come and swim in her pool during the summer; to use her apartment when noisy construction in my building was going on; and to be the recipient of numerous theater tickets. An idealizing, homoerotic transference was active, but not interpretable to this patient, who had limited capacity for self-reflection. She refused to look at herself as part of a transference in which she wanted to dominate and control me. She was not happy with the brand of tissues I kept in my office and said she would send me some of her preferred brand. A box large enough to fill a closet arrived the next day filled with tissues sufficient for 10 years and symbolized her unshed tears. Her considerable hostility was masked in charm and generosity. I had to ask her to have the box returned.

She kept testing my stance (and my dignity). I was feeling worn down having to graciously refuse and not be able to analyze with her, her many offers. Then I fell into a trap, behaving completely unlike me or the way I have conducted my practice. She was on the board of a chamber music group that was in town and had attended many of their concerts. She offered me a single ticket to a performance she said she could not attend and I dropped my guard and took it. When I arrived she was my seat partner!! I felt completely fooled and foolish. Back in session, she could not see what the problem was.

One of Catherine's many significant others, powerful in this world but not with her, was a brilliant businessman who could not say "no" to her or to his grown children. I saw him for a consultation with regard to his children hoping to make a referral. He came in and confided in me about Catherine: "I know she's a Princess, but I love her anyway."

As Freud (1914) said in "On Narcissism":

> Women, especially if they grow up with good looks, develop a certain self-contentment/which compensates them for the social restrictions that are imposed on them in their choice of object. Strictly speaking, it is themselves that such women love with an intensity comparable to that of the man's love for them. Nor does their need be in the direction of loving, but of being loved; and the man who fulfills this condition is the one who finds favor with them. The importance of the type of woman for the erotic life of mankind is to be rated very high. Such women have the greatest fascination

for men, not only the aesthetic reasons, since they are the most beautiful, but also because of a combination of interesting psychological factors. For it seems very evident that another person's narcissism has a great attraction for those who have renounced part of their own narcissism and are in search of object love.

(pp. 87–88)

Let me fast-forward to my clinical work today. The following is a bit of a digression, but I think it is the backdrop for the increasing number of "outrageous" women in our culture today. The young women I see in and out of my clinical practice (whether outrageous or not) are in perpetual motion. It is difficult for many of them to sit still or lie still in analytic treatment. Many are still single at 38 or 45, although they say they want to marry and maybe have children. Today they have a choice. Quiet moments for all are spent on computers, iPads, iPhones, and cell phones, and many are multitasking on these devices. They are on Facebook, Twitter, Instagram, etc. When not working, they are exercising vigorously: running, spinning, and walking fast. Those who have married and have babies run with jogging strollers. If their children are older, they are biking, or skiing with them. These mothers are quite concerned about staying thin and muscular and are suspicious of the food they take in, however meager it is. They often have "purge" days. They scan the Internet for problems in food and teach their babies that sweets are bad for them. (Paradoxically food stores and supermarkets are full of cupcakes and chocolate, which somehow seem to be purchased and consumed!) Babies learn early on to access their own iPhone apps and are toilet-trained tapping at iPads for distraction. Single women often have dogs to walk or run with and to cuddle with. Many have found their dogs to be more loving and loyal than the men they have dated and many are quite ambivalent about getting married and having children. As a result, they delay finding mates until pregnancy becomes a nightmare laden with fears of infertility, having a child with birth defects, multiple births, having to go through IVF, or have surrogate mothers, or adoptive mothers. I understand from those working in hospital delivery rooms that mothers giving birth are often texting their friends prior to looking at their newly born babies.

Once giving birth, with or without a partner, many have difficulty bonding with their babies and/or nursing. If their mothers are available and willing, the mothers often take over. Lactation specialists are called in to intervene. Mother-infant observation programs and "Mommy and Me" programs have bloomed to ward off the ill effects of this attenuation of the mothering instinct. Many young mothers express more concern about losing "the baby weight" than they do for the baby. After 3 or so months, mother goes back to work and the baby is handed over to a nanny or daycare. Weekends are devoted to exercise. New mothers fear losing their husbands should they retain any extra poundage. Their husbands have "made do" by watching perfect bodies on the Internet. At the same time, the terms "over parenting," "Velcro parenting," and "helicopter parenting" have come into vogue. There is much chatter about babies and children on websites.

I see in my practice women so very different from those described in our literature of the late 20th century! In a 1983 paper "The Female Superego: A Different Perspective," Bernstein, in comparing the contents of male vs. female superegos proclaimed:

> given two contents, "I should prepare dinner for my children," and "I should work for a professional paper," male and female responses would be very different. Men, in Western culture would have no conflict in this area; the commitment to work is fixed, dominant, and supercedes most other contents. For women, the relative strengths of the two contents are not so fixed, but vary according to the situation.
>
> (p. 188)

She saw the female superego as flexible, not rigid.

Bernstein went on to report her observations of women as timid and inhibited: "When associations have pointed to longings for stardom and fame, admiration and power in women, they are ashamed, timid and anxious" (p. 188). I have difficulty relating to these observations today.

What I think I am observing today is an abdication of womanliness and a seeming paucity of the "mothering" instinct. Some of this is socioeconomic and cultural. The cost of living in our cities mandates that many women work and the threat of job loss and job insecurity due to the recent economic downturn invade any domestic sense of serenity. These problems face heterosexual couples, gay and lesbian couples, and single parents alike. A number of single women have told me that they want to marry someone on Wall Street so they can feel secure. In this respect it feels as if we are back to the days of Edith Wharton!

The above represents a kind of "norm" that is the backdrop against which I have worked with a number of women. Many of the patients I have seen coming into treatment are more extreme, more aggressive, more entitled, and self-centered than I have ever witnessed.

Clinical example II

Alice came to therapy for a number of reasons. She was 30, a newly married journalist, whose husband complained about her unwillingness to have sex with him. She was quite beautiful and sexy looking, perfectionistic about her body, her hair, and her clothes. She shone. She also looked somewhat different each time I greeted her at my door. There was always a change of hairdo, of clothing style, of shoe height. A lot of shopping, visits to hairdressers, manicurists, dermatologists, and the gym were behind what she looked like, even though they were not in her associations.

In addition to her sexual inhibition, Alice reported many anxieties. She was worried about keeping up her regimen. She was careful of her diet, her need to exercise, and to keep her apartment perfect. The kitchen was HERS and her husband could not enter it (as he could not enter her body). This, by the way seemed to have been the case in Freud's household. Ernest Jones noted that Freud had only one type in mind: a gentle feminine one, yet many of the women surrounding him were outrageous. Although priding herself on her humility and her lack of obtrusiveness Freud's wife's domestic authority was unquestioned: "When in 1920, their daughter Anna wanted to change some rooms around, Sigmund wrote to her: 'I cannot force her [Martha], and have always let her have her way in the house'" (cited in Appignanesi and Forrester, 1992, p. 43).

Mother was described as perfect, a wealthy suburban housewife who had a live-in housekeeper, but by herself kept the huge house spotless and cooked elaborate meals while maintaining her perfect figure and wardrobe. Family values centered on the purchase of expensive cars (she and her younger brother had good cars from the age of 15), designer clothing, and fine jewelry. Mother insisted upon spending days with Alice purchasing clothing for her and showed a kind of disingenuous disbelief if she said "no" to anything. When Alice and her husband developed a plan to add an extension to their apartment, mother and her decorator and architect just showed up one day without asking. She presented them with an offer they could not refuse. Alice's husband felt resentful and emasculated, however, because there was no way he could have paid for such a renovation. Father was described as successful, working all the time, never expressing a separate opinion. The parents were self-made and did not realize that their children needed to be self-made too. Her younger brother was completely dominated by them and still lived at home at 28.

Alice did not feel aroused by her husband who wanted to have sex several times/week. She managed to limit him access to her body as much as she could and did not want him to even touch her. On Saturday morning she would get up and sneak off to the gym while he slept. Keeping her body and wardrobe sexually alluring was preferred to having sex. They were "scheduled" to have a baby in the next year, which would require sex. Mother was waiting with bated breath to hear about a pregnancy and to help raise the child, disenfranchizing her daughter as many of her friends were doing with their daughters.

The transference was subtle: Alice commented at least once a month about how much she enjoyed her sessions and how much she was learning about herself. Nevertheless, she put a check on the hall table at the end of each month prior to her session. (Was I a prostitute?) And after each interpretation I would make, she would agree, and then say "maybe," taking away its impact.

Freud did not use the term "spoiled," defined by McIntosh (1989) as excessive, self-centered and immature behavior, lack of consideration for other people, inability to delay gratification, demands to have one's own way, obstructive, and manipulative. The parents of spoiled children fail to enforce consistent age-appropriate limits. Materialism abounds. (See also the 2012 *The New Yorker* book essay, "Spoiled Rotten: Why Do Kids Rule the Roost?" by Elizabeth Kolbert) It is possible that children were not "spoiled" in Freud's day, although many other unhealthy child-rearing practices existed.

I have seen in psychoanalytic therapy and analysis a series of women who are single, claiming they wanted to meet men to marry, but had not dated or had sex for several years (see Lieberman, 1991). They socialized in packs of women going to bars, hotels in Florida and the Caribbean, getting drunk, and wasted. I worked with them about their fears of rejection, of sex itself, of commitment, of their perceptions of their parents', siblings' and friends' marriages, and of how they avoided meeting men in their daily lives. At this point they began to socialize and meet men; but they soon began to make outrageous demands of them.

Clinical example III

Barbara was tied by phone, e-mail, and text messages day and night to her mother, grandmother, and a series of friends, and coworkers. Endless chatter all day and in her sessions enabled her to discharge her considerable aggression toward her father who had divorced her mother and toward several men who had rejected her. This chatter was often accompanied by tears and a demand for soothing. Her self-denigration resulted in others' feeling they had to tell her she was beautiful, smart, and deserving of any man's love. She was incredibly envious of any of her friends who married, but found fault with each of their husbands and said that *she* would not settle for any of them.

As treatment went on she acquired a cat who she shared with Steve, with whom she lived. The cat was "*hers,*" a *Jewish cat*, even though Steve was not Jewish. And of course their children would be brought up Jewish. That is, although when single she said she had no self-esteem and wondered why someone would want her, as soon as someone did want her, she made outrageous demands of him as if she were a very entitled and important person. She insisted that the cat share the bed with them and she refused to have sex with Steve. Nevertheless, she had targeted Steve as a husband and became overly-involved with his friends and relatives as an attempt to win their allegiance. Needless to say, eventually he ended the relationship and she was in tears for months, repeating the cycle of being unhappy and having her mother, grandmother, her brother, coworkers, and friends console her, and buttress up her self-esteem.

Barbara then decided to increase the frequency of her sessions and at one point I suggested she try the couch. After her first session on the couch, she arrived with her cat. She thought nothing of it. I had to tell her that it was not possible to do treatment with the cat in the room.

As treatment progressed, Barbara's younger brother became engaged. Barbara became quite depressed and her efforts to discharge her envy via her telephone and digital networks were not successful. No one in her life told her that the extent of her rage at her family members was out of bounds. (I have seen many siblings blatantly envious of their engaged siblings quite consciously being destructive toward them and not chastised by parents or friends.) I had to confront her with the outrageousness of her demands on others and her feeling entitled to have things conform to her wishes only. Barbara was finally able to work on her envy. In her sessions, she finally became able to think about her brother's birth and early years when she was so jealous of him, and felt that she was neglected. I believe that a combination of empathy and confrontation enabled me to work with and to attenuate Barbara's unreasonable and outrageous demands.

Juliet Mitchell (2003) believes that psychoanalysis has placed too much emphasis on the Oedipal and the vertical and not enough on the lateral sibling relationship, both sexual and aggressive. As she notes: "Sibling displacement evokes a desire to kill or be killed" (p. 35). She goes on to suggest that: "loving one's sibling *like oneself* is neither exactly narcissism nor object-love. It is narcissism transmuted by a hatred that has been overcome" (p. 36).

I want to emphasize the commonalities between these seemingly disparate "outrageous women." They had symbiotic and idealizing relationships with their mothers, they had passive fathers, there were few if any consequences for bad behavior, and their younger brothers were weaker and unsuccessful. Each would get involved with others in meddling, and tangled ways that resulted in enactments in the treatment. I was idealized, yet controlled, charmed by them, yet rendered helpless. I want to add the "Cleopatra complex" to our lexicon.

Thinking about pathology—I can make a generalization that 40 years ago, many of the women patients I saw were on the neurotic end of the spectrum. They suffered from guilt, inhibition, harsh superegos, and led lives we might consider today to be masochistic. Today, I observe less guilt where patients who come to me are character disordered. Their aggressions are self-justified and often aided and abetted by friends and relatives. They come to treatment because of deep unhappiness. They have often killed off their relationships with the men they meet or are married to.

References

Appignanesi, L., & Forrester, J. (1992). *Freud's women.* New York: Basic Books.

Bernstein, D. (1983). The female superego: A different perspective. *International Journal of Psycho-Analysis, 64,* pp. 187–201.

Brumberg, J. J. (1997). *The body project: An intimate history of American girls.* New York: Vintage.

Friedan, B. (1963). *The feminine mystique* New York: W. W. Norton.

Freud, S. (1914). On Narcissism: An Introduction. *S.E.* XIV.

Hamburg, J. (2017). *60th reunion address.* Barnard College; New York, June 2017.

Kolbert, E. (2012, July 2). Spoiled rotten: Why do kids rule the roost? *The New Yorker,* p. 76.

McIntosh, B. (1989). Wikipedia "spoiled child syndrome."

Mitchell, J. (2003). *Siblings.* Cambridge, U.K.: Blackwell Publishing.

Riviere, J. (1929). Womanliness as a masquerade. In A. Hughes (Ed.), *Joan Riviere: The inner world of Joan Riviere: Collected papers 1920–1958* (pp. 90–101). London: Karnak (Books) Ltd.

Sandberg, S. (2013). *Lean in.* New York: Alfred A Knopf.

Schiff, S. (2010). *Cleopatra: A life.* New York: Back Bay Books; Little, Brown & Co.

Chapter 10

The male psyche

An even darker continent

My objective here is to revisit the subject of male psychology in this postmodern era. During the last 40 or so years, concurrent with an active feminist movement, a plethora of studies have appeared in the psychoanalytic literature on the subject of Female Psychology. Two supplements to the *Journal of the American Psychoanalytic Association (JAPA)* (1976, 1996) were devoted to this topic. Freud's classic writings on gender have been challenged, overruled, and rewritten. Essentially "phallocentric" theories have been thrown out. Despite some fledgling "men's movements," social psychological studies, e.g., Levinson's (1978) *Seasons of a Man's Life*, and writings that have been published in gay and "queer" journals, Freud's traditional notions of what is essentially "male" and "masculine" that is, phallic, dominant, active, directive, and focused, have not been challenged, or even very much discussed. The 2001 issue of JAPA on gender and sexuality does not deal with masculinity. Notable exceptions are a scattered literature of psychoanalytic developmental studies, e.g., those of Abelin (1971, 1975); Diamond (2004a, 2004b); Fogel and colleagues (1986); Fogel (1998); Herzog (2001); and Ross (1979), and Breen (1993) has edited an aptly titled collection of writings: *The Gender Conundrum.* Freud wrote notable papers on female psychology but not on male psychology.

There are those of course who do not even find the concept of gender to be valid. In his book, *The End of Masculinity: The Confusion of Sexual Genesis and Sexual Difference in Modern Society* (1998), Scottish sociologist John MacInnes commented that it has been impossible to define "masculinity" because "no such thing exists." He wrote: "gender, together with the terms masculinity and femininity, is an ideology people use in modern societies to imagine the existence between men and woman on the basis of their sex where in fact there are none" (p. 1). He sees gender to be like a religious fetish, lying in the imagination of its worshippers defending "men's privilege against the corrosive logic of modernity" (p. 10). He went on provocatively to note: "It has become a cliché to argue that masculinity is in crisis ... the briefest historical survey will show that masculinity has always been in one crisis or another" (p. 11).

I disagree with MacInnes. I think that "masculinity" is a valid concept, but I am uncertain about its definition since there seem to be many versions of masculinity.

Just as Freud described the female psyche as the "dark continent" many regard the male psyche as an even darker continent!

Let me quote in this context the much bedded and wedded Gloria Vanderbilt who, in her (2004) autobiography remarked: "It's a cliché, of course, but men truly are a mystery. Even now, I haven't a clue as to how they think or what goes on in their minds" (p. 10). Michael Gurian (2005) published a neurobiological explanation called *What Could He Be Thinking;* at the same time the president of Harvard University has been censured for acknowledging that male and female minds work differently.

And just as there is a wide range of what can be characterized as "female," there also exists in our culture today a broad range of what can be characterized as "male" and not simply to be relegated to the categories of perverse, perversion, or even pathological. In his book, *The Forgotten Man: Understanding the Male Psyche,* Fine (1987) commented that:

> It has been all too generally assumed that men are strong, domineering, powerful and perfectly able to take care of themselves. Little could be farther from the truth, Men are all too often weak, submissive, passive, helpless, dependent and depressed.
>
> (p. xiii)

Fogel (1986) believes that the problem for men is women: "Not only must men struggle with the real and fantasy-distorted powers of women as objects, but also with those qualities and impulses within themselves that are perceived as womanly or womanish" (p. 9).

Much has been written about what it feels like to be a woman both inside and out, but very little about what it feels like to be a man, inside and out. A literature search of writings on gender of the last 40 years might lead one to conclude that "gender is female!" In recent years, the subject of masculinity has been dealt with as it expresses itself in the female psyche as a "masculine complex." Karen Horney was responsible for this! I hope to begin to adumbrate a more differentiated spectrum of what can be regarded as "male" fantasy and action as presented in the psychoanalytic situation and the outside world as well. "Masculinity" must not just be examined clinically but as it is regarded by women and by men, by the nonclinical population and by the media (art, theater, film, television, and literature).

I take an empirical approach—examining cases of contemporary men without imposing a traditional set of constructs onto the clinical material in order to see where men are in the year 2005 (*when this was written*). It is still widely assumed in our culture that men are biologically aggressive and need to take the initiative in love and work. Men are not supposed to show emotions although both Bush Presidents have felt that it is OK to cry. From listening to my patients in these postmodern times, I have observed that today's women are still told that they will find themselves in difficulty with men if they assert themselves, e.g., calling them, asking them out, and proposing marriage that, the men will be "turned off." Yet it is obvious that little happens for many women in relationships unless they do take the initiative. Due to cultural stereotypes women hope that men will approach them ("act like men") but are thrilled and surprised when they find a man who they can communicate with ("he's like a woman"). Some men complain that women are too passive in bed and wish that they would initiate sex. On the other hand, they want women who are omnipresent, "always available," while fantasizing about two women making love, and admiring their sexual aggressiveness. (Fogel et al., 1986; Breen 1993). It is an understatement to say that there is considerable confusion about what men really want.

In my clinical work with men, I have observed that many feel "imprisoned" (rightly or wrongly) by the women in their lives. Adler (2005) has presented a paper highlighting this phenomenon. The traditional strong, domineering, and initiating male role that includes that of primary breadwinner does not seem to suit many men. The outcome for some who have bought into the social imperative to assume this role has been their direct aggression or passive aggression toward women, expressed in physical or verbal attacks on women and on their bodies, a lack of commitment and/or infidelity and poor communication. Women today are moving out of traditional constraining roles in order to better express who they are. We must ask: "What are men today really about?" The aim of psychoanalytic treatment should be to help them in this way.

In the past, it seemed that men functioned best in the world at the expense of their wives, who, in many cases, remained undeveloped. Now men need to learn to adapt to, and be satisfied with, women who are fully functioning adults while becoming fully functioning adults themselves.

To my mind, a central part of the discussion of masculinity is that of the role of the father, the man in question's father and his own role or potential role as father. The Belgian Lacanian Psychoanalyst Paul Verhaeghe (1999) has written a most provocative paper entitled: "The Collapse of the Function of the Father and Its Effect on Gender Roles." I find his observations to be so compelling that I am presenting a lengthy excerpt here. He noted that:

> Both in his case studies and in his theoretical work in general, Freud places the accent entirely on the real father. Nevertheless, there is a striking difference between real fathers in his clinical practice and the way in which he depicts the father's role in his oedipal theory. In his classic case studies, we meet a father who is living on the fortune of his wife, a second who travels in a state of total depression from one mental institution to another, a third who is utterly dominated by his wife, and a fourth who is ill but nevertheless is capable of offering his daughter in exchange to the husband of his mistress...[fathers of the Rat Man, Wolf Man, Little Hans, and Dora] The fact that these real fathers in his clinical studies turn out time and again to be total failures does not prevent Freud from cultivating the idea of the oedipal father as a feared, menacing character whose threat of castration has to be taken seriously.

(p. 133)

Verhaeghe went on to hypothesize the following:

> In order to close the gap between clinical reality and his theory, Freud invented the myth of the primal father. The myth runs as follows: once upon a time there must have been a real such father, an *Urvater*, and the phylogenetic memory of this father is stronger than any weak incarnation of it. Further, every real father, strong or weak, occupies this terrifying oedipal position owing to this collectively inherited myth.
>
> (p. 133)

Verhaeghe observed: "... the massive collapse of the father figure.... Nowadays, we are living in a period where the symbolic father as such is murdered, together with the belief in him" (p. 135).

In the scattered Freudian literature there are varied theories about how the boy uses his father on the way to becoming a man. Abelin (1971) coined the term "early triangulation," referring to the earliest role of the father at about 18 months. He observed that the toddler had to internalize the relationship of mother and father and both feel left out and as a member of a small group. Greenson (1984, in Breen 1993) saw the boy as needing to disidentify with mother and counteridentify with father and observed that:

> It is my contention that men are far more uncertain about their maleness than women are about their femaleness. I believe that women's certainty about their gender identity and men's insecurity about theirs are rooted in early identifications with the mother.
>
> (p. 258)

According to Greenson: "Each sex is envious of the opposite sex; but the male's more covert envy underneath his external facade of contempt seems to be particularly destructive in regard to his gender identity" (p. 259). For example, some of his transvestite male patients put on female underwear as part of masturbation. This was not so for females. Diamond (2004) has recently called the notion of disidentification with mother a mis-nomer. He feels that denial and disavowal are more descriptive of the painful relinquishing and traumatic loss of femininity during separation-individuation.

The time limits of this paper do not permit anything like a comprehensive review of this subject. I would like to note here the contributions of Limentani (1991) on the importance of fathers in sexual deviations; of Glasser (in Breen, 1993); Herzog (2001) on "father hunger" and a collection of papers on the importance of fathers edited by Trowell and Etchegoyen (2002).

Another part of this discussion is that of polarities: male vs. female. Does anatomy determine destiny in terms of gender role assignment as well as ideal personality traits? Written about ad nauseum is the case of women who have achieved some degree of freedom from bondage but in reality are considered less of a "woman" if unmarried, childless, aggressive in their professions, and even successful. It seems as if every other week I find an article about how difficult it is for educated professional women to find men because the men they would choose prefer secretaries and stewardesses. Men who take time out from their careers to care for their young children while their wives work have their "manhood" questioned. They are called "househusbands" or "Mr. Mom's." Clinical discussions among psychoanalysts are often "binary." Developmental charts, which are really abstractions, are used as if they represent the "normal" or the "norm," when in fact real people are organized in many varieties and combinations of traits, gender-based or not. These polarities are especially problematic when held up by psychoanalysts to be the "goals of analysis." How often in case reports do we read as criteria of termination that "she was able to marry and have children" or that "he was able to assert himself with his father," etc.

There have been some societal changes in attitudes toward men, at least in cities like New York. "Macho" has come to be regarded as a neurotic male characteristic and very masculine men are considered to have Don Juan complexes or Ernest Hemingway complexes, latent homosexuality supposedly fueling their super-masculine defensive endeavors and outlook. The term "metrosexual" has entered our vocabulary. Postmodern men have been characterized as "the new women."

I would like to demonstrate the varieties of maleness that exist in our contemporary culture by briefly describing the cases of two men who undertook courses of psychoanalytic treatment. Each presented as stereotypically male and masculine: tall, handsome, and successful in his profession, each the dominant one in the family who "took charge of everything," and the major breadwinner. Each had married a passive woman with whom he was comfortable and not challenged by. Yet Harry was suicidal and Richard was somewhat depressed. As Harry's treatment unfolded, occasional homosexual encounters were revealed as well as wishes to be with a woman with a perfect body to shore up his own sense of having a perfect body. He expressed tremendous aggression toward women with imperfect bodies. His "maleness" was characterized by muscularity. As Richard's treatment unfolded, a history of childhood seduction by an older brother was uncovered, one root of his passive-aggressive behavior with authority figures, an obsession with women's clothes, and compulsive infidelity. His anus and anal eroticism characterized his "maleness."

If you were to meet either socially or together you might think them alike: tall, handsome, educated, successful in business, and married to attractive women. But Richard was very regressed in his fantasy life, the fantasies were both homoerotic and heterosexual; Harry regressed in his real life to dangerous homoerotic contact with strangers. Each was acutely aware of the social consequences for their marriages, social and business relationships, should they act on many of their fantasies.

Each of these men had mothers who had assumed traditional constricting female roles and were ambivalently supportive of their sons' achievements.

Their fathers were overbearing, cold, distant, and did not permit their sons to challenge them. Both were the youngest child and their parents could be described as "burnt out" when each came along. Older siblings took over for the parents in pathological ways.

In each case, psychoanalytic treatment led to a cessation of ego-dystonic behavior, a renegotiation of marital roles and increased comfort in taking positions that were not stereotypically male. Resolution of conflict for each can be regarded as on a continuum.

There are many parallels here to Limentani's (1991) concept of the "vagina-man." He noted that some men "may go through life without acknowledging any difficulty with their heterosexuality" (p. 273). Their partners are beautiful, "masculine," and intellectually powerful women. [Richard's wife was experienced that way at the start of the marriage before her regression into a childish dependent form of motherhood.] The mothers of Limentani's patients treated them as a phallus and were capable of sudden rejections. The treatment revealed "a secret wish to be a woman, associated with a profound envy of everything female" (p. 274). According to Limentani, what is usually repressed is a fantasy vagina: the anus, mouth, eye, ear, and urethra are endowed with receptive qualities.

When there is cultural permission to cross gender boundaries these fantasies are more accessible. Limentani sees the vagina-man as "the male who relies on his heterosexual inclinations supported by an identification with the woman (the primal object) in order to escape from his homosexuality" (p. 277).

One hundred years ago, Freud (1905), in "Three Essays on the Theory of Sexuality" wrote that:

> in human beings pure masculinity or femininity is not to be found either in a psychological or a biological sense. Every individual on the contrary displays a mixture of the character traits belonging to his own and to the opposite sex; and he shows a combination of activity and passivity whether or not these last character traits tally with his biological ones.
>
> (p. 220)

I cannot agree more. I hope to collect more cases during the next few years to empirically discover and define that elusive concept: "masculinity."

References

Abelin, E. (1971). The role of the father in the separation-individuation process. In J. B. McDevitt & C. F. Settlage (Eds.), *Separation-individuation*. New York: International Universities Press.

Abelin, E. (1975). Some further observations and comments on the earliest role of the father. *International Journal of Psycho-Analysis, 56*(3), 293–302.

Adler, E. (2005). Morbid precipice: Male fears of being entrapped by love. Presentation at PEP CD Conference on Love. February, New York.

Breen, D. (Ed.). (1993). *The gender conundrum*. New York and London: Routledge.

Diamond, M. J. (2004). Accessing the multitude within: A psychoanalytic perspective on the transformation of masculinity at midlife. *International Journal of Psycho-Analysis, 85*(1), 45–64.

Fine, R. (1987). *The forgotten man: Understanding the male psyche*. New York: Haworth Press.

Fogel, G. I., Lane, F., & Liebert, R. (Eds.) (1986). *The psychology of men: Psychoanalytic perspectives*. New York: Basic Books.

Fogel, G. I. (1998). Interiority and inner genital space in men: What else can be lost in castration? *Psychoanalytic Quarterly, 67*(4), 662–697.

Freud, S. (1905). Three essays on the theory of sexuality. In J. Strachey (Ed. & Trans.), *The standard edition of the complete psychological works of Sigmund Freud* (Vol. 7, pp. 135–174). London: Hogarth Press.

Gurian, M. (2005). *What could he be thinking: How a man's mind really works*. London: Macmillan.

Herzog, J. M. (2001). *Father hunger: Explorations with adults and children*. Hillsdale, N.J.: Analytic Press.

Levinson, D. J., Darrow, C. N., Klein, E. B., Levinson, M. H., & McKee, B. (1978). *The seasons of a man's life*. New York: Alfred Knopf.

Limentani, A. (1991). Neglected fathers in the etiology and treatment of sexual deviations. *International Journal of Psycho-Analysis, 72*, 573–584.

MacInnes, J. (1998). *The end of masculinity: The confusion of sexual genesis and sexual difference in modern society*. Buckingham: Open University Press.

Ross, J. M. (1979). Fathering: A review of some psychoanalytic contributions on paternity. *International Journal of Psycho-Analysis, 60*(3), 317–327.

Trowell, J., & Etchegoyen, A. (2002). *The importance of fathers: A psychoanalytic re-evaluation*. London: Routledge.

Vanderbilt, G. (2004). *It seemed important at the time*. New York: Simon & Schuster.

Verhaeghe, P. (1999). The collapse of the function of the father and its effect on gender roles. *Journal of Culture and Society, 4*(1), 18–30.

Part III

Relationships

Chapter 11

Issues in the psychoanalytic treatment of single females over 30[1]

Conducting psychoanalytic treatment can be a considerable challenge when the patient is a single woman over 30 years of age seeking more effective pathways toward marriage as a life goal. The analyst must preserve intrapsychic change as the goal of treatment and the analysis of intrapsychic conflict as its task. It is desirable that an analysis be conducted in an atmosphere of "timelessness." Yet, the single woman patient may become concerned with external issues, such as the diminishing number of suitable men available to her as she gets older and the pressure of the "time-line" for having a baby. This can serve resistance purposes. Alternatively, she may join the analyst in a "timeless" exploration of intrapsychic conflict, unconsciously gratify herself through her relationship with her analyst in the regressive transference, avoid dealing with her life goals, and pass over the time-line for fertility.

Psychoanalysts have traditionally maintained the point of view that unwanted single status is the result of unresolved neurotic conflict. An additional viewpoint with which to understand single women patients is proposed: unwanted single status can in itself stimulate regression to less mature levels of development. Furthermore, prolonged single status can be internally experienced as a chronic traumatic state that is emotionally depriving, narcissistically wounding, and an impediment to the further psychological growth and development of the adult. There is no way to compensate for the absence of experiences typically shared with a partner in a good marriage over the course of the adult years or those experiences to be had by virtue of being a parent, individually as well as in interaction with others in society.

Traditional psychoanalytic theories about why people remain single will be discussed on p. 132. Reality factors are introduced here as quite pertinent to the analysis of single women. Clinical examples will be given. A syndrome that characterizes women who have been "single too long" will be described. This syndrome consists of the following symptoms: depression, low self-esteem, poor body image, proneness to shame and humiliation, lonesomeness, alienation, envy, psychosomatic complaints, and polar extremes of behavior, such as frantic man-hunting vs. social withdrawal, promiscuity vs. frigidity, and workaholism vs. work inhibition. A state of "adult developmental arrest" is postulated and is considered to apply to many of these patients. This syndrome is to be found across diagnostic lines, and it creates diagnostic confusion as it interacts with pathology not related to single status. Analyst and patient must work hard in order to assess which aspects of the patient's present pathology stem from childhood traumata and the incomplete resolution of infantile fantasy and conflict, and which aspects result from living the out-of-phase, often adolescent-type singles life in middle adulthood.

Some of the specific types of transference, countertransference, resistance, and defense that characterize this patient population in treatment are discussed. Also examined are the analyst's personal value systems with regard to issues such as: the importance of marriage as an indicator of emotional adjustment per se; sexual behavior outside marriage; and what constitutes a "suitable and appropriate mate" for an analyzed female. Recommendations for doing effective treatment with this patient population are made. Concepts from drive theory, ego psychology, self-psychology, and object relations theory are used when they seem most appropriate to describe the clinical material, for, as Pine (1988) has written: "While the drive and ego perspectives on ego functioning were more formally part of Freud's theory, psychoanalytic practice clearly deals with them all" (p. 574).

The single women over 30 discussed here typically enter psychoanalytic treatment in order to "better understand themselves" and why they have not been able to get into "stable relationships with men." The affect-laden word, "marriage," is generally not used in the first sessions. "Being single" is occasionally raised as the presenting problem, but more often than not, it is mentioned after several sessions have elapsed and after these patients have presented a long list of vague difficulties, self-accusations, and/or career-related problems to the analyst. The casual way in which the problem appears in the sessions belies the fact that many of these women patients unconsciously bring to treatment a hidden agenda: *They expect to find a husband* as an outcome of treatment. This "hidden agenda" can serve the unconscious purpose of organizing massive resistance to the goals of psychoanalytic treatment, the uncovering of unconscious fantasy and inner conflict. The dilemma of "not finding a husband" becomes a lightning rod upon which to project a galaxy of problems. This hidden agenda must be recognized and interpreted early in the treatment, for even the best-trained of analysts at times become convinced by their patients that their obtaining husbands would be the only appropriate cure for their unhappiness. The problems faced by single women over 30 who wish to marry are *not just intrapsychic.* Once women reach their late 20s and increasingly as they get older, there is a scarcity of suitable men available to them. The shortage of heterosexual men capable of a long commitment like marriage to women over 30 seems to be a fact of reality that is commonly overlooked or even denied by society. If the reports I hear are true, many analysts deny this fact as well. I consider this to be a "cultural lie." Notable exceptions are Kernberg (1976) and Person (1988). Person acknowledges this scarcity of men:

as one of the major problems that confronts women today, and contributes to the transformation of a perfectly healthy longing for love into a kind of deadly preoccupation. The frequent female obsession with love is in part the result of a demographic imbalance with profound psychological ramifications; unlike men, women live in a scarcity economy; there simply aren't enough men to go around. This problem is compounded by the fact that men often consider women less desirable as they grow older.... After a certain age women know their chances of finding love and sex are greatly reduced.

(p. 284)

A much-quoted study by Bennett and Bloom (1986) conducted at Yale and Harvard, entitled, "Why Fewer American Women Marry," reported that college-educated women at 30 have only a *20 percent* chance of marrying and those at 35 have a *5 percent* chance. These statistics seem to be the result of a number of factors, including the greater longevity of women and social norms that permit men to marry women younger and less educated than themselves. Marrying younger women is considered to be a status symbol for middle- and upper-class men. Men find it acceptable to marry women who are intellectually, socially, and professionally beneath them, whereas women usually do not find such marriages acceptable. There may even be a rise in the population of men who are overtly homosexual and of men who are unable to make commitments (see, for example, Weiss, 1987). Additionally, many men report that they are threatened by the recent advances women have made, both professionally and socially.

Developmental differences between men and women further explain this phenomenon. Kernberg (1977) has speculated that because the road of female sexual development is lonelier and more secretive, it is more courageous than the little boy's, whose male genitality is for various reasons stimulated by both parents.

Perhaps, because under optimal circumstances, the little girl has to change the first erotic object in turning from mother to father, and in the process has had to cross the boundary from pregenital to genital development earlier, more definitively, and in a lonely way, the adult woman has a potentially greater courage and capacity for heterosexual commitment than the adult man.

(p. 92)

The abundance of women who greatly need and seek male companionship has led to a situation that one divorced male patient has experienced as a "candy store." He finds that the strains and stresses of a serious commitment to one woman are not very appealing because there is so much immediate gratification available to him. Consequently, he has little motivation to work to resolve inner difficulties in the quality of his relationships in treatment or out.

Getting married in and of itself cannot be considered to be a sign of health, growth, or integration, or an indicator of readiness to terminate treatment, since pathological females do marry. As I review my practice over the years, I cannot identify the characteristics that differentiate between single and married patients that would help me understand why the first group was unable to marry. Papers abound in which are reported cases of young women whose preoedipal attachment to their mothers or oedipal attachment to their fathers was assumed by their analysts to prevent them from marrying.

Yet, there have been as many cases in which similar fixations are found in married women who enact their neuroses with their husbands.

Traditional psychoanalytic views of prolonged singlehood

In "Some Character-Types Met with in Psycho-Analytic Work," Freud (1916) described a single woman whose neurotic fantasy life prevented her from reaching her conscious goal of marriage. She fell ill when she could finally marry her lover. Freud wrote:

> At that moment she began to go to pieces. She neglected the house of which she was now about to become the rightful mistress, imagined herself persecuted by his relatives, who wanted to take her into the family, debarred her lover through her senseless jealousy from all social intercourse, hindered him in his artistic work and soon succumbed to an incurable illness.
>
> (p. 317)

Freud set the precedent for psychoanalysts to view the possibility of marriage as an unconsciously terrifying goal, laden with multiple, and overdetermined symbolic meanings. Unresolved infantile conflicts and their phase-specific core fantasies have been traditionally viewed as having explanatory value in the failure of patients to reach their conscious goal of marrying. These conflicts can stop them at any point along the way. There are those who never date, those who never have a long-term relationship, or those who, like the woman Freud described, go all the way to the altar and then stop. For some, the unconscious conflicts that stand in the way are focused on issues related to pregnancy, birth, and motherhood. They avoid marriage as a way of warding off the rest.

In the traditional psychoanalytic literature, it has been held that those who are heterosexual and consciously wish to marry and cannot are suffering from unconscious guilt over sexual and aggressive wishes toward parents and siblings. The "debt to the superego" is paid off by depriving the individual of success and happiness. Masochistic solutions are effected with concomitant suffering and the taking on of martyred life roles. Other means of expressing unconscious aggression toward one or both parents take the form of unconscious spiteful rebellion in the refusal to comply with the perceived parental demand to marry. This spiteful self-destructive tendency must be worked through over and over in treatment.

It is quite a formidable obstacle to the analysis and to marriageability since it has so many unconsciously gratifying aspects.

Traditionally, patients who have not yet married and wish to do so have been analyzed along the lines of the psychosexual stages—oral, anal, phallic, and oedipal—with progression to and regression from the various levels of fixation. Current thinking about the dynamics underlying prolonged single status might include, in addition, the possibility of strong preoedipal pathology, fear of intimacy and merger, inability to separate and individuate, and severe pathology in the integration of self and object. Bergmann (1985), in her analysis of six professional women who delayed marriage, found that their mothers did not let them outgrow the symbiotic phase. Narcissistic problems led to mother-daughter role reversal, and sexualized father-daughter ties suggested a "central psychic constellation" in which "marriage was unconsciously equated with losing a part of the self that in fantasy represented a part of the parent as well" (p. 213).

Perhaps it should be noted here that the problem of single men who wish to marry and cannot are different, due to a developmentally different set of inner fantasies and experiences. They suffer internally from unconscious conflicts and from unhappy experiences with women. However, society is not as scornful of them, and they do not suffer from a shortage of available women. Their psychoanalytic treatment does not have to include the analysis of a reality that might make their goal of ever finding a mate or ever having a child a hopeless one.

Psychosexual regression and adult developmental arrest

In my clinical work, I have found it useful to analyze single women patients in the traditional manner outlined above. It has been my observation, however, that whereas unresolved intrapsychic conflict may have historically led *some* of these women to their present dilemma, the single condition, in and of itself, along with the shortage of suitable men to interact with, providing them little or no outlet for amelioration of their condition, creates particular stress, strain, and cumulative trauma that can produce regression and/or a state of "adult developmental arrest." This latter conceptualization is an analog to the concept of "developmental arrest" proposed by Stolorow and Lachmann (1980). They spoke of environmental deficiencies, of:

> an absence of empathic responsiveness to the child's developmental requirements, extreme inconsistencies in behavior toward the child, and frequent exposure of the child to affectively unbearable sexual and aggressive scenes … (leading to the individual's remaining) arrested at, or vulnerable to regressive revivals of archaic, more or less undifferentiated and unintegrated self-object configurations.
>
> (p. 5).

The concept of "adult developmental arrest" as used here is different. The adult is more formed, more resilient than the child. However, chronic inconsistencies and disappointments, social rejections, and often bizarre sexual experiences, promises made and broken that seem to be part and parcel of single life, as well as the lack of a stable object to relate to, create for the single woman an environmental condition somewhat analogous to the one described above. The single woman whose future is uncertain and who hopes for something that may never happen can have great difficulty growing in the way normal adults can grow in the shelter and stability of a good marriage with a shared future.

Despite the so-called social advances women have made in recent years, they are still ostracized by men when they are too independent and professionally successful. Person (1988) writes that:

> Single women are still considered freaky—"losers" rather than "choosers" of their solitary state. And there are concrete liabilities in being a woman alone—among them the social devaluation that still makes the single woman less sought after by the average hostess or host, the threat of male violence that renders a woman's physical safety precarious when she is alone in certain situations, and the economic privations she suffers since she is still far from being a man's equal in earning power.
>
> (p. 283)

Very little has been said by psychoanalysts about psychic development in adults. Freud was inclined to regard adulthood as a time in which the early unconscious conflicts were *reenacted* and *relived* rather than as a time of further development. Some writers (e.g., Anthony and Benedek, 1970) have described growth in adults, outlining the process of parenthood as a developmental phase. Marriage also has been described as a developmental phase by Blanck and Blanck (1968). In normal adulthood, between the ages of 20 and 40, today's woman is usually expected and expects herself to separate from her family, to marry, to establish a home and a style of life, to bear and raise children, and to establish some kind of career life while accomplishing all of the rest. Anthony and Benedek (1970) speak of the growth potential of marriage when she writes that "each of the partners, stimulated by the ongoing psychodynamic interactions with each other, achieves another level of integration of his or her own personality" (p. 144). If a woman fails to accomplish this, damage is done to her self-esteem and to the image others hold of her. She is deprived of essential life experiences that are difficult to compensate for.

Kernberg (1976) has described sources of self-esteem and the potential for growth in married middle-aged women entering treatment. He has written that:

> women who have been able to bring up children with success, to direct a home in ways which realistically reconfirm their unconscious identification with—or triumph over—their mother image, and particularly who have had

years of gratifying sexual experiences thus gradually work through the remnants of oedipal fears and inhibitions.

(p. 231)

The unmarried woman must find in treatment alternative and often unconventional paths for inner conflict resolution.

The "singles" syndrome

In my clinical work, I have found an identifiable constellation of symptoms and complaints—the "singles" syndrome—that seems to differentiate single from married women patients over 30. This syndrome is organized around the experience of "unwanted single status," which stimulates unconscious conflicts, and it invades and curtails optimal ego functioning in the particular group of single women described here. A chronic, nagging sense of unfinished business, uncertainty about the future, and the increasing probability of failure to reach their goal of marriage and motherhood as the years pass by have a major impact on these women's sense of identity and their sense of inner stability. In this chapter, the *manifest content* of these women's complaints will be focused upon. It is recommended that the reality of their situation be addressed along with the internal unconscious, individual meanings of that particular reality.

The symptoms listed are not unique to single women. The *ideas* connected with them are—for these symptoms are experienced by these patients as being directly connected to their single status. They believe that the symptoms will disappear when they find men to marry, and, clinically, I have found that in certain cases they do disappear. The symptoms are chronic depression; bingeing and starving, obsessing that they must stay thin in order to attract men; believing that they are physically unattractive and incapable of having relationships with men; feeling ashamed about being alone; feeling punished for some crime they have not committed; feeling alienated and left out of the broader married society; feeling envious of all those who are married, and especially of all those who have children; feeling chronically ill in a variety of ways; manifesting polar extremes in behavior such as desperate man-hunting vs. total withdrawal, workaholism vs. work inhibition; and rigidity, old maidism, sphincter morality vs. promiscuity, and hyperfluidity (where anything goes).

There seems to exist a pathological interaction between an initial structure that has some weaknesses in it and a reality pressure that forces regression to more primitive and infantile phases.

These patients are as *different* as can be. They range from professional women to secretaries, from higher functioning neurotics to those with borderline conditions. Some are scholars, some hardly ever read. Some are quite beautiful, others not. Some seek men of wealth and status, others never mention this issue.

The cases presented as illustrative are not unique. They typify the many women I have treated over the years in my private practice.

Ms. A.

Ms. A., an extremely attractive, lively, and personable, professional woman of 34, came to treatment to address problems in her social and professional life. She manifested a number of dysfunctional character traits, such as childlike clinging, and histrionic attention-grabbing followed by withdrawal, which were dealt with analytically. Ms. A. is a fairly resourceful woman who has good friends, male and female, single and married. She travels, socializes, entertains, and handles her life in general in a way that might be regarded as optimal for a single woman.

She makes the following complaints: If she dates and has sexual relationships, she risks rejection and abandonment as well as some of the side effects of the single sex life, unwanted pregnancy and abortion, VD, herpes, and, most recently, AIDS. It has been extremely difficult to identify at the outset the potential for abrupt abandonment or other kinds of bizarre behavior on the part of the various men she meets. When she does not date, she suffers from loneliness, lack of affection, sexual frustration, and the feeling of being left out of the mainstream of life. She feels like a "loser." "Losing" is experienced by her on both narcissistic and oedipal levels. She experiences intense shame over her situation. Her family harasses her, especially at holiday times when embarrassing questions are asked: "How come you haven't found someone yet? Maybe if you take off some weight you'll meet someone right away." Each successful dieting phase (she is of normal weight) is followed by high expectations and severe disappointment. Oral phase pathology in particular is stimulated by her single condition. Memories of childhood loneliness and object loss around her parents' divorce are chronically relived. Feelings of helplessness are stimulated by her well-meaning friends and relatives who keep saying, "Someone as beautiful as you are should have a man," or "You'll see—right around the corner you'll meet someone." These supposedly encouraging comments are painful to her, for she has "walked around hundreds of corners" and found no one. Her reality testing is constantly put to question by comments such as, "I'm sure you're passing up good men every day," or "You're being too picky," when there seems to be hardly anyone to pick. These comments are experienced by her as a kind of "battering" and lead to depressive affect. Some aspects of the regression involved in her clinging and histrionic behavior are the result of single life stress. Ms. A. is *not* a case demonstrating adult developmental arrest.

In her excellent article on "The Single Woman in Today's Society," Margaret Adams (1971) wrote:

> single women ... are still the victims of quite outrageous stereotyping in regard to their ascribed characteristics, and their unmarried status is popularly attributed to personal failings, such as lack of sexual attractiveness (whatever that elusive quality may be), unresolved early psychosexual conflicts, narcissistic unwillingness to be closely committed to another individual, latent

lesbianism ... it is interesting to note the frequency with which psychological reasons have been adduced to explain singleness, rather than equally cogent social causes.

(p. 778)

The difficult task for both analyst and patient is to differentiate the social from the intrapsychic, the present from the past, and to acknowledge that there is trauma in *both* the adult present and the infantile past. The task is to convey to the patient that she is suffering in the present *mostly* but not *totally* because of the past and that when the past is dealt with, the present will not be so very painful.

Ms. B.

In this case, in which the patient's presenting pathology was of a much greater degree, a galaxy of unresolved issues from the past interacted with the patient's single status, furthering regression, and adult developmental arrest.

Ms. B. was a 30-year-old single woman working as an administrator when she entered analysis. She was eventually diagnosed as suffering from a masochistic character disorder with narcissistic features. She experienced low self-esteem in every area of her life and complained that her life and job were boring. She believed herself to be unattractive and ungainly, and obsessed about her small breasts and wide hips as likely to "turn off" any man. She suffered from insomnia and various nervous twitches. She described her relations with both men and women as self-destructive. She was deeply envious of several of her women friends, especially of one who had married a wealthy lawyer subsequent to analytic therapy, and demanded the same outcome of me. She obsessed about hurts from past boyfriends, current women friends, her mother, and siblings.

Contrary to Ms. B.'s experience of herself, I found her to be attractive, well-spoken, and intelligent. She did not want to work, however, at her job, at her analysis, or do anything active that would put her in a position to meet men. She spent her evenings and weekends watching television. She felt that going to a singles event would publicly label her as lonely and a loser. It was her perception that others got what they wanted automatically. She hoarded stories of women who had married well. Her siblings had married, leaving her the only single one in the family. She obsessed about gifts, for she had no man to give her anything or to buy gifts for, and quite childishly preoccupied herself with her parents' birthday gifts to her and the birthday dinners they held for her.

During her adolescence and early 20s, Ms. B. was relatively happy, capable, industrious, and enjoyed sexual relationships with men. She traveled a good deal and did not particularly concern herself with marriage as a goal, feeling confident that someone would eventually come along. As she reached the age of 30, she met fewer appropriate single men and began to date married men for some companionship and sex, but found these relationships to be ultimately painful ones. As she realized she was "being left behind," she began to regress to the passive and isolated state in which she entered treatment. There was no one to share activities with, to dress up for, to tell her she was pretty, and to plan a life with. The absence of a stimulating "other" in her life led to the regression. Years of psychological starvation were apparent in her poignant description of a married man's ordering coffee from room service during a brief affair and her gratitude when he poured a cup for her.

A lengthy analysis of Ms. B.'s character as it manifested itself in the transference, centered on the interaction of real narcissistic trauma in infancy and childhood and core unconscious fantasies from the anal-sadistic and phallic phases of her development. A type of vengeful masochistic surrender to the oedipal mother was uncovered. Ms. B. can be described as a case illustrative of "adult developmental arrest." Due to the lack of a companion, she missed important life experiences that would have enabled her to grow. She lived, as do so many urban single women, in a small studio apartment with little furniture or space to cook and entertain. She was not invited to the homes of married couples and missed being witness to the growth of babies and young children. Her single women friends would not commit to appointments or plans lest some man should call for a date. Her parents gave her last priority over her siblings, who had spouses and children. There could be no future to plan for, only today to get through. She complained that she felt like a "failure to thrive" child.

As a result of analytic treatment, Ms. B. began to recover and she became more active. She advanced professionally, utilizing her aggressive energies, which were no longer turned against herself. She began to earn money to use to travel, to entertain, to buy clothes, and to socialize. She sought relationships with her nieces and nephews in order to partially discharge maternal wishes. She is quite realistic about the real probabilities for marriage and works hard in order to meet people.

Ms. C.

This case is presented in order to illustrate aspects of the course of treatment common to this group of patients. Ms. C. is a 32-year-old professional woman with obsessional and hysterical features, whose analytic treatment was first initiated in her early 20s due to conflicts about entering a profession. As she turned 30, she became episodically anxious and depressed, feeling that her life was empty and useless. She envied young mothers walking in the streets with their children. Her relationship with her parents, with other women, and the choice of jobs she would take were organized around the vicissitudes of her love life. She alternated periods of hermit-like withdrawal in her apartment (pulling all of the shades down) with periods of organized hunting and searching for male companions. When a man was found, tremendous energy was invested in the relationship. A kind of adolescent giddiness was manifested. Family, friends, and work were decathected. Treatment became of utmost importance as the place in which to report what was happening and to assess the analyst's reaction and prognosis for the relationship. Every cough or sneeze on her analyst's part was experienced by her as a sign of approval or disapproval, of a prediction of hope or hopelessness in what had become a magical and elusive jackpot or lottery. (Considering the odds against her finding someone suitable, this metaphor was an apt one.) The analyst commented that the patient's concentration on men to the exclusion of any other topic seemed to be defensive. Various transferential reactions indicating dissatisfaction with the treatment then ensued, such as tremendous rage, or the fantasy that her analyst did not wish her to have a man or that her analyst would only let her have someone perfect who did not exist. Sometimes this was elaborated further.

Only her analyst could have a man or her analyst wished the patient to be as lonely as the analyst herself was. When the relationship was over, or Ms. C. could no longer harbor the fantasy that she had a relationship with a man who had proved to be rather unavailable from the start, a depressive period ensued in which withdrawal, feelings of humiliation, bitterness, and hopelessness predominated. Fantasies of being excluded, alienated, and deprived of what other women had, emerged. The envy was unconsciously experienced as murderous and led to further withdrawal from relationships and concurrent feelings of loneliness. She would then recover and the cycle would begin again.

During the course of treatment, the dating process, although painful, seemed to assist her to internalize an intrapsychic male-female dyad. Her relationship with her analyst provided the basis for that internalization in a milieu in which aspects of self and object representations could be verbalized and consolidated. The actual experience of being with and interacting with another and the analysis of the fantasy elements attached to it helped to build memory traces upon which to further solidify her feminine identity. The male "date" served as a displaced transference figure as well as a needed internalization.

Ms. C. terminated her treatment a better integrated individual. She carried with her some degree of unhappiness about not being married, along with the fear of remaining single throughout her life. She was considering having a child alone if she could not find a man who matched her considerable capacity for a deep, committed, and loving relationship. She regretted the fact that her 20s were spent in career development rather than finding a mate, and her love of her work was somewhat tempered by this regret.

Treatment issues specific to this patient population

In order to conduct effective psychoanalytic treatment with women who are suffering from their single status, analysts must keep in mind that the goal of treatment is "intrapsychic change," not marriage. Yet, they cannot devalue the patient's goals and must work with this issue in treatment. They must proceed along the fine line in which these patients' external goals and prime motivation for undertaking treatment is respected, without causing it to direct the focus of the treatment away from the analysis of intrapsychic issues.

Resistances and transference resistances

When patients are dating, analytic therapy can be complicated by the changing array of partners who are brought in and discussed as if they were the subject of treatment. Some patients attempt to describe and to understand their dates' dynamics rather than their own. This occurred in the treatment of the three women discussed on p. 136. This can serve as a strong resistance to treatment. The analyst's attempt to analyze the defense by saying, "You bring in your date as patient," for example, can be unconsciously experienced as confirmation of various internal transferential fantasies: mother forbids me to have any fun, father wants me all to himself, sister is jealous of me, and so on. Treatment can be more effective in dealing with this by intervening in a way that demonstrates awareness that the patient is projecting what is *inside her* onto her various dates. By teaching the patient to understand herself from this point of view, the working alliance can be strengthened. That is, the patient who consistently dates men whom she experiences to be intellectually inadequate and is contemptuous of, or the patient who consistently dates men who fear intimacy, or the patient who consistently dates men who are clinging, or who are married, is involved in a selection process reflective of inner difficulties and may be repeating something from the past. One should convey to the patient the view that meeting married men or dating men who are incapable of making commitments is not in and of itself neurotic. The neurotic aspect is the investment of energies in such unlikely candidates for marriage and the repetition of chronic experiences of frustration and disappointment. I have found it useful with some patients to intervene with confrontations such as: (1) You say that you are miserable living alone and wish only to marry; (2) Yet, you spend your time worrying about your relationship with Mr. X., who has told you that he does not plan to marry; (3) How do you understand this inconsistency?; (Or, as a variant of [2]: Yet you do nothing to try to socialize so as to increase your chances of meeting someone).

Another typically encountered strong resistance to treatment is the patient's reluctance to explore anything else but this issue. Some try to control the treatment by saying, "There are no men, so why be analyzed?" This can be handled tactfully by a statement such as, "Maybe if we let the issue of the male shortage go by for a while and if you let yourself associate more freely and get into your fantasies, something more could emerge." Another group of patients do little else but "look inside" and assume a self-blaming and self-deprecatory attitude that accounts for their being single. This can be understood erroneously by their analysts as being due to their doing insightful work. These patients are resisting a more authentic investigation of themselves, functioning via an unconscious fantasy that the punitive analyst (parent) who sees them suffer enough will be appeased and then permit them to find husbands. Single women often entertain and horrify their analysts with "war stories"—tales of the latest outrageous treatment they have suffered, often told with a combination of humor and chagrin. What appears to be catharsis in the presence of an empathic ear can often serve defensive purposes in order to avoid getting to deeper feelings of pain, depression, loneliness, and rage. It is important for the analyst to attempt to touch what is usually a rather large well of inner pain and depression. Tears and rage must be expressed if treatment of this particular group of patients is to be successful.

Transference

Subtle unanalyzed transference manifestations can lead to analytic stalemate when the analytic hour becomes the "date" or the "marriage bed" in the patient's unconscious. In such cases, the analyst is experienced as the lover and the analysis becomes the major libidinal tie. Unverbalized lies the fantasy that perhaps *after* the analysis is over, the patient will find a mate, or perhaps that the analyst, if male, will *become* the mate. In this case, the erotic gratifications of the treatment are substituted for the more frustrating task of finding these gratifications in real life. Sometimes such transferences become apparent, as when the patient tells her male analyst, "No man can ever listen to me as you can." In such a case, the transference fantasy becomes accessible to analysis. The more serious problem lies in those cases in which such fantasies are unconscious and can only be indirectly detected from the patient's lack of progress in her outside life. During the course of the treatment of most single women, a variety of different lovers are chosen as displacement figures for the analyst at different phases of the transference, further complicating the possibility of a clear understanding and interpretation of the transference.

Countertransference

Analysts must avoid making judgments about the suitability, likeability, and/or marriageability of the patient's various partners. A competition can be unconsciously set up in which male analysts see themselves as more desirable than the partners of their patients, or female analysts feel that they personally would not choose such a man, or that they *would* want him and unconsciously compete for him. Analysts can be seduced by patients' war stories and too literally buy the tales of the inadequacy of the patient's potential partners, thus joining the patient in her externalizing defense. In this case, the analyst can fall into a "transference trap" and behave like parents who keep their child for themselves and forbid the child to be sexual.

At one extreme of the analyst's countertransference, a fantasy emerges about the patient as being defective, helpless, and having something missing. The analyst tries to rescue her and becomes unconsciously involved in seeking a man for her. At the other extreme lies the fear that the patient will leave treatment if she marries. In this case, a subtle undermining of her efforts can result.

Another common type of countertransference, which must be monitored for its misuses (but can be somewhat useful if it is conscious and held in check), is the analyst's assumptions and opinions about why this or that particular patient cannot find a man (over and above the male shortage, of course). This can run the gamut from an impression of an aversive character trait or a judgment about the patient's weight, height, or clothing. It is very important, however, for the analyst to be conscious of personal as opposed to more universal tastes and to keep the former out of the treatment.

Frustrated analysts will often ask their patients to give detailed descriptions of what goes on when they meet someone, what they do to screen out men, and so on. Patients may say, for example, that they have rejected someone they met because they did not like his shoes or tie. Analysts may be provoked to imply with their statements, interpretive or confrontational that, the patients change criteria. These criteria have deeper meaning to the patient, however unverbalized, and they must be respected. They will only change as the patient deepens in self-understanding. To suggest, however the suggestion is couched in analytic terms, that the patient see someone she finds unappealing can be narcissistically wounding. Additionally, the interpretation can be taken as a suggestion or a demand and be counterproductive.

The above are some of the ways in which both analyst and patient can enter into a misalliance and avoid dealing with the patient's neurotic and narcissistic difficulties, counterproductive character attitudes, diminished functioning, and inner pain.

Summary and suggestions for treatment

Analysts working with single women patients who are seeking husbands must travel between the Scylla and Charybdis of making it a goal and yet not a goal. Patients must be made aware that analytic goals are related to intrapsychic change and, when intrapsychic change occurs, some change in external reality may be effected. Hopefully, as a result of treatment, they will be better able to love, to reach out to someone, to make an appropriate choice. Yet, analysts cannot guarantee what the world will provide. A message such as the following from Ticho (1972) must be conveyed to patients:

> A clinical distinction between treatment goals and life goals is important for the conduct of therapy, and this can be done despite their partial overlap. *Life goals* are the goals the patient would seek to attain if he could put his potentialities to use. In other words, they are the goals the patient could aim at if his "true self" (Winnicott, 1960) and his creativity were freed. *Treatment goals* concern removal of obstacles to the patient's discovery of what his potentialities are.
>
> (p. 315)

An important issue to raise here is that of whether the analyst should confront the single woman patient with the fact of the male shortage, if the patient seems to be unaware of it. If a patient is not aware of the reality situation and blames herself alone, it seems that some form of reality confrontation is in order. If this is done, the way such information, imparted by the analyst, is experienced by the patient must be explored and its effects on the transference must be analyzed. The analysis of reality and the intrapsychic reasons for not perceiving it are an essential part of any treatment (see, for example, Waelder, [1936] and Wallerstein, [1973]). Kernberg (1976), in assessing a middle-aged woman's analyzability, recommends that:

> a realistic acceptance, on the part of a woman who has never been married or is divorced, of the limited opportunities for remarrying and of the possibility of having to obtain gratification in depth from less conventional relations with men should be explored before the transference implications of these issues overshadow the real life goals.
>
> (p. 232)

The extent to which patients view themselves as at fault or as in control of the issue must be examined. Masochistic women choose to believe the problem is entirely theirs and refuse to give up this perception. Obsessional women wish to believe that it is their fault because then they can control it. If it is outside, they cannot. Keeping what was said in the section on countertransference in mind, it is possible that analysts working with single women at times subtly hint at the notion of compromise in their choice of a mate. That is, since there are so few men to go around, why not settle for someone poorer, less educated, less handsome, less "together" than the patient would have wished for if there were an abundance of men to have? The analyst must be quite aware of the patient's cultural background and of how such possibilities would be experienced by her and by others around her. Is making such a compromise a bow to reality or to neurosis? If the patient were to marry a man less well-integrated than herself, how would this affect her intrapsychically compared with living "single too long"? The analyst certainly cannot make such a decision for the patient, but the issue can be posed.

In the analysis of single females, issues of mourning and of hope must be dealt with. The patients must mourn years gone by that have not been that happily or productively spent, and they must mourn children never to be born. Today's patients who are in their mid-30s may be able to explore the possibility of becoming single mothers—a growing trend in certain subcultures. Values (monogamy vs. man-sharing, for instance) are also important to deal with in treatment. If a woman over 30 can have a stable and loving affair with a married man, is this a neurotic or a realistic solution? Does she tie up her energies in this way and keep herself unavailable to a single man were one to come along? All of this can be explored in terms of its *intrapsychic* meanings to the patient. There are no easy solutions to this very complex issue.

The approach that seems to be most appropriate employs a combination of hope and the awareness that one can lead a rather full life alone. Analysts must identify where inner conflict and/or arrested ego development stands in the way not only of their single patients' marrying, but their living comfortably alone and/or doing what needs to be done in order to find a mate.

In the first instance, living alone involves tolerating solitude, independent thinking and planning, taking the initiative to socialize and to interact with both single and married people. Doing what needs to be done involves putting oneself into social situations, being assertive with men, making oneself attractive to men, being liberal enough to deal with modern sexual mores, being able to deal with brief relationships, abandonment, rejection, decisions to end relationships, and to tolerate the mourning that ensues. It involves being able to rather quickly evaluate people and their characters. It involves taking on so-called masculine attitudes (going out alone, for example), for the woman who goes out only in the safety of her female friends will be less likely to be approached by males. The analysis of the single woman may be a lengthier one than that of her married counterpart because of the kind of life she must lead.

The analyst must continually monitor countertransference to stay in touch with what he or she would approve or disapprove of, do or not be able to do in his or her life, in order to insure that his or her own values do not get in the way. If the analyst is married, some of his or her own unresolved issues with regard to the restrictions of married life may lead to envy of the patient's potential for a full, unmarried life. The analyst might envy the social and sexual freedom of the patient, the freedom to travel where she wishes, to live and work at what she wishes—without having to account to, or compromise with, another. When the analyst can find pleasure in the single life, he or she should then be able to analyze the masochism of the patient who is suffering so very much from being single. The analyst must not be trapped either by the patient's idealization of marriage or by her defensive disparagement of that state.

Both analysts and their patients are influenced by society's attitudes. Freud's goals for a successful analysis—to free the patient to love and to work—can be taken quite concretely as getting married and having a job, rather than as the ability to marry and to hold a job if one so chooses. Many case studies in the analytic literature report that the patients have married at termination. Has ambivalence toward the opposite sex been resolved, or has an unanalyzed unconscious wish to please the analyst, parents, and friends, to save them from feeling that the patient is such a disappointment, prevailed? It is possible that some analysts do not consider their patients to be ready for termination until they have married and that this is in some way conveyed to them.

Analysts, patients, and society tend to view women without men as incomplete. Very often, a woman married to a man who is psychologically or intellectually impaired or troubled in a variety of ways receives more social acceptance than one who would not consider entering into such a marriage.

Single females who enter treatment with marriage as a goal must be asked to explore it in terms of its healthy and its neurotic meanings so that a neurotic solution does not eventuate from an unconscious pact with the analyst.

We as psychoanalysts can no longer say, as has been the custom that, when intrapsychic conflict is worked through, our single female patients will be able to find suitable men to marry. Our patients may, after psychoanalytic treatment, be more capable of having healthy, loving, and committed relationships than before. Finding suitable men to marry may be a considerable or, for some, an impossible challenge. Analysts cannot provide external solutions for patients. They must not express too much hope for their patients or therapeutic gains will be tenuous. The important interplay between reality and intrapsychic fantasy must be carefully analyzed in each case.

Note

1 Chapter 11 has been adapted from J. S. Lieberman (1991) "Issues in the psychoanalytic treatment of single females over thirty," in *Psychoanalytic Review, 78*(2), pp. 177–198. Reprinted by permission of Guilford Publications, Inc.

References

Adams, M. (1971). The single woman in today's society: A reappraisal. *American Journal of Orthopsychiatry, 41*(5): 776–786.

Anthony, E. J., & Benedek, T. (Eds.) (1970). *Parenthood: Its psychology and psychopathology.* Boston: Little, Brown.

Benedek, T. (1970). Psychobiology of pregnancy. In E. J. Anthony & T. Benedek (Eds.), *Parenthood: Its psychology and psychopathology* (pp. 137–151). Boston: Little, Brown.

Bennett, M. G., & Bloom, D. E. (1986, December 13). Why fewer American women marry. *New York Times.*

Bergmann, M. V. (1985). The effect of role reversal on delayed marriage and maternity. *Psychoanalytic Study of the Child, 40,* 197–219.

Blanck, R., & Blanck, G. (1968). *Marriage and personal development.* New York: Columbia University Press.

Freud, S. (1916). Some character-types met with in psycho-analytic work. *Standard Edition, 14,* 309–333.

Kernberg, O. (1976). *Object-relations theory and clinical psychoanalysis.* New York: Aronson.

Kernberg, O. (1977). Boundaries and structure in love relations. *Journal of American Psychoanalytic Association, 25,* 81–144.

Person, E. S. (1988). *Dreams of love and fateful encounters.* New York: Norton.

Pine, F. (1988). The four psychologies of psychoanalysis and their place in clinical work. *Journal of American Psychoanalytic Association, 36,* 571–596.

Stolorow, R., & Lachmann, F. (1980). *Psychoanalysis of developmental arrests.* New York: International Universities.

Ticho, E. (1972). Termination of psychoanalysis: Treatment goals, life goals. *Psychoanalytic Quarterly, 41,* 315–333.

Waelder, R. (1936). The principle of multiple function: Observations on overdetermination. *Psychoanalytic Quarterly, 5,* 45–62.

Wallerstein, R. (1973). Psychoanalytic perspectives on the problem of reality. *Journal of American Psychoanalytic Association, 21,* 8–33.

Weiss, S. (1987). The two-women phenomenon. *Psychoanalytic Quarterly, 56,* 271–286.

Chapter 12

Sex and the City on the couch

I have previously noted (Lieberman, 2000) that characters in film literature and television reflect back to us ourselves in a form greater and more heroic than we are, at times crazier than we are. The popular HBO (Home Box Office, Inc.) television series *Sex and the City* provides us with confirmation of this (Seidelman et al., 1998–2004). The characters and plot exaggerate the experiences of the urban single woman. Prior to my writing *Body Talk: Looking and Being Looked at in Psychotherapy* in 2000, I wrote about the special problems of conducting psychoanalytic work with single women over 30 (Lieberman, 1991, see also Chapter 11 in this book, p. 129). I see *Sex and the City* as a kind of mirror that reflects aspects of my single women patients' lives. I know that there are those who would disagree with me, those who view the story and its characters as shallow and superficial, who see the four protagonists' (Carrie, Samantha, Miranda, and Charlotte) sexual behavior as "over the top" and not to be identified with, and are turned off by the focus on beauty, designer clothes, and 500 dollar Manolo Blahnik shoes, but I disagree with them. I personally enjoy the show and relate to it. I find it to be libidinal and uplifting. I see it as a contemporary commentary on mores around finding love and mating, themes of the writings of Jane Austen and Edith Wharton. As a young woman, I read Henry James' (1881) *Portrait of a Lady* over and over and identified with the trials and tribulations of his heroine Isabel Archer. Candace Bushnell's (1996) book, upon which the series is based, may join these others.

I currently see, in once- or twice-weekly psychoanalytic psychotherapy a number of women, young and not so young, but young at heart, who have come into treatment in order to work on their relationships with men. I have found that when each new series of *Sex and the City* plays, their associations were filled with references to the show. Each week they were able to glean something from the show that related to their issues. When the show was mentioned I indicated that I saw it, which facilitated the discussion. (I take a more opaque stance with patients in analysis). In 1991 (and in Chapter 11, p. 129), I outlined the issues presented by single women (regardless of diagnosis) and characterized a syndrome that I called "single too long":

... depression, low self-esteem, poor body image, proneness to shame and humiliation, lonesomeness, alienation, envy, psychosomatic complaints and polar extremes of behavior, such as frantic man-hunting vs. social withdrawal, promiscuity vs. frigidity, workaholism vs. work inhibition...

(Lieberman, 1991, p. 178)

The expression "too little too late," rejecting men who were not initially interested in them, characterizes their maladaptive character attitudes, formed early in life, and reinforced by the single condition.

In psychotherapy, patients are encouraged to speak about shameful experiences, often forgotten, in a neutral, non-punitive, non-judgmental setting. They work to master them and to put into action new strategies of behavior and social interaction that preclude the reoccurrence of such shameful experiences. In *Sex and the City*, the protagonists experience what my patients have been trying to suppress or forget. By identifying with these attractive, strong women, their own remembering is facilitated. I believe that the show gains focus as a way for my patients to bond with me. It is something we share. I believe that this "parameter" is extremely useful and will demonstrate that in terms of what came into treatment during a few weeks in the summer of 2003, when I made these notes based on the sixth and final series of *Sex and the City* (King et al., 2003–2004).

1 Body issues

Identifications with the beautiful

Patients see that even the most beautiful of women can be "stood up," rejected, abandoned, and treated poorly. These episodes help reduce the commonly-held fantasies that beautiful women are not treated the way they are and do not suffer, that their own less than perfect looks are to blame. This show gives patients the opportunity to voice resentment about how beauty and perfection are so prized in our culture and that they are "losers." It provides a catalyst to retrieve painful memories around body issues (and those who can improve their appearance begin to do so as a result of talking about these issues). When Carrie met Big she confessed that she was in love with him and terrified that he could leave her because she was not "perfect." "Perfect" in our culture has to do with body, not morality.

2 Sexual inhibitions

For those patients who are conflicted about having sex (there are still some around!), observing the sexual freedom and exhilarating exploits of the women in the show enable them to work with me as I challenge their rigidly held beliefs (that men will not respect them, that they would be regarded as "sluts") and to explore the genesis of such ideas. I do not think that the sexual behavior in the show is meant to be a mirror of reality, but rather to give women entitlement to think about sex, to desire it, to have it recreationally as well as romantically and in the context of a loving committed relationship. So-called old-fashioned morality can be a cover for masochism and self-bashing. This can be seen in "The Catch" (Season 6, Episode 8), in which Carrie has a "fling" with the best man from Charlotte's wedding and then each blames the other for feeling "used" (Taylor, 2003). Many single women fear having sex because they will feel "used" if the man does not return.

3 Break-ups and abandonments

The episodes in which Berger breaks up with Carrie were catalysts for numerous memories of painful break-ups. First, after acting annoyed at her behavior he let her off at her house in a taxi and asked to take a break. She was flabbergasted and that he did not want to talk about it. Then she tried to go after him, rented a car to go see him in the Hamptons and then thought better of it. She knew she loved him. A week later, in "Hop, Skip and a Week" (Season 6, Episode 6), he showed up with pink carnations (her favorite) and slept with her (Engler, 2003). She woke up to an empty pillow beside her and a note on a Post-it® that said he was sorry and hoped she would not hate him. She threw the vase of flowers on the floor in anger. Water dripped like blood. For a number of my patients this act of anger felt liberating, since they would have blamed themselves in such a situation (too fat, bedroom messy, etc.).

One patient remembered a painful breakup: her boyfriend of 5 years lost his grandfather and she was not asked to the funeral in the small town in which they lived. He brought instead another girl who he had been dating while she thought they were about to become engaged. This humiliation was an unconscious reliving of her parents' breakup when she was 5. Her father had been seeing someone else, and her mother's rage was such that she stopped her from seeing him for years.

Another patient who saw these episodes recalled with tremendous guilt rejecting a man who loved her, a much older man (a colleague of her father's), who fell in love with her when she was 15 and eventually asked her father for her hand. She harbored the fantasy that she had ruined his life and her guilt was such that she hardly dated anyone during her youthful years. Although she had had a lengthy treatment with me, she was only able to tell me about this after witnessing Carrie's suffering.

4 Examining what they do in relationships

These episodes are useful as mirrors of what to do and what not to do in relationships, to examine what one can do to connect or to disconnect. In "Hop, Skip and a Week" (Season 6, Episode 6), it is obvious that Carrie and Berger are competing in their professions as writers and that Carrie is the more successful one

(Engler, 2003). He became upset at her challenging his announcement that he was going to a computer store at 9 a.m. one morning. They had a fight and then kissed and made up. But his anger was building and when he escorted her to an opening he said he did not want to come in with her, quite visibly envious of her celebrity. She smiled and went to the show and had a good time. Each patient wondered what she would have done. One said: "It would have been curtains for him." Each realized that she would have seen his egregious behavior only from her own disappointed self-perspective and would have no empathy with him.

5 Envy and its vicissitudes

A number of women enter treatment at the point at which a sibling becomes engaged (especially a younger sibling) or a best friend becomes engaged. The envy becomes difficult to master, good wishes become choked with painful affect and they see themselves as "always a bridesmaid, never a bride," the odd man out, Cinderella (all derivatives usually of oedipal level issues) but also fueled by family expectations that they will have a reaction. Mothers and grandmothers sometimes get into the act and stimulate envy rather than help to reduce it. These patients are ashamed of their feelings of envy and aggression and their wishes to do harm to the relationship. In therapy, they are helped to realize that many have similar feelings and they should talk about their aggressive wishes and fantasies rather than act them out.

In "The Catch" (Season 6, Episode 8), good friends acted out in response to Charlotte's wedding (Taylor, 2003). Samantha wore a pearl bracelet that she could not unlatch herself (living alone) and fiddled with it during the ceremony making it fall apart, interrupting the service. Carrie had too energetic sex with the best man (mentioned before) and arrived with a bent over back (deflecting attention away from the bride?).

Some patients suffer so much from envy that they cannot socialize out of fear that they will see women who are more attractive than they are. If they do go to a party, they "fall apart" and cannot talk. They are envious of ex-boyfriends' new girlfriends. In "The Catch" (Season 6, Episode 8), Miranda's ex, the father of her baby Brady, wanted her to meet Debbie, his new girlfriend (Taylor, 2003). He showed up at her apartment and she hid under the bed (couldn't look at her).

As friends begin to have children they have less and less time for and less and less in common with their single friends. There is envy of the single freedom and envy of the baby. In "A Woman's Right to Shoes" (Season 6, Episode 9), Carrie complains about spending US$2,300 on her friend Kyra's events, including the most recent baby shower (Van Patten, 2003). She remarks that Hallmark does not have cards for not having a baby, and for not finding the right guy. I have observed single women patients unable to visit the hospital or to give the new baby a gift. Carrie called Kyra and left a message that she was getting married to herself and registering for shoes at Manolo Blahnik's. Quite unlike what would really happen, she received a pair of the expensive shoes, her very first wedding present!

6 Trying to control the uncontrollable

The women in *Sex and the City* resort to superstitious thinking and use catchy phrases to try to master what is incomprehensible and uncontrollable: the odd behavior of many of the men they meet. They are trying to understand why they cannot make a good connection. Charlotte and Carrie are continually looking for a good sign of luck in love and have powerful fantasies that they are not meant to meet anyone. When Charlotte and David see one another after their breakup at a synagogue mixer and kiss, the women who witness them aver that they'll come back to the same spot the next week! My patients avidly read the wedding announcements in the *New York Times* to find out how and where people who manage to marry have met and go there with their hopes.

They soothe themselves that everything happens for a reason. The show is notable for its catchy phrases and labels: "toxic bachelors" are commitment-phobic men; and "modelizers" are men who only date models. Samantha calls it "expiration dating" when someone is in town a short time and then drops out. She is the most manic and cynical of them all, being the oldest and the one who has probably been hurt the most. She takes a superior, combative position never stopping in one place long enough to get hurt.

The scarcity of men for such women, as Person (1988) has noted: "contributes to the transformation of a perfectly healthy longing for love into a kind of deadly preoccupation" (p. 284).

Role models for the single woman

The characters are strong women, successful in their careers. Carrie is a fashion writer who gets a lot of designer clothes gratis and many perks. Samantha is a caricature of a public relations person, but is clearly good at what she does. Charlotte is an art dealer/designer. Miranda is a successful lawyer and single mother. At the point at which her baby was crying for his nanny rather than herself, she negotiated working fewer hours. When criticized by her colleagues she held her own—reminding them of her previous record of hard work. She did not accept blame, as so many women do.

These women are not settling for the wrong man. They are waiting for "Mr. Right." They are "choosers," not "losers." They enjoy what a wealthy man can provide but do not sell out or "trade up," the title of Bushnell's most recent novel. In "The Catch" (Season 6, Episode 8), Carrie declares that she would love to find a man strong enough to catch her (Taylor, 2003).

They are thoughtful and self-reflective, and at times act out not in their own best interest.

I see them as fearless in their dress, unafraid to look sexually attractive while maintaining their professional status. They seem to maintain their figures while frequenting restaurants and bars and I wonder if they ever actually eat or drink! The characters are in their late 30s to mid-40s and they are looking older than those around them. The series ended because of that, as if women older than that cannot be sexual in the city.

Friends as support

The women in the show serve as good friends to party with and to console one another. Many single women are, on the other hand, very alone and/or have poor relationships with one or several single women. This adds to the shame and perception of being a "loser." It is helpful for them to watch how these characters relate to one another (Carrie cut a romantic evening short to help Miranda give birth), and do not try to steal each other's men.

Women's groups can also be a defense from the pressure of finding a man and provide an easy retreat that is safe but counterproductive. They are helpful when the group members help each other to go out and to separate when men are present.

The women in the show have men as friends. Carrie's gay friend escorts her to parties when she is not in a relationship.

I do take issue with their "kiss and tell" reporting of every sexual exploit to the group. This seems to be the norm today. It is a defense against the possibility of the development of intimacy.

Do they search for men online? My patients are encouraged by me to use Match.com, eHarmony, Jdate, and others. A whole new type of heartbreak has emerged in this computer age as participants are able to observe the person they dated go home and start immediately a new search for someone else.

Where are their parents?

The women in the show rely on their friends and mentors. Have they separated from their parents? They do not consult with their mothers several time/day to discuss every detail of their dates as some of my patients report doing at the beginning of treatment. They are not hearing voices as are my patients, e.g., "So, what's new?"; "Go out with him one more time, maybe you'll grow to like him"; and most problematic: "Did you lose any weight?"

They do not seem fixated on their fathers either. They do not seem to be of the "My Heart Belongs to Daddy" variety.

What are single women up against?

What is reality and what is fantasy?

There seems to be a real shortage of desirable men who can make a commitment and a social norm of men who, as they grow older, wealthier, and more successful, choosing younger women with "great bodies," the bodies being of more importance than character, wit, intelligence, accomplishment, creativity, or nurturance. The therapist's task is to acknowledge that reality and to help the patient to find those men who are able to seek more authentic lives for themselves.

Person (1988) noted:

> Single women are still considered freaky—"losers" rather than "choosers" of their solitary state. And there are concrete liabilities in being a woman alone—among them the social devaluation that still makes any single woman less sought after by the average hostess or host, the threat of male violence that renders a woman's physical safety precarious when she is alone in certain situations, and the economic privations she suffers since she is still far from being a man's equal in earning power.
>
> (p. 283)

I do not believe that this has changed very much. A powerful male character in Bushnell's (2003) satire *Trading Up* says: "The truth is that—*biologically*—men choose women based on their looks ... And that's the one thing feminism will never be able to change" (p. 50). However, the popularity of *Sex and the City* may be a sign that a new kind of woman is on the scene.

References

Bushnell, C. (1996). *Sex and the city.* New York: Atlantic Monthly Press.

Bushnell, C. (2003). *Trading up.* New York: Hyperion.

Engler, M. (Director) (2003, July 27). Hop, skip, and a week [Television series, season 6, episode 6]. In *Sex and the city.* New York City: HBO.

James, H. (1881). *Portrait of a lady.* London: Wordsworth Classics.

King, M. P., Frankel, D., Engler, M., Taylor, A., Van Patten, T., Stanzler, W., & Farino, J. (Directors) (2003–2004, June 22–February 22). *Sex and the city* [Television series, season 6]. New York City: HBO.

Lieberman, J. S. (1991). Issues in the psychoanalytic treatment of single females over thirty. *Psychoanalytic Review, 78*(2), 177–198.

Lieberman, J. S. (2000). *Body talk: Looking and being looked at in psychotherapy* Northvale, N.J. Jason Aronson, Inc.

Person, E. (1988). *Dreams of love and fateful encounters.* New York: Norton.

Seidelman, S. (Director) et al. (1998–2004). *Sex and the city.* [Television series, seasons 1–6] New York City: HBO.

Taylor, A. (Director) (2003, August 10). The catch [Television series, season 6, episode 8]. In *Sex and the city.* New York City: HBO.

Van Patten, T. (Director) (2003, August 17). A woman's right to shoes [Television series, season 6, episode 9]. In *Sex and the city.* New York City: HBO.

Chapter 13

The search for love in a digital age

The prevalent use of digital communication (e-mail, Skype, dating websites, Facebook, Twitter, and Instagram) and the wealth of information about any individual to be found on the Internet, has greatly impacted not just the content of what is said between patient and analyst but has transformed their relationship in myriad ways. In certain instances, the devices used to communicate with others (cell phones, iPads, etc.) are brought into the consulting room and can serve to enhance and facilitate the treatment or to pervert it. The analyst's "anonymity" is challenged and the question of its importance in this day and age will be discussed.

In addition, the wealth of information to be found on the Internet has greatly impacted the content of what is said between patient and analyst and has in many ways transformed their relationship.

In Spike Jonze's film *Her* (2013), placed in the "near future," the main character Theodore Twombly, played by Joaquin Phoenix, falls madly in love with his phone's artificially intelligent operating system (IOS) "Samantha." She is a male fantasy object with a beautiful voice (that of Scarlett Johansson), unencumbered by the female form. After breaking the heart of a real live woman, Twombly has phone sex with Samantha. Is this a foreboding of the future for men and women seeking relationships?

In 1991, when I published *Issues in the Psychoanalytic Treatment of Single Females over Thirty* (see also Chapter 11, p. 129), we did not have frequent usage of the Internet, dating websites, e.g., Match.com, Grindr, Tumblr, Tinder, Blendr, and OkCupid, as well as instant messaging, texting, Twitter, Instagram, and, notably, Facebook. Recently a patient of mine reported feeling frustrated with a man with whom she was interacting on Match.com. She reported that all they did was text back and forth and she could not "get a handle" on him. I wondered why she did not call him to speak to him. She was aghast: "That's so *retro*!" In an age in which most everything is ordered up online, in which pen and paper are outmoded, voices are losing value as photographs are gaining value. Or the opposite. Texting, sexting are preferred ways of courting and seem preferable to face-to-face, body-to-body, visual and touch contact. In the aforementioned film *Her*, Twombly falls in love with the voice driven IOS (Ellison,

Landay, & Jonze, 2013). She is omnipresent, omni-available in ways a real woman could never be. The women on porn websites look and behave in ways real women do not.

Twenty-five years ago it took a lot of convincing on the part of psychotherapists to induce single women and men to place personal ads in *New York Magazine, New York Review of Books*, etc. They felt like "losers" who would only attract "losers." Many were loath to go to bars or even parties or benefits to meet other singles. Today "everyone does it," but online. For some, going out to bars with friends at night is part of their way of life. Trying to meet someone is experienced as less shameful than it used to be and many are willing to risk the possibility that the person they meet will be just a one-night "hookup" (formerly called a "one-night stand") rather than one seeking a permanent relationship. (There are "hookup" apps, e.g., Tumblr.) A large amount of alcohol is consumed as well as drugs (marijuana, cocaine, ecstasy, even heroin). Date-rape looms as a fearsome possibility. On a more positive note, there seem to be many more options and fewer barriers for single women to go out at night if they choose to do so and not sit home alone (by the telephone) waiting for a man to call as they used to do. They can be out and get texts or calls on their cell phones.

Today I observe that having sex early in a relationship is still conflictual for some of the women patients I see. Today they are still worried about being "used" or thought of as "sluts." They are afraid of being abandoned and betrayed by the men they have slept with. Some are afraid of contracting STDs. Having sex is still a part of a barter agreement that can be broken: "If I have sex with you, does that mean that you will call me in the morning and ask to see me tomorrow night?"

In 1991, patients brought into treatment love letters or breakup letters that were handwritten. This then moved to printouts of e-mails. Today I am read or even shown text messages on cell phones. Whereas 50 years ago, young women lived at home and their parents screened and vetted their dates, 30 years ago they lived on their own and may have discussed what their dates were like with parents and friends. Today they bring in photos and profiles, the latter possibly written by some professional. (In the film *Her*, Twombly works as a writer of love letters for an online company! [Ellison, Landay, & Jonze, 2013]) The photos on the online dating websites often give clues to potential problems not mentioned in the profiles. For example, men who post photos of themselves with their ex-wives or their mothers seem like poor prospects! I am sometimes asked to look at my patients' online profiles to see if they are posting misleading images of themselves. Usually this is very useful for the analytic work.

In 1991, dates were usually made by telephone. Women were insulted if asked out for Saturday night later than the previous Tuesday and felt that they were being "taken for granted," viewed as "easy," and "not respected." Today dates (or "hookups") are made with little advance notice and canceled easily by text message. Those who make these dates seem more ready to cancel and those asked out seem defensively ready for cancelations. I recently heard of a long-term engagement broken by a man with a text message that simply said, "Sorry."

In 1991, most of my single women patients over 30 had their own apartments and had supported themselves since they were in their early 20s. Today I hear from my patients that their families are enmeshed, that former values of autonomy and separation-individuation have been replaced by closer ties between parents and young adults. Many young women regard their mothers to be their "best friends" and are in conversation with them many times/day. (Some are also in touch with their fathers, but to a lesser degree). There are few secrets between mother and daughter. The first kiss, the first intercourse are shared. Mothers "vet" every date and since privacy is not valued mother's friends and relatives and daughter's friends know every detail. The posting of minute details of one's life as well as informative photos on Facebook and Instagram make lives into open books. Some mothers who do not have daughters who confide in them sometimes track them, and even stalk them, on Facebook. One can expect that private lives that once were the domain of the consulting room, have been aired and exposed to mothers and friends, and edited and revamped before they reach the analyst. "Give him a chance," "you are too picky" and other such "advice" results in confusion and self-doubts as well as resistance to what emerges in the treatment.

I would like to transition from this to consider the effects of this technology on my relationships with my patients. The new technology has had considerable effects on my clinical practice. In cases in which cell phones are left in bags or coats outside my office, my patients and I often hear them ringing. Neither of us can help wondering about who is invading the analytic space, why and why now. My building's lobby, my waiting area and bathroom, have become communication centers for cell phone calls, text messages, BlackBerrys, and iPhones. One patient, addicted to her e-mail, brought in her laptop, ostensibly to read her dreams to me, but I observed her sneaking a peek at her e-mail while accessing that file. All of this has involved a certain amount of management on my part. I risk being experienced as a forbidding parent, depriving an out-of-work patient the chance to receive a call from a potential employer, or an abandoned wife to receive the long-awaited call of her departed husband. At times my latent paranoia is awakened when I wonder if the cell phone casually sitting on the little table near my patient is a camera or a recording device.

In addition, my anonymity as an analyst is being challenged in unknown ways. I do not know which of my patients have "googled" me, accessed my writings or the cost of my house. When my son was married several years ago, the *New York Times* announcement was then made accessible for time immemorial on the Internet. Any patient with my name inserted into "Google Alert" would have instantly learned of this happy occasion and all my family members' names, and my son's education and the name of his business. An obsessive patient, fixated on issues of money, has let me know that he tracks from his computer at work the time of my depositing of his monthly check to me and deduces from the speed of my deposit how rich or poor I am that month!

After such invasions in my office, when I go out to take a break my very being is ignored as I walk down the street with those who make no eye contact because they are busy on their cell phones and I am bumped into by those reading their BlackBerrys or what I call "crackberrys." I would like to put the term "crackberry" into the DSM! Train and bus rides have become "busman's holidays" as I overhear all kinds of public conversations better kept private.

In my practice, I have learned about the workings of Match.com, Jdate, and eHarmony, and I have had to master new terms. Last month, two new patients came into treatment after discovering in one case of e-mail break-in, committed by her that her fiancé was having an affair, another that her boyfriend was looking at pornographic websites several times daily. (I wondered of course if that kept him safe at home and out of contact with prostitutes.) What makes a trusted lover break into her fiancé's computer and why is this stuff left around the way letters from significant others' lovers used to be left around? I thought of an older less technologically sophisticated patient who investigated her male lovers' infidelities by reading their handwritten diaries while they were in the shower. Is this old wine in new bottles or something else? What does it mean in terms of underlying dynamics?

All day long I hear about frustration and near nervous breakdown due to computers that crash and e-mails that are down. I am at a loss to analyze this, since I feel the same way when my e-mail becomes unavailable. And I wonder if the frustration my patients express with inadequate tech support from India is really displaced transference; that they are indirectly telling me they experience me as inadequate.

I am, for Discussion's sake, going to take a more positive view of all of this change. I am going to take the position and argue it that there is much psychological good to be had with all of this. Since we will keep the railroad that Freud regretted (see Chapter 14, p. 158), and children will most likely, as his did, move from their parents' towns, I think not just of telephones and e-mails, but of Skype, the Internet phone service with a video-camera that brings families together and, which is used for psychoanalysis between American analysts and Chinese patients. Camera-phone technology transmits photos of babies just born to grandparents across the sea. One young bride-to-be I know was able to include her mother in South Africa in on her wedding dress shopping trip by sending her photos of herself in the gowns and getting her mother's opinion by phone and e-mail. For better or for worse, with the new technology, parents and children who do not wish to separate do not need to do so. On the negative side of this issue, are daughters in treatment who are on their phones all daylong with their mothers and must learn to cut the psychological umbilical cord provided by the low rate calling programs for cell phones.

I work with many single women and men looking for relationships. It is true that it is sad when a woman has met a man on Jdate, feels he is right for her, then returns home from a date with him, logs on and sees that he has at that very moment returned home and has begun searching for another woman. In my day, such a woman might rather masochistically sit home by the phone for days hoping the man would call. Here rejection is instant. Is this better or worse? Internet dating seems so disembodied. Yet most send photos of themselves and those with less than perfect faces and bodies, who would not have had a chance of meeting someone in the "meat market" dating bars of past years, might actually begin a relationship based on verbal communication. I did, however, just hear of a case of a man who posted his better-looking friend's photo instead of his own! We are nostalgic for the rules of courtship in the "good old days," especially the kinds of courtship described by Henry James and Edith Wharton. But they too describe all kinds of sadomasochistic and caddish behavior.

References

Ellison, M., Landay, V. (Producers), & Jonze, S. (Director) (2013). *Her*. [Motion Picture]. LA, California: Annapurna Pictures.

Lieberman, J. S. (1991). Issues in the psychoanalytic treatment of single females over thirty. *Psychoanalytic Review, 78*(2), 177–198.

Lieberman, J. S. (2000). *Body talk: Looking and being looked at in psychotherapy*. Northvale, N.J.: Jason Aronson, Inc.

Chapter 14

The mediated gaze

An exaggerated picture of what is to come

Consider the contemporary hospital delivery room: Mother, Father, possibly both sets of Grandparents poised to photograph the birth of their baby. They have seen this baby in utero numerous times in sonograms. Some have these machines at home for more viewing opportunities. Baby is born, put on Mother's chest for his first intimate moments outside the womb. All, including Mother, are texting the photograph or video of this moment to relatives and friends, sometimes around the world. (Mother has had her hair and nails done for this photo op.) What was once a private, poignant moment of bonding has now become public. There is minimal verbal interaction and the newborn does not hear sound directed at him. Mother's gaze is what I call "a mediated gaze." She views her baby through the camera lens of her phone.

For years to come, this child will be photographed and videoed and the photos and videos sent out. His first images of Mother are of someone with a phone in her hand, and her gaze may be more fixed on the phone than on him. She will talk and text while nursing him, while wheeling him outside in his stroller. When Mother goes back to work, for sure his caretaker will be looking at her phone or talking on it. When he naps in his crib, his baby monitor will show his image, his every move and sound, to those watching in another room or transmitted to his parents' computer at work. (His caretakers will be similarly observed.) Their presence is really an absence since their attention is elsewhere. His crib, strollers, toys, clothes, diapers, supplies, and eventually, his food, will be purchased by someone looking at a screen.

In a brief period of time, the phone and its apps for babies will become an object of desire and at times the only thing that will stop his tears. He will learn soon enough how to turn it on or off and to press the apps that will access the videos, games, and music he likes. He will hear more of those sounds than the sounds of his mother's voice, if his mother is working full-time.

In order to convince him to stay in his high chair and eat, he will be given an iPad that plays cartoons to watch or puzzles to play that reward his correct choices with a funny sound. At about 2 years of age, when he begins toilet training, the iPad will keep him at the task, encouraging him to stay on the potty. Again, Mother's voice (or caretaker's voice) instructing him, rewarding him, will be in the background.

I have not yet seen drawings done by children of themselves and their families, but I predict that small rectangular objects will be hanging from the adults' hands. The influence of devices on development will increase more and more as the child grows.

At age 9 or 10, many children are given their own phones so that they can text their Mothers that they have arrived safely at school, etc. Many have their own computers to do work for school. Despite parental controls on access to the Internet, many children gain access to porn sites, send photos of themselves in scant dress or undress to friends who may distribute them and, which remain on the Internet forever. Bullying is rampant on the Internet, a topic much too broad for this chapter to consider. A very lopsided notion of others' lives often develops for those who use Facebook as their primary source of information about others. I have coined the term "Facebook envy." It seems from Facebook that everyone else is happy doing great things and having "thousands of friends" in comparison with oneself. Privacy is lacking and cyber-stalking is rampant as viewers search for someone, if not on their own wall, on the wall of someone they know. The trend to take "selfies" and post them online mirrors the desperate need for the gaze, even when it is digitally mediated.

As these children reach young adulthood they will use digitally mediated dating sites in their search for love and for instant sexual encounters, etc. The film *Her* (cited in Chapter 13) in which the lonely main character falls in love with a disembodied voice on his phone, speaks to the deepest need for a soothing voice, its intimacy (Ellison, Landay, & Jonze, 2013). This is the voice that is so lacking even from the first day of life.

After mates are found using these devices, they play a prominent role in modern marriage. Husbands and wives today go to bed with laptops, iPads, and phones or, when they happen to be in separate rooms, text one another. When television was first invented, families sat together and watched one screen, when radio was the only window on the outside world, families listened together. Prior to that, they read together by electric light or candlelight. Today, each member is on a separate device and there is no mutual topic of communication (unless it is an instruction to watch a certain episode of a series on Netflix!).

Certain families today do not sit at the kitchen table to talk out their disputes with one another. They sit facing one another and text what they are thinking. Other families, distressed by all of this, insist that phones cannot be brought to the table. Recently, I heard about weddings and even funerals where phones have been collected at the door to ensure some respect for the bride and groom, and for the dead one being memorialized.

It is paradoxical that this lack of intimacy and the widespread addiction to digital devices so canalized in our culture today can facilitate an illusion of intimacy for the lonely schizoid individual. Ms. J., possessing a prickly personality, who kills off every friendship she starts, keeps in touch with people via Facebook. By so doing, she becomes chronically envious of what she imagines are their incredible lives, but she also learns some things about what they are doing when they meet up with friends and relatives, where they travel, etc. She would not have this information because she is too envious to directly ask them herself. Mr. H., a very busy lawyer who travels much of the time for his work, also feels intimately connected with the many friends he has on Facebook even though this pseudo-intimacy ultimately does not satisfy. Intimacy involves touch, sound, smell, and sight, that is, all the senses. Not to be had with a keypad.

Just consider medical treatment today (aside from all the health apps available and Internet information available that enable some to bypass actual living doctors). Doctors' appointments are often made and confirmed online. There is often little or no touch or sight used in making diagnoses. iPads photograph you and provide the doctors with names of medications to treat symptoms and groups of symptoms. Surgeons increasingly do not use their hands to touch bodies, just to manipulate digital devices that perform the surgery.

What then are the implications for psychoanalytic treatment? The International Psychoanalytical Association website promoting the topic of Intimacy for the 2017 Congress stated:

> For psychoanalysts, intimacy is the currency of every session. It informs relationships with our patients, our theories and our own work. Intimacy transcends the individual/dyadic, animating the construction of the social, familial and cultural demands of everyday life.
>
> (IPA, 2017)

Will the psychoanalytic session become an alien space for those growing up today? Will there be enough common ground between patient and analyst to work with? Today's psychoanalyst must be aware of the ongoing deprivation from the days they were born of his younger patients, of the unmediated gaze, of the uninterrupted touch, and of the smell and sight of a constant object. The food, clothing, and toys they were given were ordered online, not selected with touch, smell, or sight. Their cribs, strollers too were ordered online. So much convenience, but with a price to pay. As Turkle (2011) has put it: "We are shaped by our tools."

In my private practice today, I have observed deep yearnings for a perfectly attuned partner on the part of those whose partners are emotionally elsewhere. One patient has retreated to "Second Life" in which he can create an avatar of himself and engage in a world of fantasy in which he can search for the closeness he does not have with his girlfriend. Willock and colleagues (2012) have amply illustrated this in an anthology of loneliness and longing.

We can only imagine what Freud would have thought about all this technology! In his 1930 monograph *Civilization and Its Discontents*, he expressed his ambivalence about the advances of his own age:

On the one hand: "If I can as often as I please hear the voice of a child of mine who is living hundreds of miles away or if I can learn in the shortest possible time after a friend has reached his destination that he has come through the long and difficult voyage unharmed." He was speaking to the positive aspects of this change ... But then he complained: "If there had been no railway to conquer distances, my child would never have left his native town and I should need no telephone to hear his voice; if traveling by ship had not been introduced, my friend would not have embarked on his sea-voyage and I should not need a cable to relieve my anxiety about him."

(p. 39)

I am not suggesting that we go back, even if we could, to a time before these devices took over our lives. Just that we identify the important role these devices have had in contributing to the sense of alienation and loneliness in many of the patients we see today.

References

Ellison, M., Landay, V. (Producers), & Jonze, S. (Director) (2013). *Her*. [Motion Picture]. LA, California: Annapurna Pictures.

Freud, S. (1930). Civilization and its discontents. *S.E.* XXI.

IPA (International Psychoanalytic Association) (2017). *Intimacy*. Retrieved June 4 2018, from www.ipa.world/IPA/BuenosAires/General_Information.

Turkle, S. (2011). *Alone together: Why we expect more from technology and less from each other*. New York: Basic Books.

Willock, B., Bohm, L. C., & Curtis, R. C. (Eds.) (2012). *Loneliness and longing*. New York: Routledge.

Part IV

Superego, gender, and body in art

Chapter 15

Violence against women in the work of women artists[1]

There are many *words* that describe the horrific treatment of women in various parts of the world. I am in this chapter going to describe and at times illustrate *visual* images in order to deepen your understanding of this difficult topic.[2] As they say: "One picture is worth a thousand words."

Most of these images are difficult to think about and to look at. The art of the 1970s and 1990s especially is very concrete and "in your face." This art does not hide behind beauty to tell its story. As I have noted elsewhere: "contemporary artists feel free to express visually ideas that were once forbidden, and to show what never before could be seen, at least in public" (Lieberman, 2000, p. 223). These artists concern themselves with issues of human conflict and human paradox. Each artwork and artist I will discuss is well-known and well-established in art history, past and present.

I intend to focus on contemporary art, but first I want to go back as far as 17th century Italy to a painting done by the great woman artist, Artemisia Gentileschi, the daughter of artist Orazio Gentileschi. This was painted when she was just 17 years old. The Old Testament tale she depicts, that of *Susanna and the Elders* (1610), is an ancient one about sexual coercion. Susanna was threatened with execution for an infidelity she did not commit unless she consented to the Elders' sexual demands. Susanna refused and was brought to trial. In the cross-examination that followed, the Elders were shown to have lied and were stoned to death. Susanna is a self-portrait of Artemisia. We see her cringing with unbearable pain under the leering looks of the two older men. They are fully dressed, giving them power, their stare gives them power and their positioning above her gives them power. She, on the other hand, is naked except for a small flimsy cloth. Her feet are red—they have been literally and figuratively placed in "hot water" and are "blushing" instead of her cheeks. Her cringe is clearly that of an adolescent girl, and seems very much like the cringe of girls we know today subject to the prurient gaze of older men. It is uncanny that Artemisia herself was raped a year after painting this picture by her father's friend Tassi, who she tried to stab in self-defense. Here too, as in the Old Testament tale, there was a trial.

Artemisia grew up in a rather lawless home characterized by overstimulation and visual traumata. Supposedly she witnessed her parents in intercourse and the bloody birth of her brother, resulting in her mother's death when she was 12. She had posed nude for her father and had seen many nude male models. At the trial, Tassi tried to present proof that she was not a virgin when he trapped her by deducing from her drawings of male men that she had "seen" male genitalia.

In that same 17th century, a number of artists depicted rape in mythological images so familiar to us that we tend to admire the art and artist and tend to ignore the violent subject matter of rape. How many of us have admired Berni-ni's *Rape of Persephone* (1622) in the Villa Borghese in Rome, its baroque grace and pure white marble evoking beauty, rather than feeling horror or indignation at her tears. Persephone was the vegetation goddess and was the daughter of Zeus. She was abducted by Pluto, the god-king of the Underworld. Similarly in the case of Poussin's (1634) *The Abduction of the Sabine Women* and Rubens' (1618) *Rape of the Daughters of Leucippus*, mass rape was considered to be part of war, all fair, and not to be thought about or challenged, very much as is the case today in too many parts of the world. We admire these paintings for their grace and beauty, ignoring the violent subject matter.

I now skip a few centuries to the 20th century, in which women artists began to have a voice about violence in their own lives as well as in others. Frida Kahlo's (1935) painting *A Few Nips: Passionately in Love,* was done after Frida read of a woman stabbed to death by her boyfriend, who alleged that he dealt her "only a few small nips" with his knife. This woman could be a stand-in for the artist herself. Frida's small body was savaged by a bus accident, her life one of physical pain. According to Knafo (2009), "Frida said two things destroyed her: the accident and Diego (Rivera, her artist husband)." Frida twice married Diego, who was double her age and three times her size, and she was deeply distressed by his numerous infidelities. (For example, he had an affair with her sister.) Just as she struggled with the many assaults to the integrity of her damaged body, so too she refused to give up on the tempestuous relationship with Diego, which was the source of so much heartache and pain" (p. 73).

In this painting, she seems to be unconsciously depicting, not just the incident of which she had read, but also the sadomasochistic bond she had with Diego by showing them both bloodied. He is clothed, wearing a hat, standing over her, clearly the powerful one. The banner says, "Unos Cuantos Pique Titos" (a few small nips), the doves ironic symbols of peace.

The rise of the feminist movement in the 1970s resulted in much politicized art. A number of 20th century women artists chose to depict violence against women in ways they said were not necessarily autobiographical. Marina Abramović, for example, in her various performances asked her audiences to abuse her, sometimes with knives, or with scissors.

To test the limits of the relationship between performer and audience, Abramović developed one of her most challenging (and best-known) perform-ances in *Rhythm 0* (1974). She assigned a passive role to herself, with the public being the force, which would act on her. Abramović placed on a table 72 objects that people were allowed to use (a sign informed them) in any way that they chose. Some of these were objects that could give pleasure, while others could be wielded to inflict pain, or to harm her. Among them were a rose, a feather, honey, a whip, olive oil, scissors, a scalpel, a gun, and a single bullet. For 6 hours the artist allowed the audience members to manipulate her body and actions. This tested how vulnerable and aggressive the human subject could be when hidden from social consequences. By the end of the performance, her body was stripped, attacked, and devalued into an image that Abramović described as the "Madonna, mother, and whore." Additionally, markings of aggression were apparent on the artist's body; there were cuts on her neck made by audience members, and her clothes were cut off of her body.

Abramović's art also represents the objectification of the female body, as she remains motionless and allows the spectators to do as they please with her body, pushing the limits of what one would consider acceptable.

The women artists I discuss next give us a window into the shattered psyches of those who have been abused and raped. Unlike the images of Artemisia, Bernini, Poussin, Rubens, and Kahlo, the men are not depicted. Ana Mendieta (1973) in *Rape, Murder Scene*, recreated the crime scene of the rape and murder of fellow University of Iowa student Sarah Ann Ottens. For the performance, spectators found Mendieta crouched, bloody and still, naked from the waist down. She did additional tableaux of rape that year. She did not announce them but let them be discovered by unsuspecting passersby. In one, she spread blood on the sidewalk and observed people walking on by, indifferent to the violence they had just seen. A number of Mendieta's performances, which she photographed depict she herself as abused, her face bloodied (*Bloody Eye* 1973). She either jumped or fell out of a window and died. Her partner, the prominent artist Carl Andre, was brought to trial, but exonerated from having committed the brutal act.

Also autobiographical are the photos and films of Nan Goldin, who had a series of sadomasochistic relationships with men. In *Nan One Month After Being Battered* (1984) she shows what was a considerable improvement upon her physical condition after she had been battered. In 1980, less horrific, she photographed her *Heart-Shaped Bruise*, as if bruises and affairs of the heart necessarily belong together. Goldin, in her ongoing film series, *The Ballad of Sexual Dependency* (1985) said that: "I wanted it to be about every man and every relationship and the potential of violence in every relationship." I find this to be sadly accepting. Nevertheless, today showings of her photos are used to effect change.

I first saw Sue Williams' (1992) autobiographical sculpture *Irresistible* on the floor of the Whitney Museum. The pain of the crouched figure and the writing on it go right to your heart. She cringes as if in a catatonic cocoon. The words of her batterer are: "... YOU DUMB BITCH. I DIDN'T DO THAT. HAVE YOU BEEN SEEING SOMEONE—HUH SLUT. I THINK YOU LIKE IT MOM. LOOK WHAT YOU MADE ME DO..."

The woman artist in my opinion whose oeuvre most poignantly depicts violence against women is Kiki Smith. Her father was the prominent sculptor Tony

Smith. His three daughters all became artists. Kiki says little about her relationship with her father. I saw *Tale* (1992) also on the floor of the Whitney Museum. A naked woman crouches on the floor, her rear end covered with excrement and leaving a long t-a-i-l that is concrete evidence of the t-a-l-e she could tell. Art critic Linda Nochlin (2015) reported a "visceral shock" when she wrote: "I still remember the intensity of the feeling, as though the bottom had dropped out of the sedate world of the gallery and my own place in it, to put it more physically, I felt it in my guts" (p. 290).

Kiki did *Bloodpool* (1992) in the same year. What could be a more wretched image than this fetal image with its prominent spine? And in the same year *Pee Body* (1992), (see Figure 15.1, p. 169) a humiliating image of an abused woman sitting on the floor surrounded by yellow glass beads (pee), a quintessential image of "abjection" as conceptualized by Julia Kristeva (1982) in her book *Powers of Horror*. (Evidently some male art critics wrote that Smith degraded art itself by calling attention to such low bodily functions as peeing.) Kristeva wrote about "abjection":

> The body's inside ... shows up in order to compensate for the collapse of the border between inside and outside. It is as if the skin, a fragile container, no longer guaranteed the integrity of one's "own and clean self" but, scraped or transparent, invisible or taut, gave way before the dejection of its contents. Urine, blood, sperm, excrement then show up in order to reassure a subject that is lacking its "own and clean self." The abjection of those flows from within suddenly become the sole "object" of sexual desire—a true "ab-ject" where man, frightened, crosses over the horrors of maternal bowels and, in an immersion that enables him to avoid coming face to face with another, spares himself the risk of castration.
>
> (p. 53)

A most compelling explanation of rape to my mind.

The early 1990s were a time of unearthing tales of violence during wartime. Judy Chicago of *The Dinner Party* fame worked on a book called *The Holocaust Project: From Darkness into Light* (1993). In *Double Jeopardy: Everybody Raped* she found that in the camps, not just the Nazis but the liberators too—American, British, and Soviet soldiers—raped women Bergen-Belsen survivors.

Kara Walker, one of our most prominent African-American women artists, chronicled in her powerful silhouettes the sexual misuse and abuse of black slave women by their white masters on Southern plantations during those infamous years of American history. In her incredible mural (1995) *The Battle of Atlanta: Being the Narrative of a Negress in the Flame of Desire* we notice a flung chicken leg. Walker's work bitingly satirizes the white man's desire for black women: "I like my coffee like I like my women, any number of combinations, 'hot, black and sweet,' 'black with a touch of cream.'" The black female body as both subject and repository of sexual fantasies, phobias, and taboos prevails

Figure 15.1 Pee Body (1992), wax and glass beads (23 strands of varying lengths, 1 in to over 15 in long); 68.6 × 71.1 × 71.1 cm (27 × 28 × 28 in).

Source: Harvard Art Museums/Fogg Museum: gift of Barbara Lee; gift of Emily Rauh Pulitzer; and Purchase in part from the Joseph A. Baird, Jr., Francis H. Burr Memorial and Director's Acquisition Funds, 1997.82 ©Kiki Smith. Photo: Imaging Department ©President and Fellows of Harvard College.

as the locus of a major portion of Walker's work with the hope that as she exposes it, it will lose its menacing power.

Fast-forward to today. Emma Sulkowicz, a performance artist, decided to not forget about and keep "hidden under the mattress" a date-rape incident at Columbia University. For her senior thesis, called *Carry That Weight* (2014–2015), she carried the offensive mattress wherever she went and even disregarded university authorities by bringing it with her to graduation. University President Lee Bollinger turned away from her, refusing to shake her hand. She was harshly criticized for creating publicity that could promote her career, but she did bring awareness to the public about the prevalence of date-rape, a backlash to the growing independence and success of young women.

I end with a glorious image of a bronze sculpture by Kiki Smith called *Rapture* (2001). It recalls the story of St. Genevieve, who saved her people from Attila the Hun. She is standing erect; the wolf is powerless, lying on the ground.

Smith also refers to the story of Little Red Riding Hood and the Wolf. She is not crouching, bent over, or beseeching. She shines in the light just as women all over the world will shine as a result of efforts such as this one.

List of images discussed in this chapter

1   Artemisia Gentileschi (1610) *Susanna and the Elders*
2   Bernini (1622) *Rape of Persephone*
3   Poussin (1634) *The Abduction of the Sabine Women*
4   Rubens (1635–1637) *Rape of the Daughters of Leucippus*
5   F. Kahlo (1935) *A Few Small Nips: Passionately in Love*
6   M. Abramović (1974) *Rhythm O*
7   Mendieta (1973) *Rape, Murder Scene*
8   Mendieta (1973) *Bleeding Eye*
9   N. Goldin (1984) *Nan One Month After Being Battered*
10   N. Goldin (1980) *Heart-Shaped Bruise*
11   S. Williams (1992) *Irresistible*
12   K. Smith (1992) *Tale*
13   K. Smith (1992) *Bloodpool*
14   K. Smith (1992) *Pee Body*
15   J. Chicago (1993) book *Holocaust Project: From Darkness into Light*
16   J. Chicago (1992) *Double Jeopardy: Everybody Raped*
17   K. Walker (1995) *The Battle of Atlanta: Being the Narrative of a Negress on the Flame of Desire*
18   E. Sulkowicz (2014–2015) *Carry That Weight*
19   K. Smith (2001) *Rapture*

Notes

1   First published as Chapter 20, "Violence against women in the work of women artists," in *The courage to fight violence against women: Psychoanalytic and multidisciplinary perspectives*, edited by Paula L. Ellman and Nancy R. Goodman (published by Karnac Books in 2017). Reprinted with kind permission of Taylor & Francis, LLC.
2   Images discussed in this chapter and listed at the end can be easily searched by entering the artist name and the title of the image into an Internet search engine.

References

Knafo, D. (2009). *Dancing with the unconscious: The art of psychoanalysis and the psychoanalysis of art*. New York: Routledge.

Kristeva, J. (1982). *Powers of horror: An essay on abjection*. New York: Columbia University Press.

Lieberman, J. S. (2000). *Body talk: Looking and being looked at in psychotherapy* Northvale, N.J.: Jason Aronson, Inc.

Nochlin, L. (2015). Unholy postures: Kiki Smith and the body. In M. Reilly, *Women artists: The Linda Nochlin reader*. New York: Thames and Hudson.

Chapter 16

The imposturous artist Arshile Gorky[1]

Arshile Gorky is considered to be one of America's foremost artists. The ideas of Gorky, a proto-abstract expressionist, were seminal influences on the works of Willem de Kooning, Mark Rothko, Jackson Pollock, and others. As a young man, he worked in a rather stilted, intellectualized painting style that was derived from European cubism. He was then greatly influenced by surrealism and developed a unique fluid style characterized by its use of biomorphic forms and lyrical color freed from line. Using a technique called automatism, in which the artist allows whatever images emerge mentally to be translated onto the canvas via his hand and the brush, Gorky was able to reach into his unconscious in a process similar to that of the analysand who says whatever comes to mind. In lieu of words, the visual images retrieved were then placed on the canvas in an order and arrangement of his own creation.

The vicissitudes of Gorky's life, as well as of his works, are of particular interest to one who is psychoanalytically trained. Gorky was not analyzed, and therefore, the nature of the comments made about him in this chapter is *entirely speculative*, as they are in most psychobiographies. His many biographers from the worlds of art, art history, and art criticism have made psychologically informed comments about him and his tendencies to imposturousness, notably Harold Rosenberg (1962, 1964), Ethel Schwabacher (1957), Diane Waldman (1981), Melvin Lader (1985), and his nephew Karlan Mooradian (1955, 1967, 1971, 1978). The psychoanalyst-critic Donald Kuspit (1987) has also written a Kohutian commentary entitled "Arshile Gorky: Images in Support of the Invented Self," that is referred to in the forthcoming discussion.

Gorky, who was born in Armenia in 1904, was beset by a series of devastating, traumatic events that began during his childhood: paternal abandonment, starvation, and exile during the Turkish genocidal attempt on the Armenians; his mother's death from starvation; and emigration to the United States at the age of 16. Nevertheless, he was able to be productive both as an artist and as a teacher throughout his life. His many friends regarded him as loveable, but with imposturous tendencies they could not begin to address. He told stories about himself that were inconsistent, with constant shifts in name, date, place, and action. His appearance was profoundly melancholy, and he always seemed to be much older than he actually was. At the age of 44 he suffered a mental breakdown and hanged himself after a series of incredible events that were most likely experienced internally as a recapitulation of his childhood Holocaust-like experiences. I regard his story as a case study of imposturousness and confirmatory of hypotheses presented earlier in this book about the antecedent personal history and psychic structure typical of imposturousness.

In this chapter, parallels are noted between certain changes in Gorky's personal identity as it developed and became more cohesive in the consistent and stable American environment and concurrent transformations in his painting style. That style evolved from a derivative and somewhat rigid one-to-one with an original, fluid, and imaginative form. Gorky's use of several "Great Artists" as idealized father figures, along with his decade of work on a series of self-portraits, in particular two versions of *The Artist and His Mother* (ca. 1929–1942, 1926–1929), (Figure 16.1) possibly facilitated a restorative process of internalization and a working through of mourning for his dead mother. One can assume that a "mourning-liberation process" (Pollock, 1989) was operative.

The series of traumatic childhood events seem to have produced in the young Gorky a profound state of identity confusion. He slavishly copied the style of other artists—not just ordinary artists, but the greats, Uccello, Ingres, and especially Cezanne, Picasso, and Miro—long past the time during which imitation is useful for an artist. An example is *Painting* (1936–1937).[2] His choice of whom to imitate was quite personal; for example, he was said to have chosen to emulate Picasso rather than Braque because he shared a sense of estrangement with Picasso. For a time, his works were indistinguishable from those of his friend John Graham. His identity confusion manifested itself: (1) in the prolonged period of copying already described; (2) in his proclivity to lying and deception; (3) in manifestations of a fraudulence bordering upon imposturousness; (4) in an opaque, covered over quality in his personality that was likened to camouflage; (5) in his idiosyncratic use of the English language, beyond the bounds one might expect in one who adopts a new language in adulthood; and (6) in a profound melancholy and seriousness that expressed his unfinished mourning of the loss of his father, his mother, his homeland, and his childhood grandiosity, a process fueled by what the psychoanalyst would reconstruct as the tremendous burden of unconscious guilt.

Art scholars have speculated that Gorky's copying of great male artists, abnegating his own personality in the process, enabled him to reach a higher-level of psychological integration. By identifying with these idealized figures, by slowly internalizing them, he was able to work through and restore the narcissistic loss of his father, who abandoned his family in an act of cowardice, and who was most likely demeaned in the eyes of his more educated, aristocratic mother. In Gorky's "surrender" to these great artists, he would make statements that indicated the adhesiveness of his identifications. For example, in speaking of Picasso, he said: "If he drips, I drip" (quoted in Rosenberg, 1962, p. 66). His identifications were more than identifications, verging on, but not precisely the

Figure 16.1 Arshile Gorky (ca. 1902–1948), *The Artist and His Mother* (1926–ca. 1936). Oil on canvas 60 × 50 1/4 in (152.4 × 127.6 cm).

Source: Whitney Museum of American Art, New York: gift of Julien Levy for Maro and Natasha Gorky in memory of their father 50.17 ©2018 The Arshile Gorky Foundation/Artists Rights Society (ARS), New York.

same as imposture and plagiarism, for he not only copied Picasso's styles but also his various signatures and placement of signatures on the canvas. He said, "I feel Picasso running in my fingertips" (quoted in Reiff, 1977, p. 215).

The inner reparation and restoration that we assume took place as a result of his working on *The Artist and His Mother* enabled Gorky in his late 30s to marry, to have children and a fine home, and to give up the mantle of suffering and poverty that he had worn all his life. He was then able to develop a unique painting style as exemplified by *The Betrothal II*, (1947) and no longer needed to draw from others in order to create.

Chronology of Gorky's life (1904–1948)

As mentioned, several biographies of Gorky's life and voluminous files of his letters and writings are available for scrutiny. Nevertheless, some basic facts, such as dates and places, appear in different form from biography to biography, creating in the researcher a sense of shaky incertitude—akin to an induced countertransference—as to exactly who this person was and exactly what took place in his life. The brief history we have pieced together from these sources is elaborated upon in the next section of this chapter.

Gorky was born in 1904 in the village of Khorkom, in eastern Armenia. His real name was Vosdanik Manook Adoian. His father, of peasant background, was a trader and carpenter, who supported Gorky's aunts and uncles, all of whom lived together under one roof. His mother, highly educated and beautiful, came from a line of exalted priests. Both parents were quite tall, supposedly the only trait they really had in common. Gorky himself grew to be 6 feet 4 inches as an adult. He had two sisters, 3 and 8 years older, and one sister 2 years younger. As a young child, his mother helped foster his artistic vision by taking him to visit various cathedrals and shrines, where he saw (and never forgot) illuminated manuscripts with their calligraphy and exotic hybrid human and animal forms. From the age of 4, he obsessively and constantly carved and sculpted wood.

At that crucial age of 4, Gorky's father left abruptly for America in order to avoid the Turkish draft. At the age of 8, now man of the house, he posed for the photograph with his mother—his sisters were not included—that served as the basis for *The Artist and His Mother*. This photograph was to be sent to his father, who was by then living in Rhode Island. In 1914 to 1915, when he was 10, the Turks seized his city and began the extermination of the Armenians. The family's house was shelled, and he, his mother, and his sisters went on a death march to the Caucasus. They lost everything. They had buried their possessions in the ground, but were never to return. The churches and manuscripts he had grown to love were also destroyed. Mother and children moved from place to place. His mother and sisters took in some sewing despite the fact that in their culture women who worked disgraced the men in the family. Gorky as man of the family had to work for the little they were to have. His two older sisters then left for America, and at the age of 15, he was to hold his mother in his arms as she died of starvation while dictating a last letter to his father in Rhode Island. He and his younger sister, dressed in rags, were helped by family friends to travel to Constantinople, then Greece, and then to the United States. After a brief stay with his father in Rhode Island, and after retrieving the photograph, he went to live in Watertown, Massachusetts, with his oldest sister and her family. He went to work in a factory, but lost his job because he spent his time drawing rather than working. At the age of 16, he took the name Gorky, a Greek word for "the bitter one." Arshile is an equivalent of Achilles. He remained in close contact with his sisters and their families throughout his life, but it is unclear how much contact he ever maintained with his father.

After studying art in Boston, he came to New York in 1925, set up a studio in Greenwich Village, and at 21 years of age taught art and published important-sounding pronouncements about his philosophy of art. For the next 10 to 12 years his works were for the most part imitations of and derivations of the works of the greats. In 1930, he moved his studio to Union Square, where he befriended Willem de Kooning, John Graham, and Stuart Davis, among other artists, with whom he interacted intensively. They debated and learned from one another about art making. His studio was noted for its immaculateness, its orderliness, and its huge stockpile of artists' supplies that put him into debt and often led to his suffering from starvation. During this period of the Depression, Gorky was noted for his impoverished look. His clothes always had holes in them. He subsisted on dough-nuts and coffee during a time when the Works Project Administration (WPA) paid him US$37 a week to do murals at Newark Airport. Constantly critical of Amer-ican values, he chose as lovers American women whom he sought to remake into deeper, more intellectual persons. In 1935, he was married briefly to a Midwestern woman, Marney George, a student of fashion art. The marriage ended when she resisted his attempts to reform her in accordance with his preferences and ideals. According to his nephew Mooradian, being an Armenian was problematic for him, and he felt blocked in praising his homeland, now under the Soviet regime.

From 1936 to 1937, he did an abstract composition called *Painting*, which was purchased by the Whitney Museum of American Art. At about that time, he completed, or shall we say let go of, *The Artist and His Mother*, which he had begun in 1926.

Life took a different turn for Gorky. He met and married Agnes Magruder, a straight, fearless, and quite beautiful young Bostonian. Perhaps he had found in her his mother imago, or more likely, he was free enough of his conflictual attachment to his mother, having mourned her death sufficiently to allow himself to love and be loved once again. Agnes seemed to give this incredibly unhappy man a center. He asked her to cook his mother's favorite recipes. Their domestic bliss resulted in their having two daughters, Maro, born in 1943, and Natasha, born in 1945. They lived in several attractive houses and finally purchased an architecturally remarkable glass house in Sherman, Connecticut.

During this period (1942–1948), his unique surrealistic style flourished. A series of one-man shows at the Julien Levy Gallery began to receive critical acclaim. However, at the height of his success, a series of tragedies occurred. A fire broke out in the chimney of his studio in 1945, destroying that year's work. He suspected his wife of having an affair with his colleague and protégé, Matta. He developed cancer and had a colostomy. In 1948, he was hurt in a car accident, breaking his neck and causing his painting arm to be temporarily paralyzed. Dark mood swings and suspiciousness ensued, alienating his wife, who, with their children, left him to go to her parents' house. Two weeks later, at the age of 44, he hanged himself.

The formative years: psychic trauma

The series of traumas that accumulated in the life of young Gorky are now described in more detail. These accounts are distillations of stories Gorky personally told friends and biographers, with all the possibilities for distortion and elaboration that exist in such tellings and that we are familiar with in the material provided us by our analysands. At the age of 4, he, his mother, and his sisters were profoundly abandoned by his father. His father put the children on a horse, told them to ride out into the field, eat lunch, and then return to their mother. He presented young Gorky with the pair of red slippers that were to be a repeated motif in his works. The children returned to find their father gone. This experience supposedly left Gorky speechless, and he refused to speak until a year later when, as he later told it, his tutor threatened to jump from a cliff unless he spoke. Coincidentally, the artist Louise Nevelson (1976), in writing of her early childhood in Russia, reported that, "I was about three when my father went to America, and my mother told me that for one half year, I didn't speak. And they thought I had become deaf and dumb" (p. 6).

From that point on, a precocious maturity as symbolized by the gift of the slippers (to "walk in his father's shoes"), was imposed upon the young Gorky, perhaps by himself, perhaps by his family, but most probably, by a combination of both. He was the responsible and only male in the family, treasured above his sisters because he was male. He was breadwinner, oedipal winner, and sibling winner. One might speculate that he experienced much unconscious resentment at his father's leaving him, depriving him of his support as a role model and as a protector against internal anxieties. One might also speculate that he developed unconscious guilt over these feelings, having been made so explicitly his mother's favorite, and that a regression to anal levels of obsessiveness and ambivalent object relations ensued.

His biographer, Ethel Schwabacher (1951), provides us with a confirmatory memory, which might well be a screen memory that partially masks an earlier event. As in much of the biographical material about Gorky, one reporter's story tends to shift slightly from another's with respect to the age at which given events supposedly occurred. Schwabacher quotes Gorky:

I remember myself when I was 5 years old. The year I first began to speak. Mother and I are going to church. We are there. For a while she left me standing before a painting. It was a painting of infernal regions. There were angels in the painting. White angels and black angels. All the black angels were going to Hades. I looked at myself. I am black too. It means there is no Heaven for me. A child's heart could not accept it. And I decided there and then to prove to the world that a black angel can be good too, must be good and wants to give his inner goodness to the whole world, black and white world.

(p. 104)

In *The Family Romance of the Artist*, Greenacre (1971) writes:

Family romance fantasies of a well-organized nature seem to emerge most clearly in the early latency period; are indicative of a marked degree of ambivalence to the parents, especially due to grossly unresolved Oedipal problems. This ambivalence seems reinforced by the ambivalence of the anal period to which good and bad, applied to the self and to the parent, appear like black and white twins in so many relationships.

(p. 507)

From Gorky's words, it may be hypothesized that the low self-esteem and the splitting mechanisms of the imposturous adult, of which Greenacre speaks, were already in place.

During latency and early adolescence, Gorky went to school as much as was feasible, but had to work to supply his family with food. We speculate once more about the emergence of feelings of guilt and a profound sense of inadequacy when his mother died in his arms, as well as a feeling of betrayal, for his mother died while writing to his father. He was disqualified in his prior attempts to place her in a hospital for homeless genocide victims because his father was still alive and believed to be capable of sending them money, which in fact he never did.

Gorky's experience of the Turkish genocide of the Armenian people was a Holocaust experience. At the age of 10, he witnessed murder, rape, starvation, pillage, thousands turning black as they died of cholera, and mounds of bodies that had to be buried in order to prevent disease from spreading. He and his family were homeless, wandering. Barefoot and in rags, Gorky and his younger sister left for America. All ties with homeland, with place and folk, were amputated. From feudal Asia Minor, they were transplanted to a Western industrial society.

The adaptive ego

How does a child survive such unspeakable traumata? Massive defenses such as splitting and dissociation are generally erected against internal pain. Certain fantasies of specialness serve a restitutive function when one is abandoned, rejected, persecuted, and rendered helpless. Gorky's heritage on his mother's side was a proud one. As has been said, she was of a long line of exalted priests. He described her as follows (quoted in Mooradian, 1978): "She was the most aesthetically appreciative, the most poetically incisive master I have encountered in all my life. Mother was queen of the aesthetic domain" (p. 104). She encouraged his artistic talent and an awareness of his Armenian heritage by taking him to see the beautiful shrines and cathedrals with their extended iconography of hybrid men and animals. She made certain he had art supplies. We speculate that in his art making, he was able to hold on to this strong mother during difficult times as if in a curative cocoon, removed from fear or pain. Gorky was, in a way, tunnel-blind to all else. Art seemed to function as his libidinal object throughout his life. A year before his death he wrote in a letter (dated January 1, 1947): "Art must always remain earnest ... must be serious, no sarcasm, comedy. One does not laugh at a loved one" (Mooradian, 1978, p. 42). Eisenstadt and colleagues (1989), in their study of parental loss and achievement, write that an overidealization of a dead parent results in an attempt to achieve, to restore. The creative product will "on the one hand, alleviate those feelings of guilt and, on the other hand, prove to all the world the individual's essential goodness" (p. 26). In their study, subtitled *Orphans and the Will for Power*, they found that a disproportionate number of those who lose parents during childhood became creative geniuses, the political leaders of the past centuries. They view parent loss as a stimulant that can "lead to the creativity necessary to resolve the issues of formation, identity, and feelings of emptiness" (frontispiece). Creativity, of course, is only one outcome of such trauma. There may be bleaker ones for the non-gifted.

Further confirmation of the theory that Gorky's art was tied up with his attachment to and identification with his mother is evident in a letter written in 1935: "Just as a woman bears children and again becomes pregnant, so I again become pregnant with new ideas and remain determined to perfect my work" (Mooradian, 1971, p. 54). In a letter of January 6, 1947, the year before he died, he wrote to his sister and her children: "Art is such a delicious food. It is nutrition and medicine wrapped in a soft bundle" (Mooradian, 1978, p. 300).

Gorky, as the only male in his family, was singled out as special. His sisters later told tales of his phallic exploits, riding an Arabian horse in the mountains. The Armenian culture held a paradoxical view of women. Women were on the one hand venerated, and they even fought in revolutionary movements. But they were also demeaned. For example, they ate separately from men. A bride entering a new household initiated conversation with her husband's family only a year after the birth of a child. Gorky as a male child was so valuable that, when there was a scarcity of food, any food his mother found was given to him rather than to his sisters; she took nothing for herself.

Those who have had such a chain of experiences usually find a rationalizing philosophy to hang onto. Gorky is quoted (Mooradian, 1978), as follows:

My life resembles our wavy sea: exploding with turbulence and tempered by sorrow, but that is not necessarily a bad thing, for storms attain certain aesthetic purity only after cleansing themselves by charging over many rocks and barriers before reaching the beauty of the soft shore.

(p. 252)

Donald Kuspit's (1987) Kohutian analysis of Gorky emphasizes the injury to his sense of self-worth:

The trauma of being uprooted, and having to put down new roots undermined Gorky's sense of self, narcissistically injured him, and necessitated fresh self-creation. Gorky had to become a new person or he would be nobody. And he could only become a new self by planting his old self in the new soil of the American landscape.

(p. 203)

The adult psyche

Although he survived, Gorky paid an enormous psychic price for this survival. He arrived in the United States at the age of 16 with a remarkable talent and a capacity to live and to work independently. However, he was to be for perhaps the next 20 or so years in a state of profound identity confusion. He had not sufficiently internalized a male role model, he had not yet, as far as we know, been able to mourn his mother's death, and he did not accept his being transplanted from one world to the other.

Harold Rosenberg (1962), the critic and his biographer, wrote of Gorky's copying of the works of the great artists: "His own work is almost a visual metaphor of the digestion of European painting on this side of the Atlantic and its conversion into a new substance" (p. 1). Gorky's rationalization was that only after an artist had "digested" the great art of the past could he hope to rival it. It was as if he lived with each artist, one at a time, in order to absorb him and incorporate him. His self-portraits were shaky, problematic, and not truly reflective of who he was, an indicator of that unstable sense of self we have come to recognize as a hallmark of unstable identifications. In 1964, Rosenberg wrote: "None of the Gorky portraits is a good likeness and in this respect his self-portraits are least good. Gorky could not grasp himself even as appearance" (p. 102). Gorky would say: "I was *with* Cezanne for a longtime and now naturally I am *with* Picasso" (quoted in Waldman 1981, p. 24). Rosenberg commented,

Until his last year, no new idea ever shows itself in Gorky all of a piece; it pokes, then recedes into the canon he is following. There is no end to his apprenticeship; yet at every stage, he reaches ahead to things of his own.

(1962, p. 48)

More problematic than characterological identity problems of imposture was Gorky's tendency toward outright lying and deception, toward what Rosenberg (1962) termed "a higher mathematics of pseudonymity which was to be characteristic of his art" (p. 42). That is, in some respects he was a true impostor, one who misrepresents himself by assuming an identity or title not his own. He took the name Arshile Gorky and passed himself off as a Russian, the cousin of a nephew of the great writer Maxim Gorky (whose name was also a pseudonym). The Armenian villager thus, became a cultivated Russian. One can speculate that Gorky, like so many artists, was motivated by underlying family romance fantasies. Greenacre (1958b) cites such cases, in which the real parents, replaced in fantasy by noble and exalted ones, were decathected and punished for their sexuality. As Diane Waldman (1981), in her catalog for the Guggenheim Museum, reflected:

> Gorky was no stranger to romantic legend, forever telling exotic and conflicting stories about his origins, posing variously as Russian, Georgian, Armenian; speaking of himself as a relative of Maxim Gorky and as a pupil of Kandinsky, a student of the Polytechnic Institute in Tiflis, a student at the Academie Julien in Paris or at Brown University, when in fact he was far too young to have undertaken such advanced studies.
>
> (p. 16)

Some of these lies were never corrected by Gorky or others. For example, after his death, an article in the *New York Times* still reported him as a cousin of Maxim Gorky and a Russian. When his younger daughter was born, she was listed as Yalda. Then her Armenian name was changed to the Russian Natasha, possibly related to some repetition of his own name change. The artist Elaine de Kooning (1951) wrote of Gorky:

> He would fabricate or embellish incidents of his personal history, shuffle a few dates in his paintings, sign his name to a couple of essays he never wrote, and pass off as his own lines from the few poems he had read. A biography was something to hide behind. He told people he was born in three different countries in three different years. He told friends he did not speak until he was 6—before that only with birds [p. 39]. His love letters to various women contained the poems of Paul Eluard, which he presented as his own.

In my attempt to understand Gorky's plagiarisms and other kinds of fraudulence as a form of imposturousness, I speculate that Gorky's superego was formed on the basis of an absent paternal introject. His own father, in a way, lied to him by not telling him of his planned departure. His father was not there in reality to inhibit (or to castrate) and could not serve to curb his son's arrogance. It does not seem like too big a leap to interpret that Gorky's search for the lost father and wishes to resurrect him within himself appear as an important dynamic in his various imitations and wishful identity fabrications.

Erikson (1968) observes that, in some cases of identity confusion, estrangement from national and ethnic origins leads to a complete denial of the true roots of personal identity, and confabulatory reconstructions of one's origins are invented. This reinvented, fantasized account of the parents as glorified covers over a death wish toward the parents who are in fact devalued (pp. 173–174). If Erikson's conclusions are applicable to Gorky's case, the artist's imposturous tendencies might account for the fate of his aggressive drive, for strong aggression and even impotent rage seem to have been stimulated by the helplessness he experienced in the face of his father's abandonment, his mother's death, and the precocious maturity that was imposed on him and that he chose to develop in an attempt to master the traumatic sense of helplessness. Another way to understand Gorky's denial of his own true identity is afforded us by Loewald's (1979) notions of authenticity and autonomy. That is, to develop an authentic sense of identity and an experience of oneself as agent can be equated unconsciously with replacing the oedipal parent as though by committing parricide. Erikson (1968) refers to imposture as a severe identity crisis in which, via the "negative identity" of imposture, there is a hateful repudiation of the most dangerous and yet the most real identifications with the parents at various critical stages of development over the life cycle.

The critic, Harold Rosenberg (1962), considered Gorky to be a paradoxical figure and was quite suspicious of him. This amateur psychologist astutely pointed to certain inconsistencies, which psychoanalysts understand as reflecting unintegrated parts of the ego, when he wrote:

> The immigrant is a self-made man; making oneself (self-creation) is not, however, far distant from making oneself up (self-disguise). When, in arriving in America, Gorky decided to become an artist, he decided at the same time to *look* like an artist.
>
> (1962, pp. 22–23)

Rosenberg (1962) described Gorky's "pleading, war-orphan" eyes and went on to write:

> that this Bohemian type, always ready to put on the neglected genius act, especially in the presence of women and important people, should be at the same time a relentless thinker and disciplined creator in a puzzle designed to baffle moralizers and mislead swindlers.
>
> (p. 24)

Psychoanalysts, however, can grasp the paradoxical closeness between feelings of authenticity as opposed to inauthenticity among the creative, a closeness that challenges some common moralizing stereotypes about truth and falsehood, honesty and deception. In general, one can discern an important connection between creation among the truly creative, such as Gorky, and the self-creation of imposturous individuals, such as Gorky. One might also speculate that Gorky never felt sure of himself, that is, was not in touch with his true self, because of significant lacunae not just in superego but in true self development, and, paradoxically, he had to cultivate his false self through his adoptive identities in order to feel authentic.

Lying helps maintain repression of painful memories. As noted earlier in Chapter 2 on lying, Fenichel (1939) describes how lying and deception could disguise unconscious fantasies and wishes; that is, they are defensively motivated. He states the rationale of the liar: "If I can make others believe the things which I know to be untrue are true, then it is also possible that my memory is deceived and what I remember as true is untrue" (p. 136). Gorky's "cover" perhaps enabled him to hold back the tide of painful childhood experiences so that he could go on with his life and his work.

Abraham (1925), Deutsch (1955), Gediman (1985), and Greenacre (1958a) describe characters who are somewhat like, but also different from, Gorky. The true impostor, as we noted, pretends under someone else's name, whereas those who are imposturous to a lesser degree—for example, as-if personalities— pretend, with great interest in imitation, under someone else's style and role, taking on the color of those who are admired and idealized. Although the true impostor suffers from serious arrests and deficits in ego development, those with lesser imposturous tendencies often behave in ways generally considered to be neurotic, such as from a need for punishment.

Continuing his self-psychological analysis, Kuspit (1987) concludes: "Gorky, moving from mentor to mentor, searching for a new identity as soon as the old one became an 'act,' was perpetually destroying himself and being reborn as someone else until finally he was reborn as himself" (p. 205).

Gorky was reported to have been highly defended: "to Gorky at that time, nothing was more fenced off than his real self" (Rosenberg, 1964, p. 100). His dealer, Julien Levy, called him a "camouflaged man," and it is of interest to note that in the early part of World War II he volunteered to teach a course on camouflage. This psychological covering over might have been an influence on his tendency to overpaint. His canvases were extremely heavy due to his painting layer on layer of image, a characteristic that art historians attribute to the scarcity of materials. Gorky's very appearance was experienced by many as staged rather than authentic. Word had got out that even his mustache and beard were his inventions to mask the real world from which he came and to create a new world in which he wished to belong. As has been said, Rosenberg described him as playing the role of the "Great Artist," according to Bohemian stereotype. Stuart Davis (1957) did not even believe that Gorky was poor, for he was the only artist who in those days had a studio. The critic Barbara Rose (1986) reported that Gorky's demeanor and intense gaze impelled one woman to ask if he were Jesus Christ, to which he replied: "Madame, I am Arshile Gorky" (p. 73).

Even in his mourning and nostalgia for his homeland, Gorky did not receive much sympathy from his friends. He induced contempt and scorn rather than sympathy in others, especially men. We wonder if he was unconsciously seeking punishment in a masochistic way. Rosenberg (1962) described his showman's use of his past as an Armenian peasant. He would sing folk songs and do shepherds' dances. His close friends eventually forbade these demonstrations in their presence. From photographs and from his letters and writings it was apparent that he was quite sad, seemed older than his age, and was never vibrant, or smiling. His immaculate shiny, colorful studio in the 1930s contrasted greatly with the dark despair and the soul-crushing isolation he experienced inside himself during those years. He forever mourned his homeland, never adapting to commercial America, feeling that although it was rich in technology, it was poor in humanism. He wrote on August 1, 1939 (Mooradian, 1971), "I always feel alone, even when I see my many friends and am among the thousands" (p. 104).

The child who once refused to speak grew up to be a compulsive talker as an adult, one of his many apparently compulsive defenses, like his arrogance, and his imposture. He spoke almost exclusively about art and his philosophy of art. He spoke while painting, while giving interviews, and while taking people to museums and galleries. His speech was strange—his letters are poetically eloquent, but difficult to understand. One might attribute this strangeness to a different thought pattern, to the translation from Armenian to English, but it seems to be something more than that. Stuart Davis (1951) described it this way: "It was no mere matter of a foreign accent, though that was present, but an earthquake-like effect on sentence structure and a savagely perverse use of words to mean something they didn't" (p. 57). This typically imposturous use of words was not just an affectation, but like so much else in Gorky's defensive armamentarium, can be understood as a narcissistically compensatory attempt. It helped him cover over a feeling of inauthenticity, perhaps related to his early entitlement fantasies, or was based on his being an oedipal winner who perhaps committed, in his imagination, a successful but premature parricide.

As Gorky became more integrated, he invented a visual language, that is, he went from verbal to visual expression of what was inside himself. As his private, internal images were placed on the canvas, he adopted the surrealist's use of enigmatic titles that were highly personal and/or titles of poems and other literary works.

The Artist and His Mother (ca. 1929–1942 and 1926–1929) and its influence on his later works

In these two transitional paintings, the first of which is illustrated in Figure 16.1, Gorky worked in a style that was quite different from the early cubist or late surrealist styles he is noted for. There are echoes of Ingres and Picasso in these portraits, polished as if they were jewels and breathtaking to behold. They show how adept he was at unifying two-dimensional and three-dimensional forms in a powerful totality. The portrait is drawn from memory and from the famous photo he took with his mother at age 8, a photo intended for his father to see. The pose is therefore not psychologically dyadic but triadic. His three sisters are excluded. He is carefully dressed. His mother, the Lady Shushenik of the priestly Armenian family, radiates with nobility and self-sacrifice. In the painting he creates a sense of intimacy absent in the photo.

Karp (1982) points out that the painting calls to mind Dietrich's (1990) "lost immortal parent complex," in which the object is both lost and immortal, frozen in space, yet not spatially bound, a beloved parent that the individual seeks or hopes will return.

Viederman (1990), in his study of Edvard Munch, examines a recurrent shape in Munch's paintings that seems to derive from a photo of the artist on his mother's lap. He reconstructs this motif as Munch's attempt to put together a coherent picture of his mother's death and to communicate this event to others. The work done is in the service of adaptation and integration. The use of the photo, in Gorky's case, can also be understood as serving a function akin to that of a transitional object.

Rosenberg (1964) calls *The Artist and His Mother* a "missing link" between the early imitative drawings and the canvases of the last phase (1942–1948): "in double portrait, Gorky reached for identity in the direction of his actual self and away from the Great Artist 'role-playing'" (p. 105). His venture into surrealism eased his communication with his childhood and loosened his concept of art and the artist so that he became closer to himself and no longer had to relate to the Great Works or resort to imposture. Waldman (1981) wrote that Gorky for the first time was able to connect with his own past and personal identity.

According to Sandler (1970), Gorky's independence was facilitated by his relationship with Andre Breton, who became another father figure to him but was not a fantasy father since they had a real relationship. The Surrealists gave him the confidence he needed to rely on his own intuition, insight, and expressiveness. One could hypothesize that the period of dependency and the protracted labor on *The Artist and His Mother* both integrated him to a greater degree and enabled him to use himself as a creative source.

Pollock (1989), in his study of the artist Kathe Kollwitz, writes that in certain individuals "great creativity may not be the successful outcome of the successfully completed mourning process but may be indicative of attempts at completing the mourning work. These creative attempts may be conceptualized as restitution, reparation, discharge, or sublimation" (p. 571).

Rosenberg (1962), wrote of the new style that then emerged: "Literally beside himself, that is, acting outside the limits of his self-consciousness, Gorky can now make manifest in his paintings and drawings psychological states he had formerly confided only in private relations. Eroticism flooded his soul of a Puritan" (p. 103). Opulent sexual imagery was especially evident in his *Garden in Sochi* series of 1940–1943 about which Gorky wrote:

The garden was identified as the Garden of Wish Fulfillment and often I had seen my mother and other village women opening their bosoms and taking their soft and dependable breasts in their hands to wash them on the rocks.

(Quoted in Rose, 1986, p. 73)

Donald Kuspit (1987) saw the works of this period as a restoration of the self-object, of the primal father-son relationship, an attempt:

to recapture, through Modernist means, the primitive spirit of 'authentic' [his own word] nature, with its miraculously generative tree symbolic of the imagination as such—he is more completely dependent than ever on self-objects. He has found his way back to his true father, to the supreme self-object.

(pp. 201–202)

Kuspit's thesis is that Gorky imagined he had done something bad by being banished from his father's garden and tried to heal this through his art.

When, in 1941, Gorky met and married Agnes Magruder, and their two daughters were born, he was finally to experience joy in his life. His domestic bliss might have been experienced by him as a reliving of the time he lived happily with his family in Armenia before he was 4 years old. He gave up his asceticism and allowed himself to have a telephone and good meals, to work outdoors, and to reacquaint himself with the joys of nature.

At this time, the series of tragic events described earlier, occurred. In February of 1945, his studio, with all the work he had done that year, was destroyed by fire. This fire might have revived, whether consciously or unconsciously, the memory of something he knew as a child. Gorky believed that he had been born with a curse, for his maternal grandmother, one year before his birth, warred against the God of the Armenians by setting fire to the family's ancestral church upon finding his young uncle's body lying in front of the church door with a Turkish dagger in his back (Mooradian, 1967). He was then diagnosed as having cancer of the colon and had a colostomy in February, 1946. These events left him psychologically, although not physically, impotent. The colostomy bag he had to wear was unpalatable to the fastidious Gorky. His work went well, but shades of paranoia were becoming manifest, as is evident in a letter to his sister of January 1, 1947: "The money-kissers are everywhere, those soulless and omnipresent flies biting the still-warm bodies of fallen heroes and appropriating the victories others have won" (Mooradian, 1978, p. 302).

Gorky began to drown himself in his work. The psychosexual regression presumably stimulated by the fire and the operation probably brought about a degree of unconscious guilt that forbade further enjoyment of his family and of the new critical acclaim being given to him. I hypothesize a regression back to imposture. In February, 1948, an interviewer (Clapp, 1948) found him to be shy and speaking without conviction. He lied again by saying that he had attended

Brown University as a young man. He complained that, "there are no more songs in the field," that everyone is a "businessman."

A series of reviews of his exhibitions at Julien Levy from 1945 to 1948 were increasingly laudatory. Clement Greenberg (in O'Brian, 1986) was at first quite critical. Then he proclaimed them to be "some of the best modern paintings turned out by an American" (p. 79). "Gorky has finally succeeded in discovering himself for what he is—not an artist of epochal stature, no epic past, but a lyrical, personal painter with an elegant, felicitous, and genuine delivery" (p. 79). And in 1948 he wrote: "Gorky is a complete hedonist, deeper in his hedonism than any French painter" (in O'Brian, 1986, p. 219). Reiff (1977), more recently wrote that:

> Gorky's late painting is expressive of a richness of pathos and mood which is poignant and yet difficult to define. It is as if a certain combination of emotional ingredients, of despair, frustration, yearning, anguish, had been distilled to result in a new essence characteristic of Gorky's art and born of his peculiar tragedy.
>
> (p. 253)

In his personal life, however, Gorky could not acknowledge or digest the extent of the tragedies he was suffering during those years (de Kooning, 1951). Waldman (1981) wrote that:

> Gorky's terrible childhood experiences may have strengthened his will to survive his grave illness and the destruction by fire of his studio and his work, or it may ultimately have contributed to his collapse. His marriage, which had been troubled, now began to disintegrate. He had endured years of poverty and lack of recognition but he could not withstand the final event in the series of tragedies that befell him.
>
> (p. 60)

Waldman refers to the car accident in New Milford, Connecticut, in June, 1948, in a car driven by his dealer, Julien Levy. Gorky's neck was broken and his painting arm temporarily paralyzed. His moods and bad temper, his lack of trust, and his doubts about his wife were so violent that she left him in mid-July, and that was the time she took the children to her parents' home. On July 12, he hanged himself in his studio. He wrote, "Goodbye My Loveds" in white chalk. Only after his death was the true value of his paintings established: they hang now in the galleries of our greatest museums.

Here ends the story of a man with an imposturous identity, often an outright liar, who appeared to be developing a well-integrated mature identity as he eventually had the courage to be authentic enough to present work that was uniquely his own. I cannot attribute his tragic suicide to later trauma alone. The later tragedies undoubtedly reactivated the earlier ones. These external events promoted an inner regression to the terrors that characterized his psychic reality all along. Although the successful imposture fueled his labors at better eventual self-integration, that very authentic self-presentation and identity might have been too much to bear. It must have symbolized a successful parricide that probably just could not be handled by the now not-so-imposturous man. As a child, he must have been just too burdened by the abandonment by his father and the deaths of those around him in the Armenian Holocaust, and especially by the oedipal victories that his later successes symbolized. The meaning of the early and late tragedies then took on traumatic proportions because they dovetailed too precisely with the terrifying demons of his inner fantasies.

Notes

1 This chapter first published as "The Imposturous Artist: Arshile Gorky," in *The Many Faces of Deceit: Omissions, Lies, and Disguise in Psychotherapy* by Helen K. Gediman; Janice S. Lieberman, 1996, Northvale, N. J.: Jason Aronson, Inc. Reprinted by permission of Rowman & Littlefield Publishing Group.
2 Images not illustrated in this chapter can be instantly accessed by inserting the artist's name and the name of the image into an Internet search engine.

References

Abraham, K. (1925). The history of an impostor in the light of psychoanalytical knowledge. In *Clinical Papers and Essays in Psychoanalysis* (pp. 291–305). New York: Basic Books, 1955.

Clapp, T. B. (1948, February 9). A painter in a glass house. *The Waterbury Sunday Republican Magazine.*

Davis, S. (1951, February). Arshile Gorky in the 1930's: A personal recollection. *Magazine of Art, 44.*

Davis, S. (1957, December 28). Handmaiden of misery. *Saturday Review, 40.*

de Kooning, E. (1951, January). Gorky: Painter of his own legend. *Art News.*

Deutsch, H. (1955). The impostor: Contribution of ego psychology to a type of psychopath. In *Neuroses and Character Types* (pp. 318–338). New York: International Universities Press, 1965.

Dietrich, D. R. (1990). *Childhood object loss, the lost immortal parent complex, and mourning.* Presented at The American Psychological Association, Boston, August.

Eisenstadt, M., Haynal, A., Rentchnick, P., & deSenarclens, P. (1989). *Parental loss and achievement.* New York: International Universities Press.

Erickson, E. H. (1968). *Identity: Youth and crisis.* New York: Norton.

Fenichel, O. (1939). The economics of pseudologia fantastica. In H. Fenichel & D. Rapaport (Eds.), *The collected papers of Otto Fenichel* (pp. 129–140). New York: Norton, 1954.

Gediman, H. K. (1985). Imposture, inauthenticity, and feeling fraudulent. *Journal of the American Psychoanalytic Association, 33,* 911–935.

Greenacre, P. (1958a). The impostor. In *Emotional growth: Psychoanalytic studies of the gifted and a great variety of other individuals* (Vol. 1, pp. 193–212). New York: International Universities Press, 1971.

Greenacre, P. (1958b). Family romance of the artist. In *Emotional growth: Psychoanalytic studies of the gifted and a great variety of other individuals* (Vol. 2, pp. 505–532). New York: International Universities Press, 1971.

Greenacre, P. (1958c). The relation of the impostor to the artist. In *Emotional growth: Psychoanalytic studies of the gifted and a great variety of other individuals* (Vol. 2, pp. 533–554). New York: International Universities Press, 1971.

Karp, D. R. (1982). Arshile Gorky: The language of art. (Doctoral dissertation, University of Pennsylvania, 1982).

Kuspit, D. (1987). Arshile Gorky: Images in support of the invented self. In *The new subjectivism: Art in the 1980s* (pp. 199–216). New York: Da Capo, 1993.

Lader, M. R. (1985). *Gorky*. New York: Abbeville.

Lieberman, J. S. (1991). Arshile Gorky: From identity confusion to identity synthesis. Paper presented at Division 39, American Psychological Association, Chicago, April, and at the New York Freudian Society, January.

Loewald, H. (1979). The waning of the Oedipus complex. *Journal of the American Psychoanalytic Association, 27*(4), 751–756.

Mooradian, K. (1955). Arshile Gorky. *The Armenian Review, 8*, 2–30.

Mooradian, K. (1967, September). The unknown Gorky. *Art News, 32*.

Mooradian, K. (1971, September–October). Arshile Gorky. *Armenian Digest*.

Mooradian, K. (1978). *Arshile Gorky Adoian*. Chicago: Gilgamesh Press, Ltd.

Nevelson, L. (1976). *Dawns and dusks: Conversations with Diane MacKown*. New York: Charles Scribner's Sons.

O'Brian, J. (Ed.) (1986). *Clement Greenberg: The collected papers and criticism II. Arrogant purpose, 1945–1949*. Chicago: University of Chicago Press.

Pollock, G. W. (1989). *The mourning-liberation process, I & II*. New York: International Universities Press.

Reiff, R. R. (1977). A stylistic analysis of Arshile Gorky's art from 1943–1948. (PhD dissertation, Columbia University, 1977).

Rose, B. (1986). *Twentieth century American painting*. New York: Spira/Rizzoli.

Rosenberg, H. (1962). *Arshile Gorky: The man, the time, the idea*. New York: Horizon.

Rosenberg, H. (1964). *The anxious object: Art today and its audience*. New York: Horizon.

Sandler, I. (1970). *The triumph of American painting: A history of abstract expressionism*. New York: Harper and Row.

Schwabacher, E. (1951). *Arshile Gorky memorial exhibition*. New York: Whitney Museum of American Art.

Viederman, M. (1990). Edvard Munch: A life in art. Presented at the Association for Psychoanalytic Medicine, New York, March 6.

Waldman, D. (1981). *Arshile Gorky (1904–1948), retrospective*. New York: Abrams.

Chapter 17

Pedophilic themes in Balthus' works

A contemporary psychoanalytic reading of art includes the study of the artwork, the artist's personal history, and the artistic and sociocultural milieu in which the art was made. To my mind, it should also include the artist's relationship with, and conscious or unconscious fantasies about, his models, his viewers, critics, dealers and, perhaps, the future owners of his work. Many 20th century artists were psychoanalytically informed and some were psychoanalyzed. Their awareness of psychoanalytic theory, its symbols and deeper meanings, impacted and influenced their work. This adds an additional layer to the understanding of their work. Some artists reacted to psychoanalysis by embracing it, for example, the Surrealists. Others reacted against it. Some tried to provoke the public and critics and obtained perverse enjoyment from the so-called "psychoanalytic" meanings ascribed to their art. Noteworthy examples are Jackson Pollack, Hans Bellmer, and the subject of this chapter, Balthus.

Image 1[1] *Thérèse Dressing* (1938) by Balthus' (1908–2001) oeuvre is an important illustration of the above. The artist's personal history and his paintings have lent themselves to much "psychoanalytic" speculation on the part of art critics and biographers. I find it entirely paradoxical and puzzling that no psychoanalyst I know of has yet written about Balthus, a major artist of the past century. Balthus protested that his works were not psychological in intent, that his young women were not intended to be erotic and that his work was not pedophilic or pornographic as it was often characterized. He said that his works had only to do with formal concerns or that his girls were "angels" (Image 2 *Katia Reading* [1968–1976]) He lamented: "The problem is that everyone sees eroticism. My pictures aren't erotic. The problem is psychoanalysis" (Weber, 1999, p. 590). At the end of his life he protested: "I never interpreted my paintings or sought to understand what they might mean. Anyway, must they necessarily mean something?" (as told to Vircondelet, 2001, p. 25). But he contradicted himself when he then said that one always paints oneself and one's personal secret history (Vircondelet, 2001). When Balthus was 6 years old (Weber, 1999), he had a birthday party. He arranged it so that his little guests made themselves dirty with chocolate cake while he managed to stay clean. In parallel fashion, his viewers have dirty thoughts while he protests that his are clean!

Balthus was familiar with Freudian theory, had some psychoanalysts as friends and was a member of a group of intellectuals in Paris that included Jacques Lacan. His friend, Jouve's wife, was a psychoanalyst who had translated Freud's (1905) *Three Contributions to the Theory of Sex*. His older brother Pierre published a work on the Marquis de Sade in a French psychoanalytic journal. It is entirely likely that Balthus was being deliberately provocative and perverse with his viewers and critics and rather disingenuous. Balthus was a self-styled rebel and rather contemptuous of those who wrote about him and his work. His wish to not be "psychoanalyzed" by those who wrote about him, that he be "a painter of whom nothing is known," which he wrote to John Russell who was gathering information for a Tate Gallery retrospective in 1968, was experienced as a challenge and a battle-cry by a number of writers. Friends and relatives feared that they would be banished if they spoke about him in a personal way.

During the course of my own research and readings in preparing this chapter, I found myself, like Weber, experiencing a roller-coaster ride of changing impressions of Balthus, impressions that were always exciting and always highly charged, although with alternating valence. I believe that many of the biographers and critics who wrote about Balthus were overstimulated by his story and his art. I found that I had to read about him in small doses.

My thesis in this chapter is that Balthus' adult personality, characterized by many as narcissistic, snobbish, deceptive and sadomasochistic, prevented others from having empathy for him or perceiving his deeper side. I believe that his aristocratic mask of "the Count de Rola" and his grandiose contempt helped him to defend against depression and prevented others from seeing a disowned and profoundly sad part of himself. Biographers emphasized Balthus' early fame and the fact that early on he was recognized as a prodigy. They overlooked the fact that as a child Balthus suffered profound abandonment on the part of his father when he was 9 years old (1917) as well as a substitute adoring father figure (the great poet Rainer Maria Rilke), who became his mother's lover when he was in his teens. Rilke abandoned them without saying goodbye because he knew he was dying. Balthus' family suffered humiliating poverty because his father had lost all that they had in a bad investment. His childlike and depressed mother moved his brother and himself from city to city in war-torn Europe. My reading of many of his artworks demonstrates that they reveal some of that history, expressing the emotions and memories he consciously denied. It is my thesis that the affect contained in his paintings is what draws us to them and makes them great, rather than their content.

In Image 4 *Golden Days* (1944–1945), the little that is known about Balthus' personal history enables us to better understand the nature of his paintings of young women in poses that have been widely regarded as "erotic." Balthus has been likened to Nabokov (1955) *Lolita* and to Lewis Carroll (who photographed young girls in erotic, seductive, and semi-undressed poses). By carefully examining the "body language" of Balthus' models (Image 5 *The Room* [1952–1954]) and using a psychoanalytic lens to examine his life, particularly what is known about his childhood and adolescence, a more complex, and articulated understanding of his works can be reached. The reports of numerous viewers are that their gaze is erotic. Was that true of the artist or not? If not, what purpose did these young models have in the artist's psychic economy? Who did they represent?

Neret (2003) quotes Jean Clair's observations of the awkward postures:

> Children in Balthus are uncertain of their bodies. They take stock of them through excess. By continuous contact with their surround, the floor on which they slither, the furniture they rub against (measuring themselves by its side) they gradually model their awareness of self.
>
> (p. 43)

Balthus' personal story is filled with contradiction and paradox. He did not want to reveal much about himself, but much can be gleaned and pieced together from the scattered facts that are in the works of his biographers and critics. I had little difficulty locating interviews and memoirs in which he told his version of his story trying perhaps to safeguard his preferred version of his history. I will present many quotes from various sources as I attempt to piece together a psychoanalytic portrait of the man. Balthus claimed that he had a happy childhood and because of that, as he told a friend when he was 14, he would like to remain a child forever. The second part of that statement has some truth to it.

Balthus was born Balthasar Klossowski in 1908 in Paris. Later on he would call himself the Count de Rola. The family had its origins in Poland and was entitled to the de Rola coat of arms. He was the second son of Baladine and Erich, artists who had come to Paris from Poland. Counted among close family friends were Derain, Bonnard, Gide, Picasso, and, most importantly, Rilke. When Balthus was 6 in 1914, the family was forced to leave Paris because they were German. They went to live in Berlin, then Berne, then Geneva, and back to Paris when Balthus was 16. There were 10 years of economic privation and financial dependence on family and friends. Balthus' parents separated when he was 9. Erich, immensely talented, a Daumier scholar as well as an artist, left the family and went to live in another city.

Baladine began an affair with Rilke, with whom she was obsessed, when Balthus was 11. The affair lasted 2 years. She had a shrine in the house dedicated to Rilke. She and her two sons existed in small apartments, sometimes sleeping in the same room. According to Rewald, Baladine openly flirted with a similarly flirtatious Pierre and Balthus found her taking morphine, which enabled her to sleep. Little is mentioned in the literature about Balthus' father or why he left. From a psychoanalytic point of view, young Balthus' fantasies about that would be important. (Herzog, 2004; Pollock, 1989) What does seem clear to a psychoanalyst is that Balthus' early adolescence was a nightmare coupled with having received great praise for his art work, being declared a genius. Art making was his salvation and his solution.

Rilke was extraordinarily supportive of Balthus' artwork, praising him lavishly. Weber (1999) noted that "Rilke's obsequiousness was boundless to the twelve-year-old boy he treated not only as a talented equal and a confidant but practically as a lover." According to his biographer Freedman (1996), Rilke's mother had wanted a daughter and he could please her by dressing as a girl. An eroticized friendship with another boy at military school led to his leaving that school. Like Balthus, Rilke's parents had also separated when he was 9.

In a letter to young Balthus, Rilke signed off with: "And as for you yourself, my dear B, ... you know—don't you—that quite frankly we love each other. To you with all my heart" (Weber, p. 44). In another letter to Balthus, "Letters to B." published in *La Fontaine* in the 1930s, he offered to the boy on his 13th birthday the secret of a nether world between February 28 and March 1 where his birthday [February 29] was hidden for 3 out of 4 years. Rilke wrote: "This discreet birthday that most often dwells as a form of the beyond, certainly gives you rights over many unknown things here below" (Weber, p. 193). Balthus noted that: "Rilke's inspiration was poetic and spiritual, and he summoned me to the place of the 'crack' to the slit that I had to pass through starting with my student years, in order to reach true reality" (Vircondelet, 2001, p. 74). "Rilke showed me nocturnal paths, giving me a taste for slipping through narrow passages to reach the Open" (Weber, p. 193). The latent homoerotic, anal erotic meanings of these fantasies that are on a manifest level about time, are quite obvious and, I believe, are embedded in numerous paintings showing boys and girls bent over with their buttocks in the air, poses that can only be explained by such fantasies (Image 6 *The Card Game* [1948–1950], and Image 7 *Game of Patience* [1943]). The similarity between Rilke's affair with Baladine and what I perceive as a homoerotic relation to her son and J. M. Barrie's 13 years prior affair with a woman with sons is noteworthy. Barrie wrote the play *Peter Pan* in 1906 in London, in which he proposed to a young boy a fantasy of eternal youth and a journey to Neverland. There were rumors of Barrie's presumed homosexual attachment to his lover's sons.

In his memoir at the end of his life, Balthus remembers accepting Rilke's advice but missing his father, resenting his mother and taking umbrage at Rilke's presence (Vircondelet, 2001, p. 84). I wonder if he was terrified by Rilke's attentions as well as narcissistically gratified. At any rate, the accusations that Balthus' gaze was pedophilic make me wonder if the artist was in his paintings reliving and working through the anxieties aroused by Rilke's gaze. With all of the "psychoanalytic" speculation in the literature, I have not come across this one, which seems so very obvious. It is my belief that he made his viewers into voyeurs. I focus here on Balthus' relationship with Rilke and less on the predominant theories that the little girls represent Balthus himself or his mother, the sight of whose genital resulted in his perversion.

In a collaboration with Rilke, who wrote the Preface, Balthus illustrated a book Image 8 *Mitsou* (1922) about the adventures of a tomcat who had left him, when he was just 14 years old. According to Rewald (1984), Balthus took some liberties with his surroundings, his illustrations giving the impression that he lived as an only child with both his parents in a large country house with servants and a garden. Balthus' rivalry with his 4 years older brother was clear. In his memoir at the end of his life he admitted that he saw Pierre's works as transparent, not luminous enough: "The paths I've chosen are more open to God's gifts. Klossowski's work is a black diamond, while I try to paint starbursts, shuddering wings and children's flesh" (Vircondelet, 2001, p. 15). At that time, Balthus also observed that: "painting Mitsou's story was a way to make our friendship eternal, a means of preserving the moment" (Vircondelet, 2001, p. 31). He was aware that art helped him with loss. The book's publisher wrote to Rilke that: "the boy's ability to translate his feelings into graphic expression is astounding and almost frightening" (Rewald, 1983, p. 13). Bonnard too lavishly complimented the boy's artworks.

Rilke arranged for Balthus' schooling and intervened when he got into trouble and tried to help the family out as much as he could. The relationship with Baladine and young Balthus energized Rilke, who had been in a slump. Balthus was witness to his mother's ecstasy with Rilke coupled with her torment over the fact that Rilke would not live with her. She spent long hours every day writing to him and would have sent her sons away if Rilke would agree, which he would not. This had been his pattern with a series of famous mistresses, including Lou Andreas-Salome. Repeating his earlier pattern, he began to withdraw from Baladine and her sons and left Balthus' mother without any explanation. They never saw him after 1925. Early that year Rilke published a poem called "Narcissus" dedicated to Balthus. He died of leukemia, which he had kept secret, a year later.

Balthus thus suffered the loss of two fathers, the psychological availability of his mother who flirted with his brother, as well as the humiliation of his family's poverty and the gypsy-like life they led going from country to country. This was in stark contrast to the praise heaped on his artwork. He held onto his art to elevate his self-esteem and to rise above the circumstances of his life at home. Balthus reported that he fantasized himself as a cat (Image 9 *The King of Cats* [1935]). Under a whip, on a tombstone slab, in English, the language of one of his nannies, he wrote: "A Portrait of H. M. The King of Cats Painted by Himself." He is quoted as saying that: "A cat is unapproachable to those it rejects" (Neret, 2003, p. 35). He felt that he secretly belonged to the world of cats and that the terrifying cat in the painting resembled him a little (Image 10 *Cat of the Mediterranean* [1949]). This is a sign he did for the Mediterranean restaurant in the Place de l'Odeon in Paris; it was inspired by a dinner he had with Picasso in Golfe-Juan. His houses were filled with cats, perhaps 30 at a time!

In Image 11 *Girl with a Cat* (1937), a child model from the 1960s reported that when painting, Balthus was completely absorbed in his work that, he would take off into his own world. When told that he did "Lolitas" Balthus replied: "I have only painted angels. Besides everything I paint is religious" (Neret, 2003, p. 54). He considered himself to be an ardent Catholic. For him painting was a way of prayer, a means to hearing God's voice (Vircondelet, 2001). This image was used for the paperback cover of *Lolita*. According to Balthus: "That's how little girls sit" (Weber, 1999, p. 31). It has been rumored that he slept with his little models. As you can see, the cat is lapping up some milk. Is this Balthus with a fantasy of cunnilingus? (Baudry private communication).

Balthus admitted in 1955 that: "I used to like shocking people, but now it bores me" (Neret, p. 13). He also was quoted as needing his chateau, "I have a greater need for a chateau than a workman has for a loaf of bread" (Lord, 1983, p. 70). At times he painted for the market and what money his works would bring him. (Image 12 *The White Skirt* [1937] an image of Antoinette, who insisted upon wearing her bra.) Weber recounts attending a major retrospective of Balthus' work in 1993 and being appalled at the elderly Count's capers with a young model. It seemed to me upon reading this that Balthus might have been playing with his public image as a pedophile.

The combination of the vast praise received so young for his artwork and the loss of his father and Rilke as well as the humiliating poverty of his family were the makings of a narcissistic personality disorder. Herzog (2004) proposes that: "a kind of narcissistic pathology featuring perverse sexuality may eventuate in the absence of paternal availability and in the presence of a disordered relationship between the parents" (p. 893). Crucial components are problems in the modulation of aggression.

Picasso and Braque both liked Balthus. Picasso visited him and told him: "You're the only painter of your generation who interests me. The others/try to make Picassos. You never do" (Vircondelet, 2001, pp. 9–10). Picasso bought Balthus' painting Image 13 *Children* (1937). For him it connoted melancholy, suspended time, death, and disappearance.

I would like to demonstrate further how Balthus' psyche and its roots revealed themselves in his work. I chose Image 14 *Figure in Front of a Mantel/Standing Nude Before a Mirror* (1955) for the cover of my book *Body Talk: Looking and Being Looked at in Psychotherapy* (2000) for its (to my mind) theme of a young girl budding into womanhood staring at herself in the mirror in order to consolidate her inner image of who she was and what she looked like. She seems too undifferentiated to be erotic. Balthus often painted the moment of "becoming," of the transformation from one state of being to another. Alternatively, Schneider (1985) cites a paper by Szabo that reads this painting as sexual in nature: "Here the man's presence is symbolic; it lies in the mantel itself and the implied fire ... the fireplace is a squat shape whose ornamentation recalls the lower torso of a man" (p. 302). Szabo also notes the likelihood that Balthus was influenced by Rilke and cites his second Sonnet to Orpheus: "... mirrors often take into themselves ... the sacred single smiles of girls." Schneider goes on to write that: "In Balthus' painting, the relation between the girl, the mirror, and the implied flame is clearly sexual, though its exact nature remains shrouded in mystery" (p. 302). I find the sexual reading of this work to be a mystery. I look at it often for it is in New York at the Metropolitan Museum of Art. The paint application and lighting make it sensual even delicious; it is perhaps more orally erotic than sexual. If anything about the fireplace it may be the slit, the Neverland promised by Rilke.

In his memoir, Balthus remarks that: "I've always had a naive, natural complicity with young girls" (Vircondelet, 2001, p. 65) and named the long list of his models. He called what Lewis Carroll (1872) referred to in *Through the Looking Glass* as that "sweet paradise of vanished splendors." He claimed that to suggest an erotic intent "is to misunderstand the particular attention I pay to the slow transformation from a cyclic state to that of a young girl, to finding the moment of passage" (p. 66).

Elsewhere he was quoted:

> I prefer anonymity. I see adolescent girls as a symbol. I shall never be able to paint a woman. The beauty of adolescence is more interesting. The future is incarnate in adolescence. A woman has already found her place in the world, an *adolescent* has not. The body of a young woman is already complete. The mystery has disappeared.
>
> (Neret, p. 36, Image 15 *Nude in Profile* [1973–1977])

Weber (1999), on some level tried to test out Balthus' sexual or nonsexual gaze when he brought his own daughters aged 9 and 11 to an opening in Lausanne. He observed:

> Without being either sexual or inappropriate, his gaze as he inhaled my daughters' appearance was passionately reverent ... never before had I witnessed a reaction of such absolute, unadulterated, undisguised engagement. The intensity was the same as in Rilke's and Baladine's letters.
>
> (p. 587)

> The expression on Balthus' face as he took in the sight of my daughters was more Turgenev than Nabokov: the departing generation drinking in the youth of the emerging one. Tender, yes; erotic, no. The lust that was there was for beauty, for a time of life, for human feeling: not for sex.
>
> (p. 588)

Weber thought that Balthus met them as equals. I think this is in stark contrast to the primitive sexuality and lustful gaze that emerges in some old men as we see in the late Picasso's work (Image 16 *The Peeing Woman* [1965]).

I believe that in his trancelike state, while he worked, Balthus was working through major losses: of his father, of his relationship with Rilke, which combined oedipal jealousy, homoeroticism, narcissistic grandiosity, and imagos of his depressed, even "dead" mother at home (Green, 1980). I speculate that if his mother was in the state described she may have sat for hours with her legs partially exposing her genitals. This early photo of his mother seems quite similar to his famous painting of *Girl in White* (Image 17 *Girl in White* [1955]). His works express to me a surreal melancholy, and other-worldliness, located somewhere between depression and emptiness. Balthus loved Mozart and when he made stage sets for "Cosi fan Tutti" alluded to "poignant pain and heartbreak hidden behind a/mask of apparent gaiety" (Vircondelet, 2001, pp. 35–36), which seems to me to be a projection of his inner state.

I believe that Balthus' supposed pedophilic gaze was an internalization of Rilke's pedophilic gaze. When he was 11, away on vacation, Balthus was joined by his mother and Rilke. He reported: "These are very strong moving memories. Rilke knew how to be on terms of great familiarity with children. A secret spell united us. He received me at his property at Valais, with its virgin landscapes that resembled Poussin's canvasses" (Vircondelet, 2001, p. 13). The fantasies such attention might have invoked and stimulated are unknown. Nevertheless, two of the best-known of Balthus' artworks contain notions of forced rape albeit of female characters. Both of these works were exhibited in his first solo exhibition in Paris at the Galerie Pierre in 1934, when he was just 26.

Image 18 *The Street* (1933) depicts a busy street in Paris in the 6th arrondissement, near where he lived. People are going about their business but seem to be sleepwalking or in a dream. The focus is on a workman carrying a large phallic-looking board. But to his left, unobserved by the crowd, is a young man molesting a girl from behind. He grips her wrist and his leg pushed beneath hers immobilizes her. Angst and malaise are conveyed to the viewer, but Balthus said it was just everyday life. Is it possible that the little girl represents himself and the man Rilke? No one was watching.

Image 19 *Guitar Lesson* (1934), (see Figure 17.1) was kept in a back room covered with a curtain and shown to a select few. Formally the pose is like that of the 1470 Villeneuve-les-Avignons "Pieta" in the Louvre. The subject is the initiation into homosexual lovemaking of a teacher and her young student, who seems to be about 12 years old, their hard, almost dead looking bodies embracing, each hurting the other. Nipple pinching is to be found in the ca. 1594 *Gabrielle d'Estrees and One of her Sisters*, an early Fontainebleu School painting. Could this be a fantasy about Rilke and himself? This painting was considered to be so scandalous that the Museum of Modern Art would not take it as late as 1977. It was sold to Mike Nichols and then to Stavros Niarchos, in whose New York bedroom it hung. In a rare moment of honesty Balthus confessed that he wanted to acquire a "sulfurous reputation" when he made this painting. The elderly Balthus reminisced: "Only once did I paint a picture as a means of provocation" (Vircondelet, 2001, p. 50). In this context Rewald noted that Balthus was called the "Freud of painting."

Weber (1999), the amateur psychoanalyst, presented this analysis:

> The ultimate personification of what Klossowski calls Sade's "*idole tyrannique*" is the teacher in *The Guitar Lesson*. Moreover, she is, generically and specifically, a mother image; by looking like Balthus, she closely

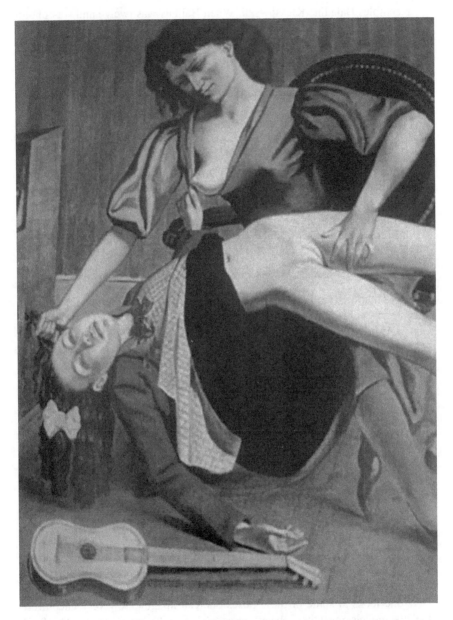

Figure 17.1 *Guitar Lesson* (1934) by Balthus. Oil on canvas 163.3 × 138.4 cm.

resembles Baladine Klossowska. When Balthus was twelve and was photo-graphed on several occasions with his mother and Rilke, he and Baladine appear strikingly similar: with identical large noses, thin mouths, deep-set eyes, hollow cheeks, and nearly the same thick black pageboy-length hair. Whatever his deliberate intentions were, Balthus made the teacher an amalgam of himself and his mother.

(p. 234)

Weber also reported that:

When I had my private viewing of "The Guitar Lesson" in Niarcho's apart-ment, the girl's flesh was so plausible that it made me feel guilty, as if I were pressing my fingers into her thighs. I could not for a minute buy Balthus' idea that these sensations reflected my own lascivious desire rather than his intentions ... The violation of a girl close in years to my own daughters was heinous.

(p. 223)

I agree that there is a boundary violation here, but I would argue that the two figures represent his fantasy of Rilke and himself. In this context I find Image 20 *Joan Miro and His Daughter Dolores* (1938) to be curious. The father is cupping his daughter's breast while standing behind her. She looks down and resigned.

Weber uses Balthus' brother Pierre's analysis of the Marquis de Sade as evidence in order to hypothesize about what happened to them as children. He reconstructed the humiliation of the mother in front of her children or by the children themselves. Balthus' paintings are replete with images of women being humiliated. In Image 21 *Andre Derain* (1936), the artist is depicted looming large in his dressing gown before the abject sleeping figure of his half nude model.

The story was told that a wealthy Connecticut woman Jane Cooley, who posed for Balthus, complained that the pain of the sittings was excruciating. She had to sit absolutely still, her back erect, at the edge of her table, and if she moved as much as half an inch he was brutal, although not physically so. It was physically so uncomfortable and he was unsympathetic and wouldn't bring her any water. By the third day she was miserable, at the edge of tears. She had not told him she was pregnant. When she did, he changed and became solicitous. He was either a gem or a monster to his models.

As one looks at some of these poses one can imagine how very uncomfort-able his models must have been: Image 22 *The Living Room* (1941–1943); Image 23 *The Card Players* (1966–1973); Image 24 *Vicomtesse de Noailles* (1936), who was a pillar of French society; and finally Image 25 *The Victim* (1939–1946). I believe that the sadomasochistic and beating fantasies so central to narcissistic pathology are embedded in these works and that in painting them he was reliving the domestic discomfort of his childhood and adolescence.

In 1946, Balthus left his wife Antoinette and their two sons in Switzerland and returned to Paris. In his abandonment of his family he repeated what his own father had done. He made a shallow excuse years later: "But life doesn't always allow us to live out all our commitments" (Vircondelet, 2001, p. 164). He did not get a divorce until he met his second wife Setsuko, a Japanese woman who was his model. As a boy he had developed an interest in the Orient from Rilke, who gave him a book on Chinese art. When he was 13, he grabbed hold of a Buddha Rilke had given his mother and refused to return it. Perhaps the adoring Oriental Setsuko represented a re-finding of Rilke.

The Count Balthasar Klossowski de Rola lived with Setsouko in the largest chateau in Switzerland, in Rossiniere. Having the chateau had oedipal significance, for he had witnessed his mother and Rilke refurbish a chateau when they were together. Balthus and Setsouko had a daughter Harumi in 1973, when he was 65. He was world famous, his aristocratic origins were doubtful and he continued to deny his mother's Jewishness. Weber (1999), found the elderly Balthus to be a "magnetic presence," the child prodigy still quite alive in the old man. He died in 2001, working until the very end of his life, in a wheelchair, his eyesight dimmed. Setsouko, an artist herself, prepared his paints. His son Stanislaus (1996) reported: "To the end he refused to accept the inevitable, never losing confidence that he would eventually recover and resume work, quite convinced that he would be granted a stay to complete his ambitious plans" (p. 18). He was planning his last piece Image 26 *The Waiting* (1995). Anticipating his death he said that "the story will continue...then I'll see my mother, Baladine, whom I loved so much" (p. 139).

I hope to have reached a deeper understanding of this man who contributed to the world important works of art that contain split-off emotions of his youth and are appreciated because they resonate with similar emotions in the viewer. Balthus' life and art are replete with themes of a search for an integrated identity, of narcissism, homoeroticism, sadomasochism, of sadness, and loss. Philippe de Montebello in the preface to the catalog (Rewald, 1984) of the Metropolitan Museum of Art retrospective appraised Balthus: "No other figurative artist of our century has expressed himself at such an intense level of consciousness, and few have plumbed so deeply the mysteries of the subconscious imagination" (p. 7).

List of images discussed in this chapter

1 *Thérèse Dreaming* (1938)
2 *Katia Reading* (1968–1976)
3 Photo of Balthus, his mother, and Rilke
4 *Golden Days* (1944–1945)
5 *The Room* (1952–1954)
6 *Card Game* (1948–1950)
7 *The Game of Patience* (1943)

  8 *Mitsou* (1922)
  9 *The King of Cats* (1935)
 10 *Cat of the Mediterranean* (1949)
 11 *Girl with a Cat* (1937)
 12 *The White Skirt* (1937)
 13 *Children* (1937)
 14 *Figure in Front of a Mantel* (1955)
 15 *Nude in Profile* (1973–1977)
 16 Picasso: *Peeing Woman* (1965)
 17 *Girl in White* (1955)
 18 *The Street* (1933)
 19 *Guitar Lesson* (1934) (see Figure 17.1)
 20 *Joan Miro and His Daughter Dolores* (1938)
 21 *Andre Derain* (1936)
 22 *The Living Room* (1941–1943)
 23 *The Card Players* (1966–1973)
 24 *Vicomtesse de Noailles* (1936)
 25 *The Victim* (1939–1946)
 26 *The Waiting* (1995)

Note

1 The artworks discussed in this chapter and listed at the end can be readily searched and found using an Internet search engine alongside the name Balthus.

References

Balthus (1921). *Mitsou: Forty images by Balthus.*(Preface by R. M. Rilke).

Balthus (2001). *In his own words: A conversation with Cristina Carrillo de Albornoz* New York: Assouline.

Barrie, J. M. (1904). *Peter Pan, or the boy who would not grow up.* London, New York: Bloomsbury Publishing Plc.

Baudry, F. (2005). Personal communication.

Carroll, L. (1872). *Through the looking glass and what Alice found there.* London: Macmillan.

Freedman, R. (1996). *Life of a poet: Rainer Maria Rilke.* New York: Farrar Straus Giroux.

Freud, S. (1905/1938). Three contributions to the theory of sex. In A. A. Brill, *The basic writings of Sigmund Freud.* New York: The Modern Library/Random House.

Green, A. (1980). The Dead Mother. In A. Green, *On private madness.* Madison, C.T.: International Universities Press, 1986.

Herzog, J. (2001). *Father hunger: Explorations with adults and children.* Hillsdale, N.J.: Analytic Press.

Klossowki de Rola, S. (1996, expanded 2002). *Balthus.* New York: Harry Abrams, Inc.

Lieberman, J. S. (2000). *Body talk: Looking and being looked at in psychotherapy.* Northvale, N.J.: Jason Aronson, Inc.

Lord, J. (1983). *Giacometti: A biography.* New York: Farrar Straus Giroux.

Nabokov, V. (1955). *Lolita.* Paris: Olympia Press.

Neret, G. (2003). *Balthus (1908–2001): The king of cats.* Koln: Taschen.

Pollock, G. (1989). *The mourning-liberation process I & II.* Madison, C.T.: International Universities Press.

Rewald, S. (1984). *Balthus.* New York: Harry Abrams, Metropolitan Museum of Art.

Rilke, R. M. (1922). Preface to *Mitsou.* Translated by R. Miller (illustrations by Balthus). New York: Metropolitan Museum of Art, pp. 12–13.

Schneider, L. (1985). Mirrors in art. *Psychoanalytic Inquiry, 5,* 283–324.

Vircondelet, A. (2001), (2002–English). *Vanished splendors: A memoir* (Balthus as told to Vircondelet). New York: HarperCollins.

Weber, N. F. (1999). *Balthus: A biography.* New York: Alfred A Knopf.

Chapter 18

Is appropriation creative?

The case of Richard Prince

Richard Prince (b. 1949) is an artist of great importance in the contemporary art world, and he has maintained that position for the past 40 years. In New York, he had important retrospectives at the Whitney Museum in 1992 and at the Guggenheim in 2007. He belongs to a category of artists (along with his former girlfriend Cindy Sherman) who have been characterized as "artist as anthropologist." His work manifests biting cultural critique and reflects and comments upon late 20th century and early 21st century popular culture in all its warts. He holds up a mirror for us to look at ourselves and our societal values. In addition, although the days of inferring the pathology of the artist through examination of the content of his or her work is over, one cannot help wondering how much Prince is expressing in his work his personal issues and how much his work reflects broader issues of American culture, as he purports. Prince is part of this culture, but stands to the side critiquing it and himself at the same time.

Prince's works enable us to think about these issues using another part of the brain, the visual brain. To my mind the difficult concrete images Prince sets before us have an impact that words do not have and are less prone to the mobilization of intellectual defenses than happens with words. In much contemporary art, the message, the idea, is more important than the aesthetics, but in truth much of Prince's work is aesthetically pleasing and some, not all, is great art making. There is at times a paradox between some of his negative, perverse images, and the rather beautiful aesthetics of his art, particularly works he had made in recent years.

Starting in the 1970s until now, there have been some interesting parallels between the history of art and the history of psychoanalysis, between art criticism and critique of traditional psychoanalytic theory and practice. Postmodern thinking has challenged notions upon which psychoanalysis was founded: the writings of Kohut, Kernberg, then the relational theorists like Greenberg and Mitchell, have led us to question the validity and worth of the very basic concepts developed by Freud. Psychoanalysis as a single method devised by Freud became many methods and his concepts were renamed and adopted by others as their own, *appropriated*. The boundary line between what was called psychoanalysis and what was called psychotherapy became fuzzy and for some, non-existent. Similarly in the art world, notions that art works are singular and unique and are the property of the artist, that art works are made of materials that will last forever, that a painting hangs on a wall, that a piece of sculpture sits on a pedestal or that paintings, drawings, sculptures, photographs, and performances are discreet and separate categories of art, were all challenged. Contemporary art has become more and more "performative": something is staged, watched, listened to, and its concrete residue, e.g., the costumes, the props, are all that remain of the event or "happening." Similarly, in the case of relational psychoanalysis, something supposedly "happens" in the analytic space between patient and analyst. (There is psychological residue, not concrete residue, except perhaps the bill and the check!)

Of course, it is debatable as to whether social and critical critique should be the province of artists, but they have taken it on. In 1970, at the height of the Vietnam War, a group of radical art historians formed a New Art Association, stating that: "We are against the myth of the neutrality of art." "We deny that esthetic experiences flow only into further esthetic experiences, for we believe that there is a firm tie between the artistic imagination and the social imagination." "We object to the study of art as an activity separated from other human concerns..." (Sandler, 1996, p. 332).

Since the 1970s, artists have commented on wars, on politics, racism, on AIDS, and more importantly is the fact that in both the art world and the psychoanalytic world, issues of gender have become the object of special focus. Richard Prince's work in particular deals with the objectification of women and of men as well, gender stereotyping as the underpinning of advertising and the media, as well as pornography. Among his most noted works (soon to be discussed) are:

1   **MARLBORO MAN COWBOY (1989)**[1]
2   **BROOKE SHIELDS CHILD "SPIRITUAL AMERICA" (1983)**
3   **BIKER CHICKS (1993)**

I write about Richard Prince because the subject matter of his work coincides with the subjects I have written about over the years: issues of deception and lying, voyeurism and exhibitionism, masculinity and femininity, and their connection to issues of basic identity, as well as the impact of contemporary culture on contemporary art. When I lectured on the 1992 Prince show as a Docent at the Whitney Museum, I did not like his work. I found it to be too aggressive, too perverse, and misogynist. Sixteen years later, I found the 2007 retrospective at the Guggenheim Museum, which included his more recent work, to be fascinating. I think that my own thinking and writing during the years that have elapsed have enabled me to better understand Prince, and I hope that I will be able to convey that understanding here.

Prince is known for his appropriation of mass cultural images and social clichés as a means of questioning assumptions about representation and identity. "Appropriation" refers to the use of borrowed elements in the construction of a new work, recontextualizing the thing that is borrowed. Marcel

Duchamp's urinal *Fountain,* Picasso's newspaper collages, and Warhol's Brillo boxes are examples. Prince incorporated appropriated texts with his re-photographs that is, photographs of photographs that are in the public domain. In his works are images as diverse as New Yorker cartoons, images of the Vietnam War, pornography and borscht-belt jokes, surfers, biker girlfriends, and hot rodders. There are large sculptures of car hoods. In the late 1980s he took car hoods and repainted them, the cars representing eroticized objects of male desire.

4   CAR HOOD (1995–1999)

I Jokes

Some of Prince's psychiatrist jokes and jokes related to gender stereotypes, sexual anxiety, family dysfunction, and problems between the sexes. It is difficult to see this from online images, but the actual Joke paintings and prints are artistically of the highest order. They are also deliberately silly, mean, and cheap. Art critic Tallman (1992) wondered: "Is he trying to mimic the rantings of an unbalanced mind or is he unbalanced himself?" He is one of the few artists whose subject matter is jokes (and sometimes cartoons). And as we all know, Freud (1905) in his "Wit and its relation to the Unconscious" wrote about the hostility expressed in cynical jokes.

A repeated joke:

> Two psychiatrists, one says to another: I was having lunch with my mother the other day and I made a Freudian slip. I meant to say please pass the butter and it came out you fuckin' bitch you ruined my life"
>
> (1991)

Art critic Tallman (1992) observed that "parapraxis" is "faulty reproduction" and Prince has made an art of faulty reproduction. This joke and many others appear over and over against minimalist backgrounds of silk-screened cartoon-like backgrounds.

Another is kind of funny: "Two friends ran into each other at the door of a psychiatrist's office. 'Are you coming or going?' The other replied: 'If I knew I wouldn't be here.'"

Another is sad: of a male torso boxing, set among doodles of a stove: "Do you know what it means to come home at night to a woman who will give you a little love, a little affection, a little tenderness? It means you're in the wrong home, that's what it means."

5   PSYCHIATRIST JOKE (1987)

And this one, often repeated with various surrounding images, colors, etc., "I went to a psychiatrist: He said, 'Tell me everything.' I did, and now he's doing my act." He alludes to a lack of basic trust, to forgeries of the self that are at the heart of his art making.

Prince's thinking is slippery, about sliding identities and themes. Multiple readings are possible. I ask and you may be also asking: Is this the work of a shallow huckster or of a keen observer of the dark side of the human psyche?

II Re-photography

6   MAN LOOKING BOTH WAYS (1977–1978)

In the mid-1970s he worked for Time-Life doing clippings. He looked at movie stills and started to see commercial ads in magazines as freeze-frames for movies. He took photographic images already out there in the public domain and photographed them himself and presented them as his artwork. They have the blurry quality of dreams. Like dreams they are not the real thing but are simalcrae of the real thing. A series of photographs are in multiples as if repetitions make something more real. There are parallels here to the concept of the "repetition compulsion" and the need to repeat on the part of patients and of analysts to repeat their interpretations.

Again, this is called "re-photography": existing photographs of other artists are stolen, scavenged, appropriated, and ready-made. We are made to doubt our basic assumptions about the authority of photographic images, ownership of public images, the nature of invention, and the fixed identifiable location of the author.

7   THREE WOMEN LOOKING IN THE SAME DIRECTION (1980)

Sandler, (1996) writes that Prince separated images from their media context. He revealed how models' stereotypical poses were used for exploitative purposes in a consumer society. "Viewers were led to understand how images could be manipulated in order to seduce and deceive the public" (p. 325). He was unveiling and exposing the truth of American life, the falsities that were at its foundation.

In a story Prince used, he described a character who could have been himself. According to Sandler:

> His own desires had very little to do with what came from himself because what he put out (at least in part) had already been out. His way to make it new was *make it again* and making it again was for him and certainly, personally speaking, *almost* him.
>
> (p. 326)

I ask: Is this just theft, art plagiarism, or merely contemporary art technique? Is he speaking about a collective false self?

III Masculinity

I have noted (Lieberman, 2006) that male psychology has been neglected by psychoanalysts. Today we ask: is there one masculinity or many? Gender roles have broken down and informed parenting in the past 30 years has encouraged this. Still, old stereotypes and binary classifications remain. Prince used images of various men to work out the various roles he as a man would play.

According to Phillips, the curator of the 1992 Guggenheim Museum show:

> Like Cindy Sherman, who explores codified images of femininity, Prince selects and therefore controls the roles he plays, developing them as a series of surrogate self-portraits: model, cowboy, surfer, race car driver, rock n' roller, patient, salesman, son, lover, stand-up comic, drunk, cheat, husband, brother, father, super-hero—all of them roles that examine masculine identity and deconstruct the authenticity of masculinity. Unlike Sherman, he doesn't restage these portraits: masculinity is embedded in the found image—in the gestures and actions that are its signs.
>
> (1992, p. 35)

She sees Prince's works as a "targeted deconstruction of masculinity."

Commenting on Prince's work in the same show curator Spector (2007) asserts that "his own identification with the various machismo stereotypes that he invokes suggests that the critique is a deeply personal one" (p. 53). The males and females he depicts are exaggerations—the exaggeration is performative. He anticipated the ideas of the 1990s that all identity is performative, rather than stable, natural, ontologically determined. Spector cites Judith Butler's thesis that gender roles are socially constructed and the acts culturally determined. She asks:

> Does this make Prince a feminist? Not in the classical sense. The crisis he probes in his work is broadly speaking, more existential. With his rotating cast of personalities, which range from the delinquent to the heroic, Prince asks what really lies behind the mask, prior to the role-playing.
>
> (p. 53)

Is he trying to decipher his socially constructed definition as a man? He uses other images connoting transvestitism, androgyny, and homoeroticism.

Joke: "I met my first girl, her name was Sally. Was that a girl, that's what people kept asking." This painting and its joke were cited in the *New York Times* article entitled: "What makes a woman a woman?" about the gender ambiguous South African runner Caster Semenya (Orenstein, 2009).

8   RICHARD AND CINDY (1980)

In 1984, Prince and Sherman donned similar wigs and posed as each other. Both dressed in the same black suits, wore the same red wig, made up their faces so they became androgynous, hybrid versions of themselves. By striking the same pose they created confusion as to gender identity and personal identity. Is it Cindy Prince or Richard Sherman? (Spector, 2007).

Prince also posed by himself in a suit wearing eye makeup and lipstick (1985).

9   COWBOY WITH CATTLE (1999)

The cowboy series from 1980–1992 was Prince's most famous grouping of re-photographs. These were taken from Marlboro cigarette ads, the image of the Marlboro man, the ideal figurine of masculinity, the real American man. These men had 10-gallon hats, boots, horses, lassos, spurs, and were set in the Western United States in arid landscapes flanked by cacti and sunsets. The cowboy was considered to be the archetypal alpha male, the American symbol of individualism and free will. (Even Freud, certainly no lover of American culture, went to cowboy movies on Saturday afternoons!)

Brod (1995), in an essay on masculinity as masquerade, noted:

> Like the American cowboy, "real" men embody the primitive, unadorned, self-evident, natural truths of the world, not the effete pretenses of urban dandies twirling about at a masquerade ball. The masquerade was women's.
>
> (p. 13)

10   COWBOY WITH HAT (1999)

Lewis (1992) noted that: "if there are any cowboys left in this country, they are not Marlboro men. The image just hovers there, separated umpteen times from nothing, like the shadow of a ghost" (p. 65). Prince shows how false the media is in depicting "fake" cowboys. He is playing with the reality that these images are of people imitating the real. His works raise the question of what is real, what is a real cowboy?

11   COWBOY WRESTLING HORSE (1997–1998)

I have written (Lieberman, 2006) that Prince's image of the cowboy was iconic for traditional masculinity. The man is action-oriented, with little thinking, or doubting. He is physically erect and sure of himself as he masters his horse, a symbol of his environment (or perhaps, his own instinctual nature). The irony is that when the iconic film *Brokeback Mountain* (Ossana, Schamus, & Lee, 2005) was released, sensitively depicting a homosexual relationship between the cowboys, the iconic cowboy of Richard Prince will never again be the stand-in for "macho man" and will more clearly reflect the complexity of masculinity in the 21st century.

IV Identity

We psychoanalysts often observe in our clinical work that gender issues often mask deeper underlying issues of identity. Prince was born in the Panama Canal

Zone in 1949. He grew up near Boston and attended college in Maine. He has told as many stories about his parents as identities that he has assumed. One is that they were Office of Strategic Services' spies, that his father was a psychopath, a gunrunner. Kuspit (1992) speculated that the tough characters Prince puts before us are surrogates for his father. "Prince describes him as 'one of those imaginative criminals who wakes up in the morning and almost makes a resolution to perform some sort of deviant or antisocial act even if it's just kicking the dog'" (p. 96).

In Chapters 16 and 17, I examined the chronic perverse lying and multiple, alternative biographies presented by Arshile Gorky and Balthus. Prince belongs with them. It is interesting to discover how many artists have created false identities for themselves, the art making perhaps, a creation of a different world from the one they are trying to disown. Just as we psychoanalysts have been the object of perverse transferences, a number of artists have had perverse relationships with their viewers, their dealers, and their collectors.

Disappearing is a theme for Prince. In 1987, he made two paintings out of disappearing ink. Two collectors bought them for US$15,000. One never knew since he immediately put the work in storage. What greater commentary on the art market and a perverse relationship to his collectors!

By the way, a cowboy print sold at auction for US$3,401,000 and a nurse painting for US$4,745,000!

Prince has written and published using undercover identities, e.g., Fulton Ryde. In 1977, he went underground and created his artistic alter-ego John Dogg, who had his own exhibitions. (Those familiar with Marcel Duchamp's life and work know of his alter-ego, Rose Selavy). This was the time Prince crossdressed and did the portraits with Cindy Sherman. And Duchamp began to crossdress after having drawn a mustache on the postcard face of the Mona Lisa.

Prince's artistic identity is also split. He has many vocations: photographer, painter, writer, gallerist, impresario, and photo editor. According to Phillips (1992), he is shadowy: "he provides clues, false leads, and always covers his tracks to throw off the scent" (p. 38).

This of course is reflected in his Joke: "I never had a penny to my name, so I changed my name."

V Misogyny and porn

As we know, Freud's struggle with misogyny has been well-documented (Lotto, 2001). When writing about conducting clinical work with racism, homophobia, and misogyny, Moss (2001) has observed that: "we can easily feel deprived of secure points of identification, and find ourselves driven back and forth between fleeting states of alienation, excitement and moral condemnation" (p. 1319). The sector of Prince's work that is the most problematic for me has to do with images that are misogynist and/or pornographic, many taken from images out there in pop culture. Prince claims that he reproduces these images so that we can think about their meaning in our culture. I question, as do many, whether by presenting them, even if in art galleries, museums, and art books, he just helps to perpetuate these negative images and stereotypes.

Prince used cartoons and borscht-belt jokes to expose hidden malevolence, perversity, and anger.

Joke: "What does it mean when you get home and your wife treats you with love and affection? Your in the wrong fucking house, that's what it means."

Joke: "I'm always kidding about my wife, says the bartender. Every time I introduce her to anybody, they say, 'Are you kidding?'"

12 SPIRITUAL AMERICA (1983)

Prince is most infamous for one of the biggest stunts of his career. In 1983, when Brooke Shields was 17 and just becoming famous, a photograph of her taken when she was 10, surfaced. The image was pirated from a photo by commercial photographer Gary Gross, taken of the 10-year-old girl with her mother's consent. Her mother had paid Gross US$450 to take the picture. Prince exhibited the image in a gallery he rented on the Lower East Side of New York that he ironically called "Spiritual America," using Alfred Stieglitz' 1923 name for a photo of a gelded workhorse's groin, itself a critique of American puritanical ethos.

Prince went into hiding and was not to be found. The art world was angry because he made the gallery into an extension of the lowest level of media fascination. The gallery was in a dimly lit room shown against a brick wall. Shield's mother was not happy about it.

Shield's oiled body is standing in a bathtub and it is ambiguous as to whether she is a boy or a girl. Her face is made up like a mature woman, the aim being to induce pornographic pleasure.

An art critic described her: "The pose she adopts is a combination of the coyness, availability, awkwardness, and knowingness, exposure and concealment. Like most pedophilic representations, a child is made to adopt a deliberately inflexible, artificially aesthetic posture" (Brooks, 1992, p. 88).

Visitors felt compliant in a crime. Not only was the image stolen, but Prince subverted the sanctity of the gallery context as a neutral space.

Brooks proclaimed that:

> Prince's action was criminally simple: by exhibiting the photo he made it an overt cover for a range of non-aesthetic responses, from mild curiosity, to scoptophilia. By opening the gallery for the sole reason of showing this one photo, Prince ensured that there would be no other reason for visiting the gallery other than to see a picture of the naked Brook Shields as a child.
>
> (p. 90)

According to Spector (2007), Prince was accused of misogyny. Around this time feminist film theory infiltrated art criticism. "Spectatorship is a gendered

activity, and any depiction of the female form is, thus, inescapably compromised..." "there was ... a profound suspicion of visual pleasure" (p. 49).

> Richard Prince's 'Spiritual America' is a dystonic topic where contradiction
> reigns. It is at once a country—our country—and a state of mind, in which
> fiction shapes reality, travesty reveals essential truths, and beauty resides in
> the tawdry and illicit.
>
> (p. i)

I wonder whether this is a cultural critique expressing how young girls can be
used and abused for the prurient male gaze. Is it an aggressive perverse act on
the part of the artist hell-bent on making the viewer uncomfortable, complicit in
a crime, or even exposing the prudery of the viewer?

Prince described it as "an extremely complicated photo of a naked girl who
looks like a boy made up to look like a woman. For me, she had the perfect
body."

This troubling image and its controversial history encapsulate the contrary
images of the American psyche: Puritan ethics vs. a yearning for recognition,
even at the price of transgression and degradation.

13 GROWNUP BROOKE SHIELDS

In 2005, Brooke Shields posed for Prince clad in a string bikini and mired in a
nitrogen fog.

The controversy lingers on. In 2009, the famous image of 10-year-old Brooke
was to be in a Tate Modern show in London. Scotland Yard came to the museum
and took it away, confiscating all the show's catalogs. The Museum lost half a
million dollars in revenue from these catalogs. To my amazement the British of
all people thought this was "kiddie porn," whereas the photo was displayed in
the Guggenheim for months in New York with no reaction. For the exhibition,
the photo of the "Grownup Brooke Shields" was put in the place formerly occu-
pied by the photo of herself as a 10-year-old.

VI Bikers and their chicks

14 BIKER CHICK (1993)
15 GIRLFRIEND (1993)

Prince used this series to pay homage to the "sex, drugs and rock 'n' roll" aspect
of American life; the bizarre types of people found in different subcultures and
found in different magazines. He re-photographed magazine images of the
motorcycle-obsessed, hot rod enthusiasts, surfers, and lovers of heavy metal
music to demonstrate the rebellious side of American culture.

Prince feels identified with the bikers and their sexual desire for half-naked
"chicks." He is the "artist as consumer," the American vision (Spector, 2007).
The girl on the bike poses naked because there is a man she wanted to please.

He used the images that showed the rankest and the most pathetic exhibitionism. These images were very much assailed by critics and feminists. He was not criticized for his images of fashion models and elegant women.

16 GANG OF WOMEN (2000)
17 CELEBRITIES (1986)
In these series, Prince was appropriating images from a lower register, socioeconomic, and in terms of the reproductive aspects of the photos.

VII Nurse paintings

18 DEBUTANTE NURSE (2004)
This series is inspired by the covers of cheap pulp romance novels sold at newspaper stands and delis. Prince scanned the covers with his computer and then with inkjet printing transferred the images to canvas and used acrylic paint.

I have found myself to be in conflict looking at these paintings. The nurse is the object of the male gaze and often of the "dirty old man's" sexual fantasies. Despite all of these feminist objections, I found in myself a contradictory aesthetic response. Up close, the painting is sumptuous, luscious. Prince paints like a modern day Renoir. As was noted earlier, these paintings have commanded upwards of US$4,000,000.

According to Spector (2007): "Prince conflates the various sociosexual stereotypes embodied by the figure of the nurse: Good Samaritan, naughty seductress, old battle-ax, and devil incarnate. He depicts each figure as both vamp and victim, undone by desire" (p. 53).

Each nurse has a name like Surfer Nurse, Naughty Nurse, Millionaire Nurse, and Dude Ranch Nurse. They all wear caps and their mouths are covered by surgical masks. In some, the red lips bleed through the masks.

VIII De Kooning paintings

19 DE KOONING PAINTING (2007)
In this series of paintings, not as sumptuous as the Nurse Paintings, Prince does not do a photograph appropriation, but rather appropriates an artist's painting style. Both homage and desecration blend elements from de Kooning's famous women series with figures cut from pornographic magazines. The resulting hermaphroditic creatures are hybrids on a number of levels, merging the male with the female and painting with photography.

De Kooning too was similarly accused of loving women and hating them, presenting them as alluring, and terrifying.

Kuspit (2004), in his tirade against postmodern art, called *The End of Art*, surprisingly does not mention Prince, but the book seems to be about artists like him. Kuspit argues that art is over because it has lost its aesthetic impact. Art has been replaced by "postart," a term invented by Alan Kaprow, as a new visual category that elevates the banal over the enigmatic, the scatological over the sacred, cleverness over creativity. He finds it empty and stagnant.

Jim Lewis (1992), typical of most critics makes the argument that: "of course it's trash; that's much of the point" (p. 77).

You may or may not agree with him. You must agree that this art is reflective of our culture and of the problems of the contemporary psyche and therefore of interest to the psychoanalyst.

Prince left New York City in 1996. He lives upstate in New York and has a house in Rensselaerville, three hours from New York City. He is married and has a daughter. He plays golf at an expensive club in Bridgehampton. He is also a rare book collector.

His house on 80+ acres is like a museum. He is quoted as saying: "Art is not an expression of personality, but an escape from personality. Only those who have personality and emotions and sensitivity know what it means to want to escape from these things" (Spector, 2007, p. 313).

List of images discussed in this chapter

1   Marlboro Man Cowboy (1989)
2   Brooke Shields Child "Spiritual America" (1983)
3   Biker Chick (1993)
4   Car Hood (1995–1999)
5   Psychiatrists joke (1987)
6   Man Looking Both Ways (1977–1978)
7   Three Women Looking in Same Direction (1980)
8   Richard and Cindy (1980)
9   Cowboy with Cattle (1999)
10   Cowboy with Hat (1999)
11   Cowboy Wrestling Horse (1997–1998)
12   Spiritual America (1983)
13   Grownup Brooke Shields (2005)
14   Biker Chick (1993)
15   Girlfriend (1993)
16   Gang of Women (2000)
17   Celebrities (1986)
18   Debutante Nurse (2004)
19   De Kooning Painting (2007)

Note

1   The artworks discussed in this chapter and listed at the end can be readily searched and found using the artwork title and Richard Prince's name in an Internet search engine.

References

Brod, H. (1995). Masculinity as masquerade. In A. Perchuk & H. Posner (Eds.), *The masculine masquerade: Masculinity and representation.* Cambridge, M.A.: The MIT Press.

Brooks, R. (1992). Spiritual America: No holds barred. In L. Phillips, *Richard Prince.* Whitney Museum of American Art: Distributed by Harry N. New York: Abrams, Inc.

Freud, S. (1905). Wit and its relation to the unconscious. In A. A. Brill (Ed.), *The basic writings of Sigmund Freud.* New York: The Modern Library/Random House.

Kuspit, D. (1992). Richard Prince's psychopathic America. *Artforum, 5*, 93–96.

Kuspit, D. (2004). *The end of art.* Cambridge, U.K.: Cambridge University Press.

Lewis, J. (1992). Outside world. In L. Phillips, *Richard Prince.* Whitney Museum of American Art: Distributed by Harry N. New York: Abrams, Inc.

Lieberman, J. S. (2006). Masculinity in the twenty-first century. *Journal of the American Psychoanalytic Association, 54*, 1059–1066.

Lotto, D. (2001). Freud's struggle with misogyny. *Journal of the American Psychoanalytic Association, 49*, 1289–1314.

Moss, D. (2001). Racism, homophobia, misogyny. *Journal of the American Psychoanalytic Association, 49*, 1315–1334.

Orenstein, P. (2009, September 13). What makes a woman a woman? *The New York Times Magazine*, p. 11.

Ossana, D., Schamus, J. (Producers), & Lee, A. (Director) (2005). *Brokeback Mountain* [Motion Picture]. United States: River Road Entertainment.

Phillips, L. (1992). *Richard Prince.* Whitney Museum of American Art: Distributed by Harry N. New York: Abrams, Inc.

Sandler, I. (1996). *Art of the postmodern era: From the late 1960's to the early 1990's* New York: HarperCollins.

Spector, N. (2007). Nowhere man. In *Richard Prince* New York: Guggenheim Museum Publications, pp. 20–57.

Tallman, S. (1992). The psychopathology of everyday life: Prince Prints. *Arts Magazine, 3*(92), 13–14.

Wikipedia. (2018). *Richard Prince.* [online], Wikipedia Foundation, Inc.

Chapter 19

Afterword

I am writing this several months after I began this book when I wrote the preliminary introduction. It is still perhaps, even a more unsettling time in the United States and the world. The different political parties are fighting with each other, with one another, and many with our president. It is difficult to feel secure about any of our institutions. We are threatened from the outside by North Korean nuclear threats and from within by homegrown terrorists, school shootings, homophobia, racism, and economic uncertainties.

Mieli and Bratsis (2018) coined the term "Trumpism" to describe as a symptom of our times. They proposed that we are experiencing the return of America's dark side, the return of the repressed racism, xenophobia, and misogyny of our ignoble past.

For psychoanalytic patients, neurotic fantasies of having their hopes and dreams destroyed have elements of reality attached to them, making it difficult for me, their analyst, to help them to differentiate realistic anxiety from neurotic anxiety. The ongoing climate of deception, obstruction of justice, sexual harassment, and pedophilia has, as I said in the Introduction, "made healthy people sick and sick people sicker." Climate change has also unsettled daily life with its odd unexpected temperature and precipitation fluctuations. My role is to help my patients to keep their inner balance, work on their dreams, fantasies, and conflicts, to help them to see how the past is affecting the present, so that they become stronger in the face of this pathological environment.

I believe that I must surrender a certain amount of neutrality and think along with my patients about their paths and decision-making in the outside world while guiding them in their exploration of their inner worlds.

This book has for the most part been written with theoretical underpinnings from Freud and Ego Psychology and to a lesser extent Self-Psychology and Kleinian theory. Many other theorists are prominent at the moment and their ideas could shed more light on this subject matter: Bion, Lacan, and Laplanche. So, in addition to the constant change in the outside world, we add constant change in the psychoanalytic world of theory and technique. The digitalization of life has rapidly expanded creating an overstimulating overload of information and misinformation. And more and more, psychoanalytic treatment is being carried out with phones and screens. The long-term effects of this on the minds of children and adults have yet to be seen.

Such are the issues of this particular moment in time.

Reference

Mieli, P., & Bratsis, P. (2018). *Trumpism: The symptom of our times.* Presentation at the Association for Psychoanalytic Medicine, New York. February 6.

Index

Page numbers in *italics* denote figures.